Foreword

D0781660

You have in your hand the second edition of *Preparing for Your ACS Examination in Organic Chemistry, The Official Guide* designed to help students prepare for examinations produced under the auspices of the Division of Chemical Education (DivCHED) of the American Chemical Society (ACS). The first edition of this guide was published in 2002. In 1998, the first study guide for general chemistry students was published; in 2009, a study guide for physical chemistry was added to the collection of guides.

As is common for materials produced by ACS Exams, we called on colleagues in the chemistry education community to help us put this second edition together. The first edition of this guide was written and produced under previous Director, I. Dwaine Eubanks and previous Associate Director, Lucy T. Eubanks. Their time and effort was utilized by many, many students who used the first edition since 2002. In this second edition, we have utilized many of their underlying principles while updating a substantial portion of the guide to provide a guide aligned to current textbooks and curriculum as well as a better representation of what may be expected on an ACS Exam. This effort was in no way accomplished solely by the four authors, rather was a collective effort with special thanks to our expert editing team and student volunteers. Specific acknowledgments noting each contributor is listed in the *Acknowledgments*.

As a discipline, chemistry is surely unique in the extent to which its practitioners provide beneficial volunteer service to the teaching community. ACS exams have been produced by volunteer teacher-experts for more than eighty-five years. Other projects of the Examinations Institute benefit from the abundance of donated time, effort, and talent. The result is that invariably, high-quality chemistry assessment materials are made available to the teaching and learning community at a fraction of their real value.

The three *Official Guides* that have been released so far are intended to be ancillary student materials, particularly in courses that use ACS exams. The care that goes into producing ACS exams may be lost on students who view the exams as foreign and unfamiliar. The purpose of this series of guides is to remove any barriers that might stand in the way of students demonstrating their knowledge of chemistry. The extent to which this goal is achieved in this new edition of the organic chemistry study guide will become known only as future generations of chemistry students sit for an ACS exam in organic chemistry.

We wish them the best.

Jeffrey R. Raker
Kristen L. Murphy

Milwaukee, Wisconsin
February, 2020

Acknowledgements

We thank the unselfish dedication of hundreds of volunteers who contribute their time and expertise to make ACS Division of Chemical Education exams possible. It is from the reservoir of their work that we have drawn inspiration and examples to produce this book to help students who will be taking an ACS exam. We gratefully acknowledge the efforts of all the past Organic Chemistry Exam Committee members.

This *Official Guide* benefited from the thoughtful and careful writing and editing of our writing team:

Patricia J. Kreke	Mount St. Mary's University
Olga Rinco Michels	Luther College
Matthew J. Mio	University of Detroit Mercy
Jeffrey R. Raker	University of South Florida

This *Official Guide* also benefited from the careful proofreading by several colleagues. We extend our special thanks to these faculty members:

Kevin L. Caran	James Madison University
Evy Colon-Garcia	Pikes Peak Community College
Mary Robert Nahm Garrett	Berea College
Joseph J. Grabowski	University of Pittsburgh
Jamie Ludwig	Rider University
Shirley Lin	United States Naval Academy
Ginger Shultz	University of Michigan
Daniel A. Turner	The Ohio State University
Jay Wackerly	Central College

Students also participated in the development of this *Official Guide* through using this guide in draft form and sharing their experiences back to us to aid in providing the student-user perspective. We extend our special thanks to these students from these institutions:

Northwestern University	Milwaukee School of Engineering
Luther College	University of South Florida

The personnel of the ACS Division of Chemical Education Examinations Institute played a central role in helping us to produce *Preparing for Your ACS Examination in Organic Chemistry: The Official Guide.* A very special thank you for all of the work involved is owed to our staff members:

Julie Adams	Cherie Mayes

While all of these reviewers have been very helpful in finding problems large and small, any remaining errors are solely our responsibility. You can assist us in the preparation of an even better product by notifying the Exams Institute of any errors you may find.

Jeffrey R. Raker
Kristen L. Murphy

Milwaukee, WI
February, 2020

Table of Contents

Toolbox: Foundational Concepts and Approaches to Problem Solving

Chapter Summary:

This chapter will focus on foundational concepts and skills from your organic chemistry coursework that you will use throughout this study guide and likely on your exam. The material in this chapter should not be considered a comprehensive list of preparatory material, but a list of important concepts that will be referenced throughout.

Specific topics in this chapter are:
- Ionic and covalent bonding
- Chemical formulas and molar mass
- Chemical equation balancing and stoichiometry
- Solubility and intermolecular interactions
- Oxidation/reduction
- Thermochemistry
- Trends on the periodic table: valence, electronegativity, atomic/ionic size
- Acid/base theory

Additionally, this chapter will include supplemental information in sections at the end of this chapter for preparation for your exam, including:
- Sample instructions
- Sample datasheet and periodic table
- How to use this book

Where to find this in your textbook:

The material in this chapter typically aligns to "General Chemistry Review" or "The Basics" in your textbook. The name of your chapter may vary.

Practice exam:

There are practice exam questions aligned to the material in this chapter. Because there are a limited number of questions on the practice exam, a review of the breadth of the material in this chapter is advised in preparation for your exam.

How this fits to the big picture:

The material in this chapter aligns to the Big Idea of Atoms (I), Bonding (II), Structure and Function (III), Intermolecular Interactions (IV), Chemical Reactions (V), Energy and Thermodynamics (VI), and Equilibrium (VIII) as listed on page 13 of this study guide.

Study Questions (SQ)

SQ-1.	Identify the covalent compounds.	NaBr I	CH₄ II	KMnO₄ III	ICl IV

(A) I and II   **(B)** III and IV   **(C)** II and IV   **(D)** I and III

Knowledge Required: (1) Identification of covalent and ionic compounds. (2) Recognition of metals and nonmetals.

Thinking it Through: From the prompt, you recognize that you need to determine the different kinds of bonding in compounds. You know that covalent compounds are comprised of atoms making covalent bonds. To form a covalent bond, you need two or more nonmetal atoms to share electrons. You recall that this contrasts with ionic bonds, where a nonmetal gains (an) electron(s) to become an anion while a metal loses (an) electron(s) to become a cation. The electrostatic attraction between the anion and cation forms an ionic bond. Finally, you know that metallic bonding exists when only metallic atoms are present.

You identify from the possible atoms in the answer options that sodium (Na), potassium (K) and manganese (Mn) are all metals while bromine (Br), carbon (C), hydrogen (H), iodine (I), oxygen (O) and chlorine (Cl) are all nonmetals. Thus, all the answer options contain either ionic or covalent bonds.

Choice **(C)** is correct. Methane (CH_4) and ICl both contain only nonmetals. The atoms in these molecules will share electrons and form covalent bonds.

Choices **(A)** and **(D)** are not correct. Both include **I** in which sodium (a metal) combines with bromine (a non-metal). This will create an ionic bond, and thus the compound, overall, will not contain only covalent bonds.

Choice **(B)** is not correct. It includes **III** which contains a potassium cation being attracted to the polyatomic anion permanganate (MnO_4^-), which will create an ionic bond, not a covalent bond. Thus, **III** will not contain only covalent bonds.

Practice Problems: **PQ-1** and **PQ-2**

SQ-2.	What is the molecular formula and molar mass of this compound?	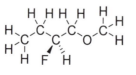

(A) $C_5H_{11}OF$, 106 g·mol⁻¹   **(B)** $C_5H_{12}FO$, 107 g·mol⁻¹

(C) C_2H_6OF, 65 g·mol⁻¹   **(D)** C_2H_6FO, 65 g·mol⁻¹

Knowledge Required: (1) Determining a molecular formula from a given molecular structure. (2) Determining a molar mass from a given molecular structure.

Thinking it Through: You know that bond-line or skeletal drawings in organic chemistry make assumptions about the number of carbon and hydrogen atoms present. You recall that each end or kink in the chain represents one carbon atom. You also know that a neutral carbon atom will form four bonds with other atoms, and that any "missing" bonds are bonds to hydrogen atoms. You also know that organic molecular formulas list atoms present in the order of "CHNOPS," with all other elements listed after these in alphabetical order.

You are first asked to determine the molecular formula of the compound. You count the number of carbon (C) atoms represented (5), you note the presence of one fluorine (F) and one oxygen (O), and then count the number of hydrogens (H) both indicated (6) and implied (5), for a total of 11 hydrogen atoms. You may find it easier to do this by drawing the molecule with all its atoms indicated:

The molecular formula is therefore: $C_5H_{11}OF$.

You are next asked to determine the molar mass of the compound. You remember that to calculate the molar mass of a compound, you use the molecular formula to total the atomic masses (from the periodic table) of all atoms present. You multiply the atomic mass of an atom by the number of that type of atom present and then sum all of these masses together.

Choice (A) is correct because it contains the correct molecular formula, the atoms in the molecular formula are listed in the correct order, and the correct sum of the molar masses is given (106 g·mol⁻¹).

Choice (B) is not correct because the number of hydrogen atoms is incorrect resulting in an incorrect molar mass.

Choice (C) is not correct because the choice contains an incorrect number of carbons and hydrogens in the molecular formula, resulting in an incorrect molar mass calculation for the structure. This choice is the result of not expanding the bond-line structure, and ignores the carbons and hydrogens not explicitly shown.

Choice (D) is not correct because there is an incorrect number of carbons and hydrogen atoms in the molecular formula and the atoms in the molecular formula are out of order.

Practice Problems: PQ-3 and PQ-4

A note throughout the study guide: A true bond line structure would not have the methyl group indicated (structure on the left) but for ease of viewing in some questions the authors have chosen to include terminal methyl groups (structure on the right). You will likely encounter both types of structures on ACS and other standardized exams.

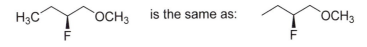

Also note that "g·mol⁻¹" is equivalent to "g/mol". The former is commonly used on ACS Exams; the latter may be used in this guide and in your textbook.

SQ-3.	What needs to be added to balance the chemical equation?

$$CH_3Br + {}^{\ominus}OH \longrightarrow CH_3OH$$

(A) hydroxide, to the product side   (B) bromide, to the product side

(C) bromine, to the product side   (D) bromide, to the reactant side

Knowledge Required: (1) How to balance chemical equations.

Thinking it Through: You are asked in the prompt to consider what atoms or species are needed on either the left or right side of the chemical equation in order to balance the reaction. You know that balancing chemical equations requires making sure an equal number and type of atoms are present on both sides of the reaction arrow: the left (or reactant) side and the right (or product) side. You also know that charges on each side of the reaction arrow must be equal for a chemical equation to be balanced.

To balance atoms and charge, you note that both a bromine (Br) and a negative charge are missing from the right hand (or product) side of the equation. You note that the number of carbons (1) and hydrogens (4) is balanced on the reactant and product side of the equation.

Choice (B) is correct because a negatively charged bromine (called a bromide ion) is needed on the product side of the equation.

Choice (A) is not correct because the addition of hydroxide (OH⁻) to the equation would not balance the number of bromine atoms.

Choice (C) is not correct because though it balances the atoms by adding a bromine it is not balancing the charge.

Choice (D) is not correct because the bromide (Br⁻) is needed on the product side of the chemical equation for the reaction to be balanced.

Practice Problems: PQ-5 and PQ-6

SQ-4. Which organic compound is most soluble in water?

(A) *n*-hexane

H_3C~~~~CH_3

(B) methylene chloride

$H-\overset{Cl}{\underset{Cl}{C}}-\overset{}{\underset{H}{C}}$

(C) ethyl acetate

$H_3C-\overset{O}{\underset{H_2}{C}}-OCH_3$

(D) ethanol

H_3C~~~~OH

Knowledge Required: (1) Solubility of organic compounds. (2) Recognition of intermolecular interactions.

Thinking it Through: From the prompt you recognize that you need to determine the relative solubility of the compounds in water, and thus you recognize you will need to identify intermolecular interactions present between the molecules themselves, and between the molecules and water.

Water is very polar and hydrogen bonds extensively with itself and other compounds having the ability to accept or donate hydrogen bonds. Because "like dissolves like," and "like" in this case refers to similar intermolecular interactions, you realize that the most soluble compound would be a compound that can both donate and accept hydrogen bonds or is highly polar.

To consider the polarity of a molecule, you look for polar bonds in the molecule and then decide if those polar bonds are additive based on shape and direction of the dipoles or if the polar bonds cancel. *n*-Hexane has no polar bonds, so it is not polar. Nonpolar molecules are not soluble in water.

Methylene chloride (or dichloromethane) is polar. The Cl–C–Cl bond angle in methylene chloride is approximately 109.5° and thus the two Cl–C bond dipoles are added and do not cancel each other out entirely. Though polar, methylene chloride is not capable of accepting or donating hydrogen bonds.

You note that both ethyl acetate and ethanol contain C–O bonds, which are polar. The three-dimensional orientation of these polar bonds lead to overall molecular polarity. Only ethanol, however, has hydrogen bond donating capabilities. The requirement for a hydrogen bond donor is a hydrogen bonded to a fluorine, oxygen or nitrogen; ethyl acetate does not have such hydrogen bond donation ability. The oxygen atoms on the ethyl acetate can accept a hydrogen bond from water, but because ethyl acetate is not also a hydrogen bond donor, it will be less soluble in water than ethanol.

Choice **(D)** is correct because ethanol is polar and can donate and accept hydrogen bonds.

Choices **(B)** and **(C)** are not correct because while they are both polar, neither has hydrogen bond donation ability like the compound in Choice **(D)**.

Choice **(A)** is not correct because the compound is non-polar.

Practice Problems: **PQ-7** and **PQ-8**

SQ-5. Is this an oxidation or reduction reaction?

$H_3C-\overset{O}{\overset{||}{C}}-CH_3 \xrightarrow[\text{EtOH}]{\text{NaBH}_4} H_3C-\overset{OH}{\underset{}{CH}}-CH_3$

(A) oxidation, because of the oxidation state of the carbonyl carbon

(B) reduction, because of the oxidation state of the carbonyl carbon

(C) oxidation, because of the oxidation state of the carbonyl oxygen

(D) reduction, because of the oxidation state of the carbonyl oxygen

Knowledge Required: (1) Definition of an oxidation reaction and a reduction reaction.

Thinking it Through: Based on the given starting material, reagents, and product, you are asked to determine if the reaction is an oxidation or reduction reaction. You recall that the definition of such a reaction type is based on whether the starting material (i.e., the reactant) is oxidized or reduced. You note that the second part of the answer choices require you to determine "why" the reaction is an oxidation or a reduction.

You note there are two ways by which you could solve this problem. First, you could calculate the oxidation state of the carbonyl carbon and decide whether it is oxidized or reduced. If you chose this method, the oxidation state of the carbonyl carbon on the left is +2, while the oxidation state of the carbonyl carbon on the

right is 0. You recall that a decrease in the oxidation number means a gain of electrons, and a gain of electrons is a reduction (a loss of electrons would be an oxidation).

The other method by which you could choose whether this reaction is a reduction or oxidation is by remembering that if you increase the number of hydrogen atoms (or decrease the number of oxygen atoms) bonded to a carbon, that carbon atom is reduced; while if you increase the number of oxygen atoms (or decrease the number of hydrogen atoms) bonded to a carbon atom, that carbon is oxidized. Using this method, you note from the structures in the given reaction that the number of hydrogen atoms bonded to the carbonyl carbon is increased (and the number of bonds to the oxygen atom is decreased) and therefore this is a reduction reaction.

Choice **(B)** is correct.

Choices **(A)** and **(C)** are not correct because this is not an oxidation reaction.

Choice **(D)** is not correct because the oxidation or reduction is of the carbonyl carbon and not the carbonyl oxygen, as the carbonyl oxygen does not change oxidation states (i.e., always –2 unless bonded to another oxygen atom).

Practice Problems: **PQ-9** and **PQ-10**

SQ-6. The primary reason the chemical equilibrium lies to the right side is because:

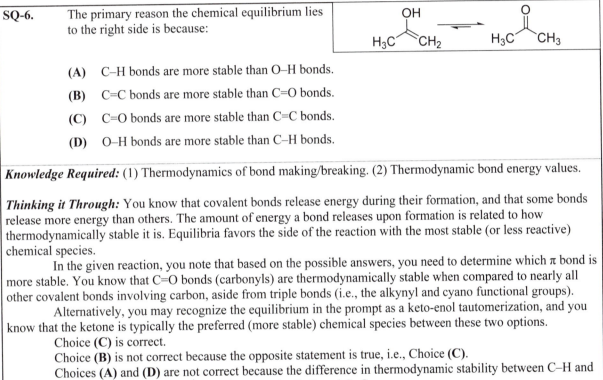

(A) C–H bonds are more stable than O–H bonds.

(B) C=C bonds are more stable than C=O bonds.

(C) C=O bonds are more stable than C=C bonds.

(D) O–H bonds are more stable than C–H bonds.

Knowledge Required: (1) Thermodynamics of bond making/breaking. (2) Thermodynamic bond energy values.

Thinking it Through: You know that covalent bonds release energy during their formation, and that some bonds release more energy than others. The amount of energy a bond releases upon formation is related to how thermodynamically stable it is. Equilibria favors the side of the reaction with the most stable (or less reactive) chemical species.

In the given reaction, you note that based on the possible answers, you need to determine which π bond is more stable. You know that C=O bonds (carbonyls) are thermodynamically stable when compared to nearly all other covalent bonds involving carbon, aside from triple bonds (i.e., the alkynyl and cyano functional groups).

Alternatively, you may recognize the equilibrium in the prompt as a keto-enol tautomerization, and you know that the ketone is typically the preferred (more stable) chemical species between these two options.

Choice **(C)** is correct.

Choice **(B)** is not correct because the opposite statement is true, i.e., Choice **(C)**.

Choices **(A)** and **(D)** are not correct because the difference in thermodynamic stability between C–H and O–H is less significant than the difference between the C=O and C=C.

Practice Problems: **PQ-11** and **PQ-12**

SQ-7. Which bond is the most polar?

(A) C–O   (B) C–N   (C) C–F   (D) C–C

Knowledge Required: (1) Trends from the periodic table: valence, electronegativity, atomic/ionic size

Thinking it Through: You are asked in the prompt to consider several bonds to determine which is the most polar. You know that covalent bond polarity is determined by the difference in electronegativity between the two atoms that comprise the bond. You also know that electronegativity, i.e., the chemical property that describes the tendency of an atom to attract a shared pair of electrons towards itself, increases for an element as its position on the periodic table is closer to fluorine, commonly referred to as the most electronegative element.

In this question, you notice that carbon is involved in all the answer options, and thus, you must only identify which element has the largest difference in electronegativity value compared to carbon.

Choice (**C**) is correct because of the given atoms bonded to carbon, fluorine has the largest electronegativity difference with carbon.

Choices (**A**) and (**B**) are incorrect because although there is a reasonable difference between the electronegativity of carbon and oxygen/nitrogen, that difference is not as great as the C–F bond.

Choice (**D**) is incorrect because there is no electronegativity difference between two carbon atoms.

Practice Problems: **PQ-13** and **PQ-14**

SQ-8. Which species in the equilibrium is the strongest acid?

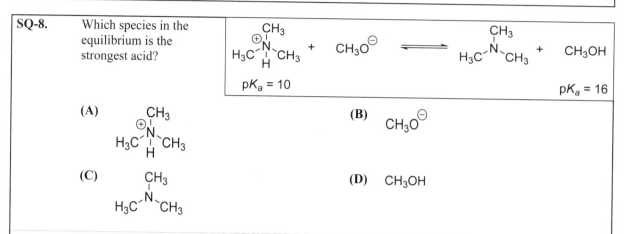

(**A**)

(**B**) $CH_3O^{\ominus}$

(**C**)

(**D**) CH_3OH

Knowledge Required: (1) Brønsted-Lowry acid/base theory. (2) Proton transfer based on pK_a. (3) Understanding of pK_a values.

Thinking it Through: You recall that the Brønsted-Lowry definition of acids and bases correspond to whether the species are proton (i.e., hydrogen cation) donors (acids) or acceptors (bases). Proton transfer reactions take place when a Brønsted-Lowry base uses a lone pair of electrons to make a new bond with a proton, creating the conjugate acid of the base. Electrons in the bond between the acidic proton and the heteroatom, are left behind on the heteroatom, such that the original acid is converted into its conjugate base.

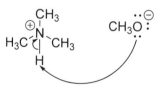

You also know that pK_a is used to indicate the strength of acids where smaller pK_a values correspond to stronger acids. Finally, you recall that equilibria prefer stability, and thus an equilibrium will always favor the side of the more stable acid and base pair, which corresponds to the weaker acid and base pair.

Choice (**A**) is correct because the species has the lowest pK_a.

Choices (**B**) and (**C**) are not correct because they are Brønsted-Lowry bases.

Choice (**D**) is not correct because the species does not have the lowest pK_a.

Practice Problems: **PQ-15** and **PQ16**

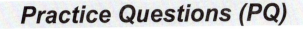
Practice Questions (PQ)

PQ-1. Which reagent is organometallic?

(A) H₃C–O–CH₃   **(B)** 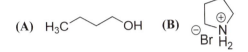   **(C)** $H_3C\!\!\equiv\!\!^{\ominus}$ $^{\oplus}Na$ **(D)** $KMnO_4$

PQ-2. Which compound is NOT ionic?

(A) H₃C⌒⌒OH   **(B)**    **(C)** H₃C⌒⌒O⁻ ⁺Li   **(D)** K_2CrO_7

PQ-3. What is the molecular formula of the structure?

   (A) C_5H_3BrNO **(B)** $C_6H_{10}NOBr$ **(C)** C_5H_3NOBr **(D)** $C_6H_{10}BrNO$

PQ-4. What is the molar mass of the structure in g/mol?

$$H_3C\!\!\equiv\!\!N$$

   (A) 28   **(B)** 29   **(C)** 40   **(D)** 41

PQ-5. What needs to be added to balance the chemical equation?

  (A) methylthiolate (CH_3S^-), to the reactant side   **(B)** chloride (Cl^-), to the product side

  (C) chloride (Cl^-), to the reactant side   **(D)** methylthiolate (CH_3S^-), to the product side

PQ-6. What needs to be added to balance the chemical equation?

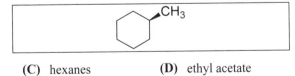

  (A) water, to the reactant side   **(B)** water, to the product side

  (C) chloride, to the reactant side   **(D)** chloride, to the product side

PQ-7. Which solvent is LEAST likely to dissolve the compound?

  (A) water   **(B)** acetone   **(C)** hexanes   **(D)** ethyl acetate

PQ-8. Which structure would engage in strong dipole-dipole interactions and not stronger intermolecular forces?

PQ-9. This reaction is termed a reduction because

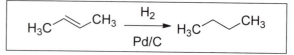

    (A) the oxidation number of two carbon atoms decreases.

    (B) the number of hydrogens decreases.

    (C) a transition metal catalyst is used.

    (D) the number of double bonds decreases.

PQ-10. This reaction is termed an oxidation because

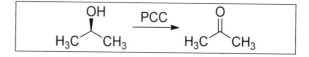

    (A) the number of hydrogens increases.

    (B) the oxidation number of the central carbon atom increases.

    (C) PCC reagent is used.

    (D) the number of double bonds increases.

PQ-11. Which bond has the highest dissociation energy?

    (A) C–C   **(B)** C=C   **(C)** C≡C   **(D)** C–H

PQ-12. Which compound has the most negative $\Delta H_f°$?

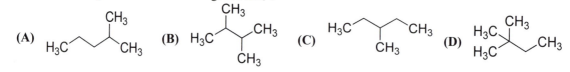

PQ-13. Which species has an INCORRECT formal change on the oxygen atom?

    (A)   **(B)**   **(C)**   **(D)**

PQ-14. Which is the most polar bond?

    (A) C–H   **(B)** C–Cl   **(C)** C–B   **(D)** C–I

PQ-15. Which statement best describes why the acid/base equilibrium lies to the left?

$$H-\!\!\!\equiv\!\!\!-H \;+\; CH_3S^{\ominus} \;\rightleftharpoons\; H-\!\!\!\equiv\!\!\ominus \;+\; CH_3SH$$

$pK_a = 25$ $pK_a = 10$

    (A) The stronger acid is on the left.   **(B)** The weaker acid is on the right.

    (C) The weaker acid is on the left.   **(D)** The weaker base is on the right.

PQ-16. How many curved arrows are needed to describe the mechanism?

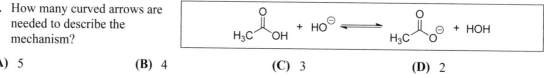

    (A) 5   **(B)** 4   **(C)** 3   **(D)** 2

Answers to Study Questions

SQ-1.	C	SQ-4.	D	SQ-7.	C
SQ-2.	A	SQ-5.	B	SQ-8.	A
SQ-3.	B	SQ-6.	C		

Answers to Practice Questions

PQ-1.	C	PQ-7.	A	PQ-13.	A
PQ-2.	A	PQ-8.	D	PQ-14.	B
PQ-3.	B	PQ-9.	A	PQ-15.	C
PQ-4.	D	PQ-10.	B	PQ-16.	D
PQ-5.	A	PQ-11.	C		
PQ-6.	B	PQ-12.	D		

How to use this book

You have an ACS exam coming up and might be feeling a bit overwhelmed by it. You might be worried that the exam will be very different from the ones you are used to and will be on material you haven't covered. The first thing to do is to R-E-L-A-X. The ACS exam you are going to take was written by chemistry faculty from around the country who all teach organic chemistry courses. The truth is that most organic chemistry courses, like most organic chemistry textbooks, are very similar. There is a set of common topics that almost every course covers. What makes courses different are the level of detail of coverage of the topics. Some instructors have favorite topics that they cover in depth and some that they only briefly cover due to time. The good news is that the exam you are going to take was written to be applicable to this wide variety of topic coverage and depth of topic coverage. The committees that write these exams do not look for the most minute details; instead the topics covered are the foundational ones that are common to most courses, and you should recognize them. Due to the variations in courses, described above, you might see a few questions about topics that are not as familiar to you. That is fine, relax!

As you use this study guide, and study chemistry in general, you should focus on the underlying concepts present in a question. Remember that there are many ways to ask a question about predicting the products of reactions. If you focus on identifying the underlying concept/topic being asked about in the question, you will be able to handle any "surface" differences in the way the question is asked. After you complete a problem, and before you go onto the next question, take a minute to think about other ways the problem could have been asked. For example, what if you had been given the information in the answer and had been asked for some information that was given to you in the original question? When you stop and think like this, you have moved beyond working problems to actual studying.

The chapters in this study guide are arranged in the same order as many common chemistry textbooks. Topics typically covered in the first semester are in chapters (1–10) and typical second semester topics are in chapters (11–16). Each chapter begins with a brief summary and a list of topics covered. This list of topics should correspond to the topics covered in your course. Following this you will be told where the material might be found in your chemistry textbook. There is not much variation in chapter titles between books, so you should be able to find the relevant material no matter what book you have. This is an important point; this study guide is not intended to be a replacement for your textbook. It is a supplement specifically designed to assist you to prepare for the ACS exam. The introductory material ends with a mention of online practice exam problems and how the material in the chapter fits into the bigger picture of chemistry concepts.

Following this introductory material, you will find worked Study Questions. The best way to use these would be to cover up the detailed solution and try to answer the question/work the problem. Only after you have tried the question should you move to the discussion of the solution. The worked-out solution is written to model the thinking that could be used to answer the question correctly. Sometimes, this involves solving the problem without looking at the multiple-choice options (i.e., numerical problems), other times this involves an analysis of each choice (i.e., selecting a correct statement). At the end of each study question, you will find an explanation of why each incorrect choice is wrong and which practice problems at the end of the chapter correspond to the study question. There are as many as 30 practice problems at the end of each chapter.

Remember that this study guide was written to give you practice with ACS exam-type questions as you review the chemistry content. As you review, you are likely to find topics that you need to go back to your textbook and notes to review and you will find some topics that you have a very good grasp of. Don't let the thought of a BIG ACS exam scare you; if you have been working throughout the course and put in some quality study time, you will be fine!

Sample Instructions

You will find that the front cover of an ACS Exam will have a set of instructions very similar to this. This initial set of instructions is meant for both the faculty member who administers the exam and the student taking the exam. You will be well advised to read the entire set of instructions while waiting for the exam to begin.

TO THE EXAMINER:
This test is designed to be taken with a special answer sheet on which the student records his or her responses. All answers are to be marked on this answer sheet, not in the test booklet. Each student should be provided with a test booklet, one answer sheet, and scratch paper; all of which must be turned in at the end of the examination period. The test is to be available to the students only during the examination period. You must collect and account for all exam booklets at the end of the examination. For complete instructions refer to the Directions for Administering Examinations. Only nonprogrammable calculators are permitted. ***All electronic devices with photo-taking capability are prohibited.*** Norms are based on:

Score = Number of right answers
70 items - 110 minutes

TO THE STUDENT:
DO NOT WRITE ANYTHING IN THIS BOOKLET! Do not turn this page until your instructor gives the signal to begin. A periodic table and other useful information is on page 2. When you are told to begin work, open the booklet and read the directions on page 3.

Be sure to notice that scoring is based **only** on the number of right answers. There is no penalty for making a reasonable guess even if you are not completely sure of the correct answer. Often you will be able to narrow the choice to two possibilities, improving your odds at success. You will need to keep moving throughout the examination period; it is to your advantage to attempt every question. Do not assume that the questions become harder as you progress through an ACS Exam. Questions are generally grouped by topic rather than difficulty.

Note for the exam in the example, the data sheet and periodic table are in the exam. For other exams it could be on a separate datasheet or occasionally be on the last page of the exam.

Next, here is a sample of the directions you will find at the beginning of an ACS exam.

DIRECTIONS

- When you have selected your answer, blacken the corresponding space on the answer sheet with a soft, black #2 pencil. Make a heavy, full mark, but no stray marks. If you decide to change an answer, erase the unwanted mark very carefully.
- Make no marks in the test booklet. Do all calculations on scratch paper provided by your instructor.
- There is only one correct answer to each question. Any questions for which more than one response has been blackened **will not be counted**.
- Your score is based solely on the number of questions you answer correctly. **It is to your advantage to answer every question.**

Pay close attention to the mechanical aspects of these directions. Marking your answers without erasures helps to create a very clean answer sheet that can be read without error. As you look at your answer sheet before the end of the exam period, be sure that you check that every question has been attempted, and that only one choice has been made per question. As was the case with the cover instructions, note that your attention is again directed to the fact that the score is based on the total number of questions that you answer correctly. You also can expect a reasonable distribution of **A**, **B**, **C**, and **D** responses, something that is not necessarily true for the distribution of questions in *The Official Guide*.

A C S
Exams

PERIODIC TABLE OF THE ELEMENTS

1																	18
1 H 1.008	2											13	14	15	16	17	2 He 4.003
3 Li 6.941	4 Be 9.012											5 B 10.81	6 C 12.01	7 N 14.01	8 O 16.00	9 F 19.00	10 Ne 20.18
11 Na 22.99	12 Mg 24.31	3	4	5	6	7	8	9	10	11	12	13 Al 26.98	14 Si 28.09	15 P 30.97	16 S 32.07	17 Cl 35.45	18 Ar 39.95
19 K 39.10	20 Ca 40.08	21 Sc 44.96	22 Ti 47.88	23 V 50.94	24 Cr 52.00	25 Mn 54.94	26 Fe 55.85	27 Co 58.93	28 Ni 58.69	29 Cu 63.55	30 Zn 65.39	31 Ga 69.72	32 Ge 72.61	33 As 74.92	34 Se 78.96	35 Br 79.90	36 Kr 83.80
37 Rb 85.47	38 Sr 87.62	39 Y 88.91	40 Zr 91.22	41 Nb 92.91	42 Mo 95.94	43 Tc	44 Ru 101.1	45 Rh 102.9	46 Pd 106.4	47 Ag 107.9	48 Cd 112.4	49 In 114.8	50 Sn 118.7	51 Sb 121.8	52 Te 127.6	53 I 126.9	54 Xe 131.3
55 Cs 132.9	56 Ba 137.3	57 La 138.9	72 Hf 178.5	73 Ta 180.9	74 W 183.8	75 Re 186.2	76 Os 190.2	77 Ir 192.2	78 Pt 195.1	79 Au 197.0	80 Hg 200.6	81 Tl 204.4	82 Pb 207.2	83 Bi 209.0	84 Po	85 At	86 Rn
87 Fr	88 Ra	89 Ac	104 Rf	105 Db	106 Sg	107 Bh	108 Hs	109 Mt	110 Ds	111 Rg	112 Cn	113 Nh	114 Fl	115 Mc	116 Lv	117 Ts	118 Og

58 Ce 140.1	59 Pr 140.9	60 Nd 144.2	61 Pm	62 Sm 150.4	63 Eu 152.0	64 Gd 157.3	65 Tb 158.9	66 Dy 162.5	67 Ho 164.9	68 Er 167.3	69 Tm 168.9	70 Yb 173.0	71 Lu 175.0
90 Th 232.0	91 Pa 231.0	92 U 238.0	93 Np	94 Pu	95 Am	96 Cm	97 Bk	98 Cf	99 Es	100 Fm	101 Md	102 No	103 Lr

Please note that the periodic table changes to keep current with recent discoveries.
The periodic table you use may vary from the table shown here.

Big Ideas

Big Ideas – ACS Exams Anchoring Concepts Content Map (ACCM)

Studies of past ACS Exams have shown that while individual tests vary somewhat in their content, overall the coverage of big ideas in chemistry is fairly broad when looked at with the lens of the ACCM. What is listed below are anchoring concepts or "big ideas" (in **bold**). These are followed by statements which provide more detail on how these big ideas are explained or included in the undergraduate curriculum. These are included in this guide as these big ideas apply to all levels of chemistry in the undergraduate program, and it can be useful to see how the specific chapter or content area you are studying fits into the bigger picture of your undergraduate program. Towards that end, at the beginning of each chapter in this guide, you are provided with the specific big idea covered in that chapter.

I. **Atoms**
    A. Atoms have unique chemical identities based on the number of protons in the nucleus.
    B. Electrons play the key role for atoms to bond with other atoms.
    C. Atoms display a periodicity in their structures and observable phenomena that depend on that structure.
    D. Most information about atoms is inferred from studies on collections of atoms often involving an interaction with electromagnetic radiation.
    E. Macroscopic samples of matter contain so many atoms that they are counted in moles.
    F. Atoms maintain their identity, except in nuclear reactions.
    G. Ions arise when the number of electrons and protons are not equal, and can be formed from atoms.

II. **Bonding**
    A. Because protons and electrons are charged, physical models of bonding are based on electrostatic forces.
    B. Because chemical bonds arise from sharing of negatively charged valence electrons between positively charged nuclei, the overall electrostatic interaction is attractive.
    C. When chemical bonds form, the overall energy of the bonding atoms is lowered relative to free atoms, and therefore energy is released.
    D. To break a chemical bond requires an input of energy.
    E. A theoretical construct that describes chemical bonding utilizes the construction of molecular orbitals for the bond based on overlap of atomic orbitals on the constituent atoms.
    F. Covalent bonds can be categorized based on the number of electrons (pairs) shared. The most common categories are single, double, and triple bonds.
    G. Metallic bonding arises in many solids and fundamentally involves the sharing of valence electrons among many positively charged "cores" over extended distances.

III. **Structure and Function**
    A. Atoms combine to form new compounds that have new properties based on structural and electronic features.
    B. Models exist that allow the prediction of the shape of chemicals about any bonding atom in a molecule.
    C. Theoretical models are capable of providing detail structure for whole molecules based on energy minimization methods.
    D. Symmetry, based on geometry, plays an important role in how atoms interact within molecules and how molecules are observed in many experiments.
    E. Three-dimensional structures may give rise to chirality, which can play an important role in observed chemical and physical properties.
    F. Reactions of molecules can often be understood in terms of subsets of atoms, called functional groups.
    G. Periodic trends among elements can be used to organize the understanding of structure and function for related chemical compounds.
    H. Many solid state, extended systems exist, and geometric structures play an important role in understanding the properties of these systems.

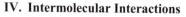
IV. Intermolecular Interactions

A. Intermolecular forces are generally weaker, on an individual basis, than chemical bonds, but the presence of many such interactions may lead to overall strong interactions.

B. For large molecules, intermolecular forces may occur between different regions of the molecule. In these cases, they are sometimes termed noncovalent forces.

C. Intermolecular forces can be categorized based on the permanence and structural details of the dipoles involved.

D. For condensed phases that are not structures of extended chemical bonds, the physical properties of the state are strongly influenced by the nature of the intermolecular forces.

E. The energy consequences of chemical reactions that take place in condensed phases (solution) usually must include intermolecular forces to be correctly/completely explained.

V. Chemical Reactions

A. In chemical changes, matter is conserved and this is the basis behind the ability to represent chemical change via a balanced chemical equation.

B. Chemical change involves the breaking or forming of chemical bonds, or typically both.

C. Chemical change can be observed at both the particulate and macroscopic levels, and models exist that allow the translation between these two levels of observation.

D. There are a large number of possible chemical reactions, and categories have been devised to organize understanding of these reaction types.

E. Many chemical properties of elements follow periodic trends that can be used to strategically design reactions to achieve desired outcomes.

F. Chemical change can be controlled by choices of reactants, reaction conditions, or use of catalysts.

G. Controlling chemical reactions is a key requirement in the synthesis of new materials.

VI. Energy and Thermodynamics

A. Most chemical changes are accompanied by a net change of energy of the system.

B. Many chemical reactions require an energy input to be initiated.

C. The type of energy associated with chemical change may be heat, light, or electrical energy.

D. Breaking chemical bonds requires energy; formation of chemical bonds releases energy.

E. The forces that are associated with energy change in chemical processes are electrostatic forces.

F. In accord with thermodynamics, energy is conserved in chemical changes, but the change of form in which the energy is present may be harnessed via natural or human-made devices.

G. Thermodynamics provides a detailed capacity to understand energy change at the macroscopic level.

H. The tendency of nature to disperse, particularly in terms of energy distribution, is embodied in the state function called entropy.

I. Energy changes associated with nuclear chemistry are many orders of magnitude larger than those of classical chemical changes.

VII. Kinetics

A. Chemical change can be measured as a function of time and occurs over a wide range of time scales.

B. Empirically derived rate laws summarize the dependence of reaction rates on concentrations of reactants and temperature.

C. Most chemical reactions take place by a series of more elementary reactions, called the reaction mechanism.

D. An elementary reaction requires that the reactants collide (interact) and have both enough energy and appropriate orientation of colliding particles for the reaction to occur.

E. Catalysis increases the rate of reaction and has important applications in a number of subdisciplines of chemistry.

F. Reaction products can be influenced by controlling whether reaction rate or reaction energy plays the key role in the mechanism.

VIII. Equilibrium

A. Both physical and chemical changes may occur in either direction (e.g., from reactants to products or products to reactants).

B. When opposing processes both occur at the same rate the net change is zero.

C. For chemical reactions, the equilibrium state can be characterized via the equilibrium constant.
D. When the equilibrium constant is very large or small, products or reactants, respectively, are primarily present at equilibrium. Systems with K near 1 have significant amounts of both reactants and products present.
E. If perturbed, a system at equilibrium will respond in the direction that tends to offset the perturbation.
F. Thermodynamics provides mathematical tools to understand equilibrium systems quantitatively.
G. Equilibrium concepts have important applications in several subdisciplines of chemistry.

IX. Experiments, Measurement, and Data
A. Quantitative observation of matter can be made at a wide range of distance scales and/or time scales.
B. Because there are a large number of compounds, a system of naming these compounds is used.
C. Experimental control of reactions plays a key role in the synthesis of new materials and analysis of composition.
D. Chemical measurements are based on mass, charge, or interaction with electrons or photons.
E. Observations are verifiable, so experimental conditions, including considerations of the representativeness of samples, must be considered for experiments.
F. Fidelity of inferences made from data requires appropriate experimental design.
G. Chemistry experiments have risks associated with them, so chemical safety is a key consideration in the design of any experiment.

X. Visualization
A. Many theoretical constructs are constructed at the particulate level, while many empirical observations are made at the macroscopic level.
B. The mole represents the key factor for translating between the macroscopic and particulate levels.
C. Macroscopic properties result from large numbers of particles, so statistical methods provide a useful model for understanding the connections between these levels.
D. Quantitative reasoning within chemistry is often visualized and interpreted graphically.

A C S
Exams

Chapter 1 – Structure: Shape and Stability

Chapter Summary:
        This chapter will focus on the structure and shape of organic molecules. This includes common representations such as the bond-line formula for molecular structure and representations used for orbitals, hybridization, and VSEPR shapes. This chapter also covers dipole moments, the effects of resonance on stability, and introduces carbocations and radicals.

        Specific topics covered in this chapter are:
- Bond-line formula
- Molecular orbital theory
- Orbitals and hybridization
- VSEPR theory and molecular structure
- Dipole moment
- Resonance
- Carbocation and radical stability

        Previous material that is relevant to your understanding of questions in this chapter include:
- Electronegativity and polar bonds *(Toolbox)*
- Lewis structures *(Toolbox)*
- Valence electrons *(Toolbox)*

Where to find this in your textbook:
        The material in this chapter typically aligns to "Introduction to Organic Chemistry" or "Bonding and Molecular Structure" in your textbook. The name of your chapter may vary.

Practice exam:
        There may be practice exam questions aligned to the material in this chapter. Because there are a limited number of questions on the practice exam, a review of the breadth of the material in this chapter is advised in preparation for your exam.

How this fits to the big picture:
        The material in this chapter aligns to the Big Ideas of Bonding (I) and Structure and Function (III) as listed on page 13 of this study guide.

Study Questions (SQ)

SQ-1.   What is the bond-line formula for $(CH_3)_3C(CH_2)_5CH_2Br$?

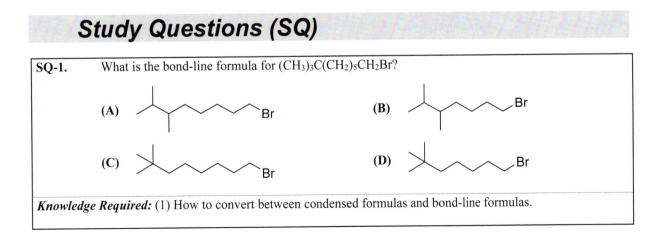

Knowledge Required: (1) How to convert between condensed formulas and bond-line formulas.

Thinking it Through: First, you notice that the condensed formula shows parentheses around CH_3 followed by a subscript of 3. You remember that this means that there are three $-CH_3$ groups attached to the next atom, in this case a carbon, and thus making a *t*-butyl group. This eliminates choices **(A)** and **(B)** as possible correct answers as the terminal group of these molecules are isopropyl groups ($-CH(CH_3)_2$). Next, you notice that there are parentheses around CH_2 indicating that there are five consecutive $-CH_2-$ groups in the molecule. Finally, you notice that after the five $-CH_2-$ groups there is a CH_2 group with a bromine atom attached. This means that after the *t*-butyl group, there are six more carbons plus the bromine atom. You can eliminate choice **(D)** because it only has five carbons after the *t*-butyl group on the left.

   Choice **(C)** is correct.

   Choices **(A)** and **(B)** are not correct because they do not contain a *t*-butyl group at the left terminus. Choice **(D)** is not correct because the chain contains the wrong number of carbons.

Practice Problems: **PQ-1, PQ-2, PQ-3,** and **PQ-4**

SQ-2. How many hydrogen atoms are bonded to the indicated carbons in this bond-line formula?

  (A) Carbon-**I** has 0 hydrogen atoms; carbon-**II** has 1 hydrogen atom.

  (B) Carbon-**I** has 0 hydrogen atoms; carbon-**II** has 2 hydrogen atoms.

  (C) Carbon-**I** has 1 hydrogen atom; carbon-**II** has 1 hydrogen atom.

  (D) Carbon-**I** has 1 hydrogen atom; carbon-**II** has 2 hydrogen atoms.

Knowledge Required: (1) Hydrogen atoms implicitly shown in bond-line formulas.

Thinking it Through: You recall that with bond-line formulas, hydrogen atoms bonded to carbon atoms are not explicitly shown. You also remember that an uncharged carbon atom typically has four bonds. Examining the given molecule, you note that carbon-**I** has two bonds to other carbons in the ring and a bond to an $-OH$ substituent. Because it is uncharged, carbon-**I** must have one additional bond to a hydrogen atom. Carbon-**II** has a bond to the cyclohexane and a bond to an isopropyl group. Because it is uncharged, carbon-**II** must have two additional bonds to hydrogen atoms.

   Choice **(D)** is the correct answer.

   Choice **(A)** is not correct because it has the incorrect number of hydrogen atoms on both indicated atoms. Choice **(B)** is not correct because it has the incorrect number of hydrogen atoms on carbon-**I**. Choice **(C)** is not correct because it has the incorrect number of hydrogen atoms on carbon-**II**.

Practice Problems: **PQ-5**

SQ-3. Which structure is the same as this molecule?

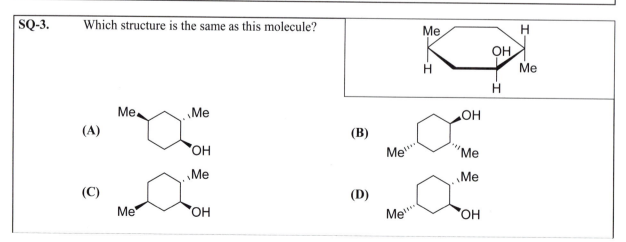

Knowledge Required: (1) How to convert between Haworth projections and bond-line formulas.

Thinking it Through: To solve this problem, first, you note the arrangement of the substituents on the cyclic structure given. You notice that if the carbon with the alcohol is listed as number 1, then moving around the ring counterclockwise, the methyl groups are on carbon-**2** and carbon-**5**.

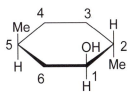

   Choices (**A**) and (**B**) can be eliminated as possible answers because one of the methyl groups has been moved to carbon-**4**.
   When you examine choices (**C**) and (**D**), you remember that the filled wedge means "up" from the page and the dashed wedge means "down" from the page. In the original structure, the alcohol and the methyl on carbon-**5** are both pointing "up;" the methyl on carbon-**2** is pointing "down." Choice (**D**) is not correct because it shows both of the methyl groups oriented in the same direction "down" on dashed wedges.
   Choice (**C**) is correct because it shows the correct orientation and substitution pattern for the substituents on the ring.
   Choices (**A**) and (**B**) are not correct because they show the wrong substitution pattern for the substituents. Choice (**D**) is not correct because it has the wrong orientation for its substituents.

Practice Problems: **PQ-6** and **PQ-7**

SQ-4. Which MO diagram correctly illustrates the placement of six π electrons for benzene in the ground state electron configuration?

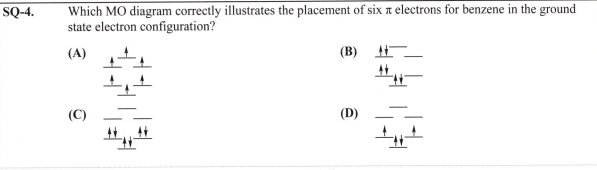

Knowledge Required: (1) How to construct molecular orbital diagrams.

Thinking it Through: To solve this question, you recall the rules for filling orbitals. First, the Aufbau rule: start by filling the lowest energy orbital. All of the options have electrons in the lowest energy orbital; however, choice (**A**) is eliminated because the lowest energy orbital is not filled.
   Second, the Pauli Exclusion Principle: no orbital may hold more than two electrons and they must be of opposite spin.
   The third rule, Hund's rule states that when filling degenerate orbitals (i.e. orbitals of the same energy), each orbital receives one electron, then, the degenerate orbitals receive a second electron of opposite spin. Following this rule, you eliminate choice (**B**), since one of the bonding molecular orbitals has no electrons.
   Choice (**C**) is correct because the electrons are paired and in the lowest energy orbitals.
   Choice (**A**) is not correct because the electrons are not paired and in the lowest energy orbitals. Choice (**B**) is not correct because the electrons are not in the lowest energy orbitals. Choice (**D**) is not correct because there is an insufficient number of electrons in the orbitals.

Practice Problems: **PQ-8, PQ-9,** and **PQ-10**

SQ-5. Which diagram depicts the orbital diagram for the valence electrons for a nitrogen atom after hybridization to the sp^3-hybridized state?

(A)   (B)

(C)   (D)

Knowledge Required: (1) How to construct molecular orbital diagrams.

Thinking it Through: To solve this problem, you first remember that an uncharged nitrogen atom has five valence electrons. All of the energy diagrams contain five electrons.

Next you recognize that the question asks for the hybridized energy diagram, which means that an s orbital and three p orbitals have combined to make four sp^3 orbitals, which are degenerate. Choices (C) and (D) both depict four degenerate orbitals.

Next you remember the rules for filling orbitals with electrons. Hund's rule indicates that for degenerate orbitals, each orbital receives a single electron before the electrons are paired up. You eliminate choice (D) because two orbitals contain pairs of electrons while another degenerate orbital is empty.

Choice (C) is correct because there are four degenerate orbitals and are filled following Hund's rule.

Choices (A) and (B) are not correct because the energy diagrams do not depict four degenerate hybridized orbitals. Choice (D) is not correct because the degenerate orbitals are not filled following Hund's rule.

Practice Problems: **PQ-8, PQ-9,** and **PQ-10**

SQ-6. What are the hybridization states of the indicated atoms?

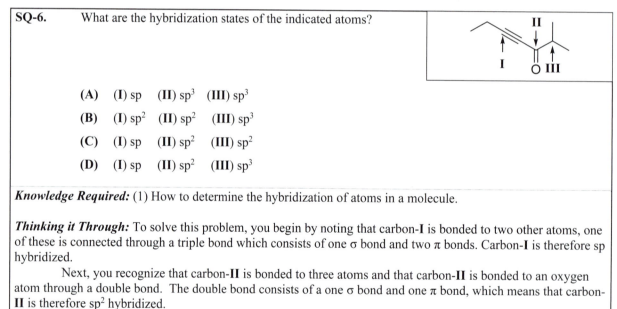

(A)   (I) sp   (II) sp^3 (III) sp^3

(B)   (I) sp^2 (II) sp^2 (III) sp^3

(C)   (I) sp   (II) sp^2 (III) sp^2

(D)   (I) sp   (II) sp^2 (III) sp^3

Knowledge Required: (1) How to determine the hybridization of atoms in a molecule.

Thinking it Through: To solve this problem, you begin by noting that carbon-**I** is bonded to two other atoms, one of these is connected through a triple bond which consists of one σ bond and two π bonds. Carbon-**I** is therefore sp hybridized.

Next, you recognize that carbon-**II** is bonded to three atoms and that carbon-**II** is bonded to an oxygen atom through a double bond. The double bond consists of a one σ bond and one π bond, which means that carbon-**II** is therefore sp^2 hybridized.

Finally, you note that carbon-**III** is bonded to four atoms, three carbons and one hydrogen. Carbon-**III** is therefore sp^3 hybridized.

Choice (D) is correct.

Choice (A) is not correct because it incorrectly lists carbon-**II** as sp^3 hybridized. Choice (B) is not correct because it incorrectly lists carbon-**I** as sp^2 hybridized. Choice (C) is not correct because it incorrectly lists carbon-**III** as sp^2 hybridized.

Practice Problems: **PQ-11, PQ-12, PQ-13, PQ-14, PQ-15,** and **PQ-16**

SQ-7.   What are the VSEPR shapes (molecular geometries) associated with atoms **I**, **II**, and **III**, respectively?

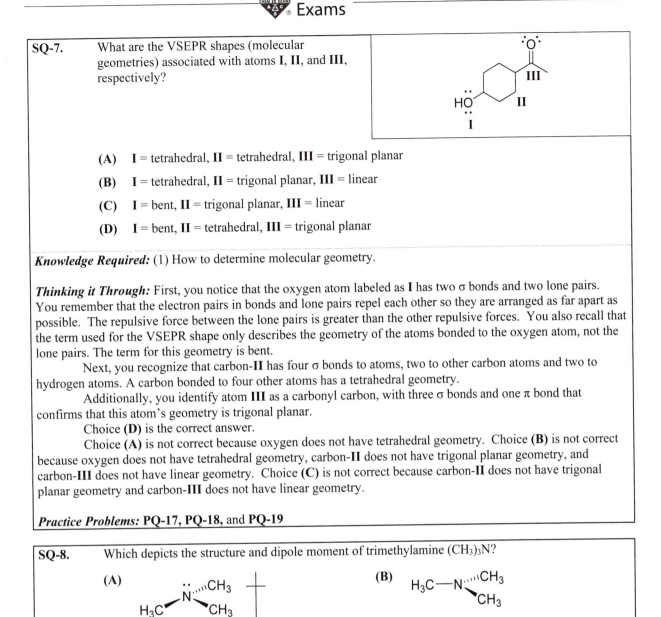

(A)   **I** = tetrahedral, **II** = tetrahedral, **III** = trigonal planar

(B)   **I** = tetrahedral, **II** = trigonal planar, **III** = linear

(C)   **I** = bent, **II** = trigonal planar, **III** = linear

(D)   **I** = bent, **II** = tetrahedral, **III** = trigonal planar

Knowledge Required: (1) How to determine molecular geometry.

Thinking it Through: First, you notice that the oxygen atom labeled as **I** has two σ bonds and two lone pairs. You remember that the electron pairs in bonds and lone pairs repel each other so they are arranged as far apart as possible. The repulsive force between the lone pairs is greater than the other repulsive forces. You also recall that the term used for the VSEPR shape only describes the geometry of the atoms bonded to the oxygen atom, not the lone pairs. The term for this geometry is bent.

Next, you recognize that carbon-**II** has four σ bonds to atoms, two to other carbon atoms and two to hydrogen atoms. A carbon bonded to four other atoms has a tetrahedral geometry.

Additionally, you identify atom **III** as a carbonyl carbon, with three σ bonds and one π bond that confirms that this atom's geometry is trigonal planar.

Choice (**D**) is the correct answer.

Choice (**A**) is not correct because oxygen does not have tetrahedral geometry. Choice (**B**) is not correct because oxygen does not have tetrahedral geometry, carbon-**II** does not have trigonal planar geometry, and carbon-**III** does not have linear geometry. Choice (**C**) is not correct because carbon-**II** does not have trigonal planar geometry and carbon-**III** does not have linear geometry.

Practice Problems: **PQ-17**, **PQ-18**, and **PQ-19**

SQ-8.   Which depicts the structure and dipole moment of trimethylamine $(CH_3)_3N$?

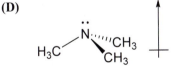

(B)   No net dipole moment.

Knowledge Required: (1) How to determine molecular geometry. (2) How to determine polar bonds and molecular dipole moments.

Thinking it Through: In solving this problem, you recall that uncharged nitrogen atoms make three bonds and have one lone pair of electrons.

Next, you remember that to determine dipole moment, the molecule should be drawn in its correct VSEPR shape. Given its hybridization state, sp^3, and its three bonds, for the molecule $(CH_3)_3N$, the correct structure is trigonal pyramidal.

You also remember that the net dipole moment of a molecule is a vector quantity built from the addition or cancellation of the bond dipoles in a molecule. In this molecule all of the C–N bonds are polar with the δ^- end of the dipole vector pointing toward the nitrogen atom. The addition of these three vectors create a dipole moment through the N-atom with the δ^- end pointing away from the methyl groups as shown in Choice (D).

Choice (D) is correct because it depicts the correct number of lone pairs, the correct VSEPR geometry, and the correct dipole moment.

Choice (A) is not correct because it depicts an incorrect VSEPR structure and the wrong dipole moment. Choice (B) is not correct because the nitrogen atom needs a lone pair and does not have a trigonal planar geometry; in addition, the correct molecule has a dipole moment. Choice (C) is not correct because the nitrogen atom should only have one lone pair.

Practice Problems: **PQ-20, PQ-21,** and **PQ-22**

SQ-9. Which structure is NOT a resonance structure of this molecule?

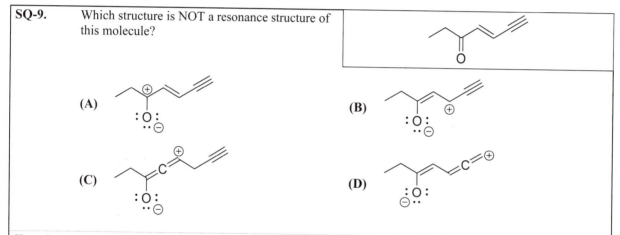

(A)

(B)

(C)

(D)

Knowledge Required: (1) How to construct resonance structures.

Thinking it Through: To solve this problem, you recall that the primary rule for drawing resonance structures is that electrons move, not atoms. You begin by recognizing the important resonance structure of a carbonyl, depicted in Choice (A), which shows the negative charge on the oxygen and the positive charge on the carbonyl carbon. Once you draw this structure, you can move π electrons toward the positive charge.

In this resonance system, we see choices (A), (B), and (D). Choice (C), therefore is NOT a resonance structure of the original molecule

Choice (C) is correct because this structure is NOT a resonance structure of the original molecule. Additionally, in order to transform from the molecule given in the prompt to the molecule in choice (C), a hydrogen atom would need to move and thus violate the primary rule for drawing resonance structures.

Choices (A), (B), and (D) are not correct because they are all resonance structures of the original molecule.

Practice Problems: **PQ-23, PQ-24,** and **PQ-25**

SQ-10. Which resonance structure contributes the most to the overall structure of the molecule?

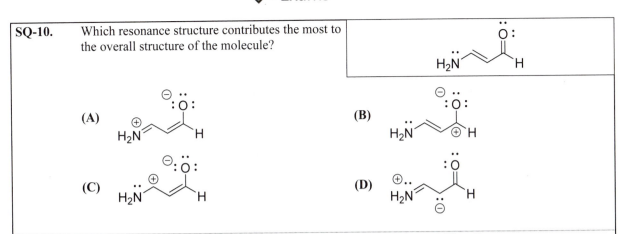

(A)

(B)

(C)

(D)

Knowledge Required: (1) How to construct resonance structures. (2) Relative stability of resonance structures.

Thinking it Through: To solve this question, you consider the possible resonance contributors. You remember that the key factor in priority of resonance contributors is that all atoms have full octets. You recognize that in choices **(B)** and **(C)**, that the carbocations do not have a full octet. Considering the structures in choices **(A)** and **(D)**, you note that all of the atoms have a full octet. To differentiate between the two, you consider the stability of the negative charge and recognize that the negative charge is more stable on the more electronegative oxygen atom.

Choice **(A)** is correct because all of the atoms in this resonance structure have a full octet and the negative charge is on the oxygen.

Choices **(B)** and **(C)** are not correct because the carbocations do not have a full octet. Choice **(D)** is not correct because the negative charge is on the less electronegative carbon atom.

Practice Problems: **PQ-25** and **PQ-26**

SQ-11. Rank these radicals in order of stability from least stable to most stable.

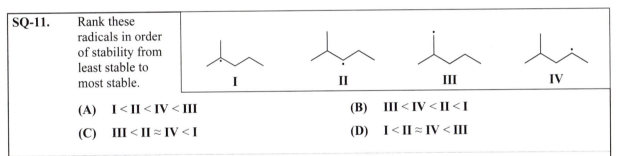

| I | II | III | IV |

(A) I < II < IV < III   **(B)** III < IV < II < I

(C) III < II ≈ IV < I   **(D)** I < II ≈ IV < III

Knowledge Required: (1) Relative stability of radicals.

Thinking it Through: You recall that radicals, like carbocations, are electron deficient. Thus, hyperconjugation, which stabilizes carbocations, also stabilizes radicals. Hyperconjugation is related to the number of alkyl substituents on an atom, making alkyl groups electron donating; therefore, a 3° carbon radical is stabilized by three electron donating groups and is more stable than a 2° or 1° radical. Choices **(B)** and **(C)** list the tertiary radical as most stable.

Next you consider the stability of 2° radical in molecule **II** and the 2° radical in molecule **IV**. There are no other electron-donating groups present to make **II** or **IV** differ in stability. This eliminates choice **(B)**.

Choice **(C)** is then correct.

Choices **(A)** and **(D)** are not correct because they incorrectly rank the 1° radical as most stable. Choice **(B)** is not correct because it does not list the two 2° radicals at the same approximate energy.

Practice Problems: **PQ-27,** and **PQ-28**

SQ-12. Which cation is most stable?

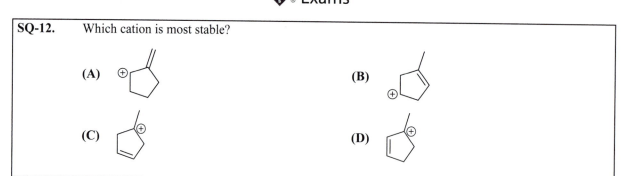

(A)

(B)

(C)

(D)

Knowledge Required: (1) Relative stability of carbocations.

Thinking it Through: To solve this problem, you first notice that the carbocations in Choices **(A)** and **(D)** are stabilized through resonance structures. You recall that resonance increases stability.

On the left, choice **(A)** has two resonance contributors: a 2° allylic carbocation and a 1° allylic carbocation. Choice **(D)** on the right has two resonance contributors: a 3° allylic carbocation and a 2° allylic carbocation. Because of the stability of its contributors (3° and 2°), choice **(D)** is more stable.
     Choice **(D)** is correct.
     Choice **(A)** is not correct because its resonance contributors are not the most stable. Choice **(B)** is not correct because it is a 2° carbocation and is not resonance stabilized. Choice **(C)** is not correct because it is a 3° carbocation and is not resonance stabilized.

Practice Problems: **PQ-29,** and **PQ-30**

Practice Questions (PQ)

PQ-1. What is the equivalent bond-line formula for the molecule, $HOCH_2CH(CH_3)(CH_2)_3CH(CH_3)_2$?

(A)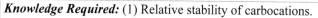

(B) HO

(C) HO

(D) HO

PQ-2. What is the equivalent structure for this molecule using a bond-line formula?

$$CH_2CH_3$$
$$CH_3$$
$$(CH_3)_2CH(CH_2)_3CHBrCHCH_3$$

(A)

(B)

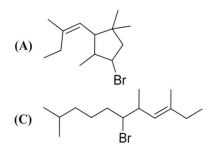
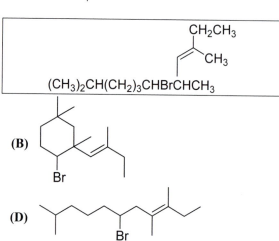

(C) Br

(D) Br

PQ-3. What is the equivalent condensed structural formula for this molecule?

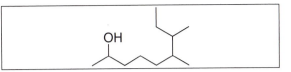

(A) $CH_3C(OH)(CH_2)_3CH_2CH(CH_3)CH_2CH_3$

(B) $CH_3CH(OH)(CH_2)_3CH_2CH(CH_3)CH_2CH_3$

(C) $CH_3CH(OH)(CH_2)_3CH(CH_3)CH(CH_3)CH_2CH_3$

(D) $CH_3CH(OH)(CH_2)_3CH(CH_3)CH(CH_3)CH(CH_3)_2$

PQ-4. What bond-line formula is equivalent to $(CH_3)_3C(CH_2)_4CH_3$

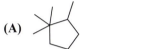 (A)   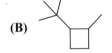 (B)   (C) 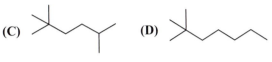 (D)

PQ-5. How many hydrogen atoms are bonded to carbons **I**, **II**, and **III** in this bond-line formula?

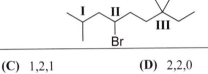

(A) 1,1,0   (B) 1,1,1   (C) 1,2,1   (D) 2,2,0

PQ-6. Which structure is equivalent to this molecule?

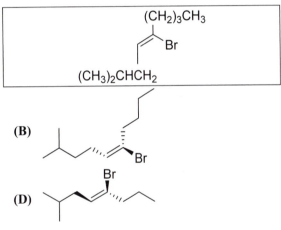

(A)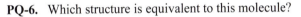

(B)

(C)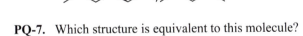

(D)

PQ-7. Which structure is equivalent to this molecule?

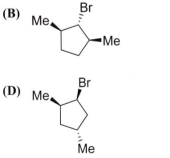

(A)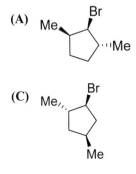

(B)

(C)

(D)

PQ-8. Which diagram depicts the atomic orbital diagram for the valence electrons for a carbon atom after hybridization in methane (CH_4)?

(A) ↑ | ↑ ↑ ↑ ___

(B) ↑ | ↑ ↑ ↑ ↑

(C) ↑ | ↑ ↑ ___ / ↑↓

(D) ↑ | ↑ ___ ___ / ↑↓

PQ-9. Which of these four molecular orbitals filled with four electrons is in a ground state configuration?

(A) ↑ | ↑ / ↑ / ↑ / ↑

(B) ↑ | ___ / ↑ / ↑ / ↑↓

(C) ↑ | ___ / ___ / ↑↓ / ↑↓

(D) ↑ | ___ / ___ / ↑↓ / ↑↓

PQ-10. Which diagram depicts the atomic orbital diagram for the valence electrons of a ground state O-atom before hybridization?

(A) ↑ | ↑↓ ↑ ↑ / ↑↓

(B) ↑ | ↑↓ ↑↓ ↑ / ↑↓

(C) ↑ | ↑↓ ↑↓ ↑↓ ↑

(D) ↑ | ↑↓ ↑↓ ↑ ↑

PQ-11. Identify the hybridization states of the indicated atoms.

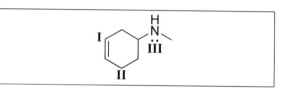

(A) (I) sp; (II) sp^2; (III) sp^3

(B) (I) sp^2; (II) sp^2; (III) sp^2

(C) (I) sp^2; (II) sp^3; (III) sp^2

(D) (I) sp^2; (II) sp^3; (III) sp^3

PQ-12. What are the hybridization states of the indicated atoms?

(A) (I) sp; (II) sp^2; (III) sp

(B) (I) sp^2; (II) sp^2; (III) sp^2

(C) (I) sp^2; (II) sp^2; (III) sp

(D) (I) sp^2; (II) sp^3; (III) sp

PQ-13. What hybrid orbitals are used to form the sigma bond between the indicated carbon atoms (indicated with stars)?

(A) sp^2 and sp

(B) sp^2 and sp^2

(C) sp^2 and sp^3

(D) sp^3 and sp^3

PQ-14. What hybrid orbitals are used to form the sigma bond between carbon-**I** and carbon-**II**, respectively?

(A) sp^3 and sp^2

(B) sp^2 and sp^2

(C) sp^3 and sp

(D) sp^2 and sp

PQ-15. What are the hybridization states of the indicated atoms?

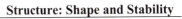

(A) (**I**) sp; (**II**) sp^2; (**III**) sp^2

(B) (**I**) sp^2; (**II**) sp^2; (**III**) sp^2

(C) (**I**) sp^3; (**II**) sp; (**III**) sp^3

(D) (**I**) sp^3; (**II**) sp^2; (**III**) sp^2

PQ-16. The double bond in 2-butene consists of

(A) one π bond.

(B) two π bonds.

(C) two σ bonds.

(D) one σ bond and one π bond.

PQ-17. What are the VSEPR shapes (molecular geometries) associated with the indicated atoms **I**, **II**, and **III**, respectively?

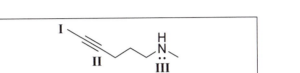

(A) **I** = linear, **II** = linear, **III** = trigonal planar

(B) **I** = linear, **II** = trigonal planar, **III** = tetrahedral

(C) **I** = tetrahedral, **II** = linear, **III** = trigonal pyramidal

(D) **I** = tetrahedral, **II** = linear, **III** = trigonal planar

PQ-18. What is the VSEPR geometry for atoms **I** and **II**, respectively?

(A) tetrahedral and tetrahedral

(B) tetrahedral and trigonal pyramidal

(C) trigonal planar and trigonal planar

(D) trigonal planar and trigonal pyramidal

PQ-19. Which of these molecules have one or more atoms with trigonal planar geometry?

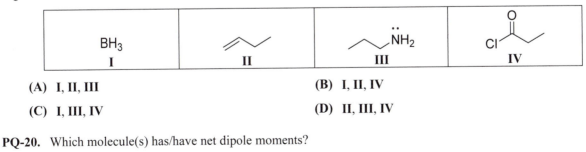

| BH$_3$ | | $\overset{..}{N}H_2$ | O |
| **I** | **II** | **III** | **IV** |

(A) **I, II, III**

(B) **I, II, IV**

(C) **I, III, IV**

(D) **II, III, IV**

PQ-20. Which molecule(s) has/have net dipole moments?

(A) BF$_3$, CH$_3$CH$_2$OH, and CCl$_4$

(B) CH$_3$CH$_2$OH and CCl$_4$

(C) BF$_3$ and CCl$_4$

(D) CH$_3$CH$_2$OH

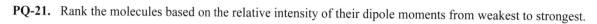

PQ-21. Rank the molecules based on the relative intensity of their dipole moments from weakest to strongest.

(A) $CHCl_3 < CH_2Cl_2 < H_2O < CH_3CH_2OH$

(B) $CHCl_3 < CH_2Cl_2 < CH_3CH_2OH < H_2O$

(C) $CH_2Cl_2 < CHCl_3 < H_2O < CH_3CH_2OH$

(D) $CH_2Cl_2 < CHCl_3 < CH_3CH_2OH < H_2O$

PQ-22. Which figure depicts the structure and net dipole moment for NF_3?

(A)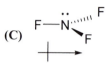

(B)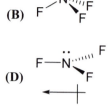

(C)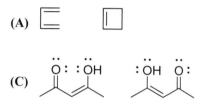

(D)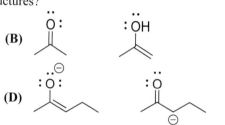

PQ-23. Which structures represent a pair of resonance structures?

(A)

(B)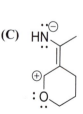

(C)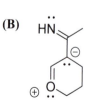

(D)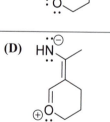

(C continued)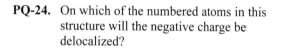

(D continued)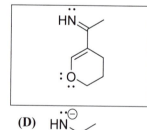

PQ-24. On which of the numbered atoms in this structure will the negative charge be delocalized?

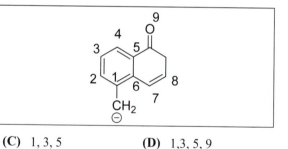

(A) 2, 4, 6

(B) 2, 4, 6, 8

(C) 1, 3, 5

(D) 1, 3, 5, 9

PQ-25. Which is NOT a resonance contributor for this molecule?

(A)

(B)

(C)

(D)

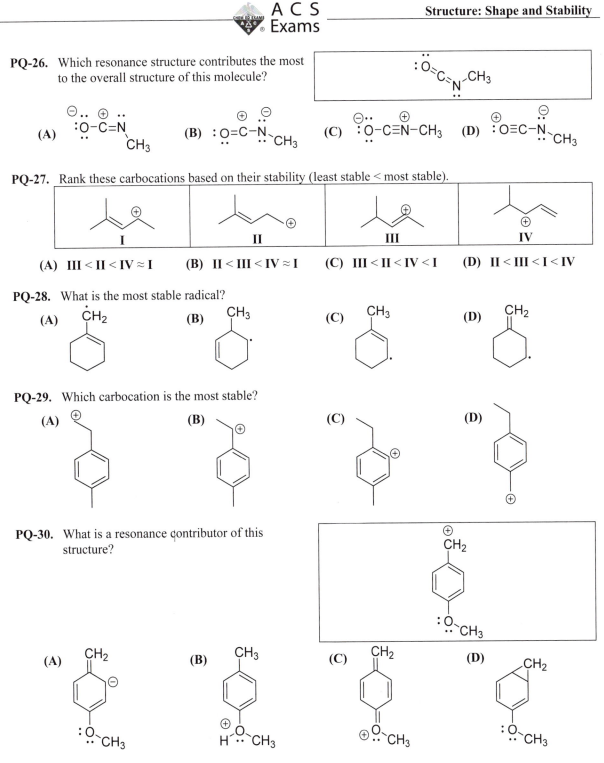

PQ-26. Which resonance structure contributes the most to the overall structure of this molecule?

(A)   (B)   (C)   (D)

PQ-27. Rank these carbocations based on their stability (least stable < most stable).

I   II   III   IV

(A) **III < II < IV ≈ I** (B) **II < III < IV ≈ I** (C) **III < II < IV < I** (D) **II < III < I < IV**

PQ-28. What is the most stable radical?

(A)   (B)   (C)   (D)

PQ-29. Which carbocation is the most stable?

(A)   (B)   (C)   (D)

PQ-30. What is a resonance contributor of this structure?

(A)   (B)   (C)   (D)

Answers to Study Questions

SQ-1.	C	SQ-5.	C	SQ-9.	C
SQ-2.	D	SQ-6.	D	SQ-10.	A
SQ-3.	C	SQ-7.	D	SQ-11.	C
SQ-4.	C	SQ-8.	D	SQ-12.	D

Answers to Practice Questions

PQ-1.	B	PQ-11.	D	PQ-21.	B
PQ-2.	C	PQ-12.	C	PQ-22.	B
PQ-3.	C	PQ-13.	C	PQ-23.	D
PQ-4.	D	PQ-14.	D	PQ-24.	B
PQ-5.	A	PQ-15.	D	PQ-25.	A
PQ-6.	A	PQ-16.	D	PQ-26.	C
PQ-7.	D	PQ-17.	C	PQ-27.	C
PQ-8.	B	PQ-18.	D	PQ-28.	C
PQ-9.	C	PQ-19.	B	PQ-29.	B
PQ-10.	A	PQ-20.	D	PQ-30.	C

Chapter 2 – Structure: Nomenclature and Functional Groups

Chapter Summary:

This chapter will focus on how to name organic structures using fundamental IUPAC rules. Also included in this chapter are questions related to identifying major organic functional groups, how the structure of those functional groups determines intermolecular forces present, and how those intermolecular forces are used to predict physical properties.

Specific topics covered in this chapter are:
- Nomenclature of parent chains and substituents
- Major organic functional groups
- Intermolecular forces present in functional groups and molecular structure
- Relative boiling points and solubility

Previous material that is relevant to your understanding of questions in this chapter include:
- Bond-line structures (*Chapter 1*)
- Molecular shape (*Chapter 1*)
- Intermolecular forces (*Toolbox*)

Where you might see related material in upcoming Study Guide chapters:
- Nomenclature and functional groups will be embedded in problems throughout the study guide, Structural Isomers (*Chapter 3*), chapters associated with the second semester organic chemistry course (e.g., *Chapter 13* and *14: Carbonyl Chemistry*), and the cumulative full-year examination.

Where to find this in your textbook:

The material in this chapter typically aligns to "Families of Organic Compounds" and "Functional Groups" in your textbook. The name of your chapter may vary.

Practice exam:

There may be practice exam questions aligned to the material in this chapter. Because there are a limited number of questions on the practice exam, a review of the breadth of the material in this chapter is advised in preparation for your exam.

How this fits to the big picture:

The material in this chapter aligns to the Big Idea of Structure and Function (III) and Intermolecular Forces (IV) as listed on page 13 of this study guide.

Study Questions (SQ)

SQ-1.	What is the IUPAC name for this compound?	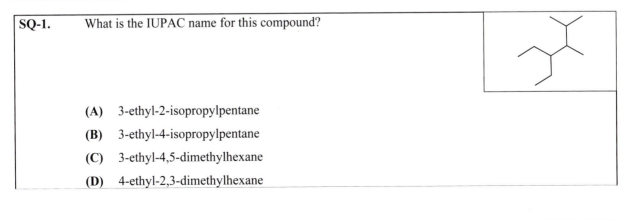

    (A) 3-ethyl-2-isopropylpentane

    (B) 3-ethyl-4-isopropylpentane

    (C) 3-ethyl-4,5-dimethylhexane

    (D) 4-ethyl-2,3-dimethylhexane

Knowledge Required: (1) IUPAC rules for alkyl parent chains and branches.

Thinking it Through: Based on the question prompt, you recognize that you have to apply the IUPAC rules for naming compounds. The first rule you apply is to find the parent chain, i.e. that is the longest chain of carbon atoms. You note that the longest carbon chain has six carbon atoms. You note that there are multiple ways that you can number the six carbons in the parent chain; however, you recognize that due to symmetry in the molecule, among the possible numbering schemes, some are identical. You then number the chain starting at the end of the structure such that the substituent is on the lowest possible numbered carbon:

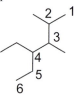

You then identify substituents and where they are located. You note that there are methyl groups at carbon-**2** and carbon-**3**, and an ethyl group at carbon-**4**. Because there are two methyl groups, you place the "di-" prefix before methyl in the name. To formulate the complete structure name, you order the substituents in alphabetical order ignoring the "di-" prefix necessary to denote two methyl groups: 4-ethyl-2,3-dimethylhexane.
　　　　Choice (**D**) is correct.
　　　　Choice (**A**) is not correct because the name is based on a shorter chain than the actual parent chain and was numbered in the wrong direction. Choice (**B**) is not correct because the name is based on a shorter chain than the actual parent chain. Choice (**C**) is not correct because the parent chain is numbered incorrectly.

Practice Problems: **PQ-1**, **PQ-2**, **PQ-3**, **PQ-4**, and **PQ-5**

SQ-2.　　　Which structure has the IUPAC name 1-bromo-3,3-dimethylcyclopentene?

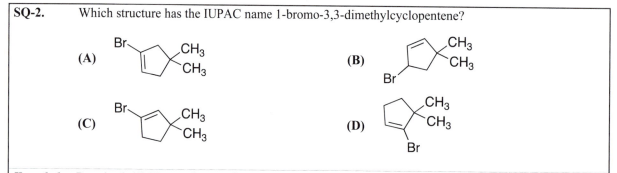

Knowledge Required: (1) Nomenclature of cycloalkenes. (2) Nomenclature of halide and alkyl substituents.

Thinking it Through: You notice that the name has the term "cyclo", meaning the parent chain will be a ring. You also see that the end of the name is functionalized with "ene", indicating the presence of a double bond in this five-membered ring. For a cycloalkene without an additional functionality, you recall that the "1" designation is not needed in the name; however, you will want to note the first carbon when determining where the other substituents are connected to the parent chain (and you know to start with 1 at the double bond).

　　　　You then place a Br group on carbon-1 and two methyl groups on carbon-3. You now have the final, correct structure:

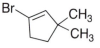

　　　　Which is choice (**C**).
　　　　Choice (**A**) is not correct because the methyl groups are on the wrong carbon; the correct name of this structure is 1-bromo-4,4-dimethylcyclopentene. Choice (**B**) is not correct because the double bond position

changes the numbering of the substituents; the correct name of this structure is 5-bromo-3,3-dimethylcyclopentene. Choice (D) is not correct because the bromine is on the wrong carbon; the correct name of this structure is 2-bromo-3,3-dimethylcyclopentene.

Practice Problems: **PQ-6**, **PQ-7**, **PQ-8**, **PQ-9**, and **PQ-10**

SQ-3.   Citalopram is a common medication used to treat depression. What functional groups are present in citalopram?

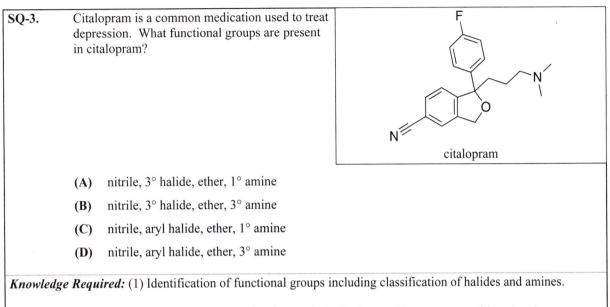

citalopram

(A)   nitrile, 3° halide, ether, 1° amine

(B)   nitrile, 3° halide, ether, 3° amine

(C)   nitrile, aryl halide, ether, 1° amine

(D)   nitrile, aryl halide, ether, 3° amine

Knowledge Required: (1) Identification of functional groups including classification of halides and amines.

Thinking it Through: As you consider the molecule, you look for the familiar structures of functional groups. Two groups are identified in all of the options: a nitrile (RCN) and an ether (ROR′).

$$R\!-\!\!\equiv\!\!N \quad \text{(nitrile)}$$

$$R\!\diagdown\!{}^{O}\!\diagup\!R' \quad \text{(ether)}$$

The other two functional groups are identified as a halide (RX) and an amine (RNH_2). Next, you consider the classification of these functional groups. You recall that halides are classified based on the carbon bonded to the halide, which may be 1°, 2°, 3°, or aryl, and amines are classified by the number of carbons bonded to the nitrogen, which may be 1°, 2°, 3° or 4°. Based on these classification schemes, the halide is an aryl halide and the amine is 3°. Choice (D) is correct.

Choice (A) is not correct because the halide and amine are classified incorrectly. Choice (B) is not correct because the halide is classified incorrectly. Choice (C) is not correct because the amine is classified incorrectly.

Practice Problems: **PQ-11**, **PQ-12**, **PQ-13**, **PQ-14**, and **PQ-15**

SQ-4.   Which compound is capable of exhibiting both dipole-dipole and hydrogen bonding interactions?

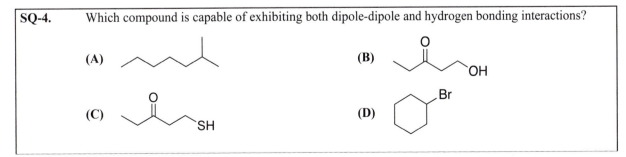

Knowledge Required: (1) Recognition of intermolecular interactions based on structural features.

Thinking it Through: In solving this problem, you inspect the kind of bonds present in each structure. You first need to identify whether a given bond between two atoms is polar or nonpolar. You recall that polarity is generated when two atoms, with differences in electronegativity, are covalently bonded. Bonds between H and highly electronegative atoms F, N, and O exhibit hydrogen bonding. In addition, you recall that C–H and C–C bonds, which are common in organic structures, are viewed as nonpolar bonds, because their atoms have little or no difference in electronegativity.

You recall that dipole-dipole interactions between molecules arise from the presence of polar bonds in both molecules. You note that choices **(B)**, **(C)**, and **(D)** include polar bonds. You also note that hydrogen bonding interactions are present in choice **(B)** where oxygen is bonded to hydrogen. Therefore, choice **(B)** is correct because it can exhibit both dipole-dipole and hydrogen bonding interactions.

Choice **(A)** is not correct because it cannot exhibit any polar bonds. Choice **(C)** is not correct because it cannot exhibit hydrogen bonding interactions. S–H is not polar enough to be considered a hydrogen bond. Choice **(D)** is not correct because it cannot exhibit hydrogen bonding interactions.

Practice Problems: **PQ-16**, **PQ-17**, **PQ-18**, **PQ-19**, and **PQ-20**

SQ-5. Rank these compounds from lowest to highest boiling point.

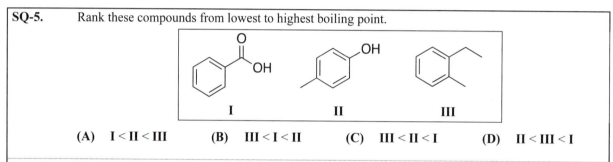

(A)   I < II < III   (B)   III < I < II   (C)   III < II < I   (D)   II < III < I

Knowledge Required: (1) Identifying intermolecular interactions present in a molecule. (2) Relative strength of intermolecular interactions. (3) Effect of intermolecular interactions on physical properties.

Thinking it Through: In order to solve this problem, you need to determine which intermolecular interactions are present in each molecule, recall how intermolecular interactions are related to boiling point, compare the intermolecular interactions between three molecules, and rank the molecules based on their relative intermolecular interactions, which in turn is related to relative boiling points.

First, you consider each of the molecules:
- **I** has intermolecular interactions of hydrogen bonding, dipole-dipole interactions, and London dispersion forces.
- **II** has intermolecular interactions of hydrogen bonding, dipole-dipole interactions, and London dispersion forces.
- **III** has intermolecular interactions of London dispersion forces.

Second, you recall that hydrogen bonding is the strongest intermolecular interaction, followed by dipole-dipole interactions, and lastly London dispersion forces, for molecules of the same size. The stronger the intermolecular interactions a molecule has, the higher the boiling point, i.e. more energy is required in order to break stronger intermolecular interactions for the phase change between liquid and gas. Molecules **I** and **II** have all three of these forces; whereas, molecule **III** only has London dispersion forces. You can conclude that **III** will have the lowest boiling point.

Because the **I** and **II** have the same set of intermolecular interactions, you evaluate each of the forces to determine if one is stronger. The two molecules have hydrogen bonding with one hydrogen bonding donor; molecule **I** has two hydrogen bonding acceptor sites (i.e., two oxygen atoms) and molecule **II** has one hydrogen bonding acceptor site (i.e. one oxygen atom). At this point, you can conclude that molecule **I** has a higher boiling point than molecule **II**. You consider the dipole-dipole interactions, as well, to further confirm your ranking. The carboxylic acid functional group has a larger dipole moment (i.e., two carbon-oxygen polar bonds that are directed in the same direction) compared to the alcohol functional group. Thus, your comparison of the dipole-dipole interactions provides additional support that molecule **I** has a higher boiling point than molecule **II**.

Thus, you conclude that the ranking of boiling points from lowest to highest is **III** < **II** < **I**. The correct answer is choice **(C)**.

Choice **(A)** is not correct because it is the reverse order of the boiling points. This ordering could arise from inverting the relationship between boiling point and intermolecular forces. Choice **(B)** is not correct because it inverts the relative boiling point of molecule **I** and molecule **II**. This ordering could arise from not comparing the relative boiling point of the compounds having the same set of intermolecular forces. Choice **(D)** is not correct because compound **III**, having neither dipole-dipole interactions nor hydrogen bonding capabilities, has the lowest boiling point.

Practice Problems: **PQ-21**, **PQ-22**, **PQ-23**, **PQ-24**, and **PQ-25**

SQ-6. Which compound is the most soluble in water?

    (A) propanol   **(B)** butanol

    (C) pentanol   **(D)** hexanol

Knowledge Required: (1) Intermolecular interactions between molecules. (2) Relative strength of intermolecular interactions. (3) Effect of intermolecular interactions on physical properties. (4) Nomenclature of alcohols.

Thinking it Through: In order to solve this problem, you need to determine what intermolecular interactions are present in water and each molecule, recall how intermolecular interactions are related to solubility, compare the intermolecular interactions between water and each molecule, and rank the molecules based on their relative intermolecular interactions, which in turn is related to relative solubility.

Each molecule is an alcohol and thus is capable of hydrogen bonding and dipole-dipole interactions with water. Thus, intermolecular forces are not the key determinate for solubility of these molecules.

Each molecule has a different carbon chain length: propanol has $CH_3CH_2CH_2-$, butanol has $CH_3CH_2CH_2CH_2-$, pentanol has $CH_3CH_2CH_2CH_2CH_2-$, and hexanol has $CH_3CH_2CH_2CH_2CH_2CH_2-$. Alkyl chains are nonpolar and therefore hydrophobic and are not soluble in polar solvents such as water. Alkyl chain length for this series is predictive of solubility, with the smallest chain being the most soluble.

Therefore, choice **(A)**, propanol, is the most soluble.

Choices **(B)**, **(C)**, and **(D)** are less soluble than propanol in water because of increased alkyl chain length.

Practice Problems: **PQ-26**, **PQ-27**, **PQ-28**, **PQ-29**, and **PQ-30**

Practice Questions (PQ)

PQ-1. What is the IUPAC name for this compound?

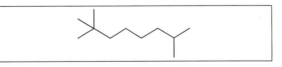

    (A) 1,1,1,6-tetramethylheptane   **(B)** 1-*tert*-butyl-4-isopropylbutane

    (C) 2,2,7-trimethyloctane   **(D)** 1-*tert*-butyl-4-isopropyloctane

PQ-2. What is the IUPAC name for this compound?

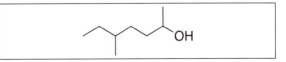

    (A) 1-methyl-4-ethyl-pentanol   **(B)** 1,4-dimethyl-1-hexanol

    (C) 3-methyl-6-heptanol   **(D)** 5-methyl-2-heptanol

PQ-3. What is the IUPAC name for this compound?

(A) 1-*tert*-butyl-2-butanol

(B) 5,5-dimethyl-3-hexanol

(C) 2,2-dimethyl-4-hexanol

(D) 1,1,1-trimethyl-3-pentanol

PQ-4. Which structure is 4-isopropyl-2,5-dimethylheptane?

(A)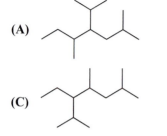

(B)

(C)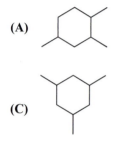

(D)

PQ-5. Which structure is 1,3,5-trimethylcyclohexane?

(A)

(B)

(C)

(D)

PQ-6. What is the IUPAC name of this structure?

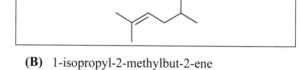

(A) 2,5-dimethylhex-2-ene

(B) 1-isopropyl-2-methylbut-2-ene

(C) 2,2,4,4-tetramethylbut-1-ene

(D) 2,5-dimethylhex-5-ene

PQ-7. What is the IUPAC name of this structure?

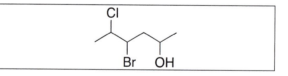

(A) 4-bromo-5-chlorohexan-2-ol

(B) 3-bromo-2-chloro-hexan-5-ol

(C) 3-bromo-4-chloro-2-methyl-pentan-1-ol

(D) 3-bromo-2-chloro-5-methyl-pentan-5-ol

PQ-8. Which structure is 4-bromohex-1-en-3-ol?

(A)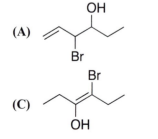

(B)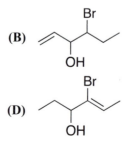

(C)

(D)

PQ-9. What is the IUPAC name of this structure?

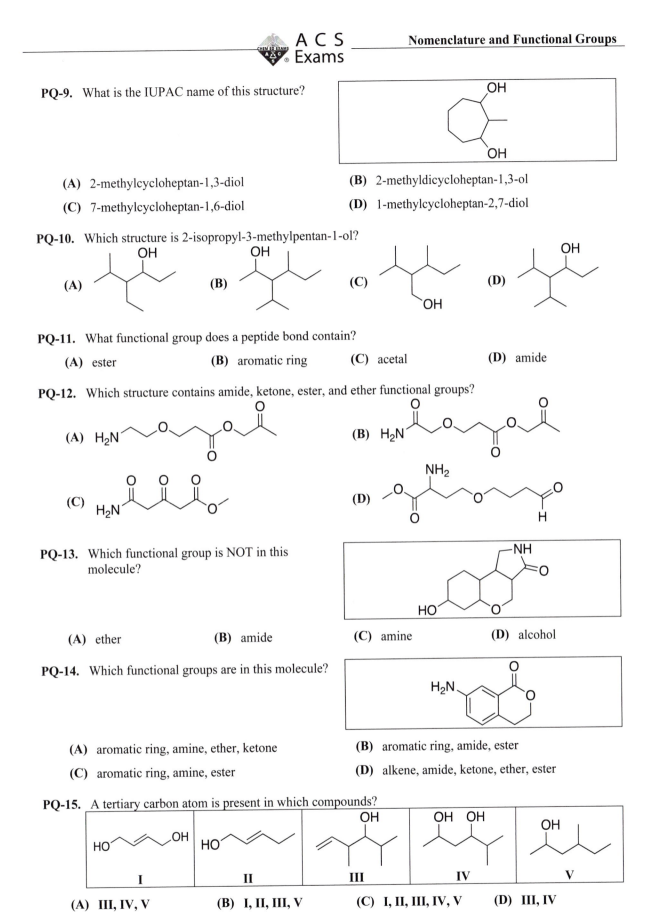

(A) 2-methylcycloheptan-1,3-diol

(B) 2-methyldicycloheptan-1,3-ol

(C) 7-methylcycloheptan-1,6-diol

(D) 1-methylcycloheptan-2,7-diol

PQ-10. Which structure is 2-isopropyl-3-methylpentan-1-ol?

(A) (B) (C) (D)

PQ-11. What functional group does a peptide bond contain?

(A) ester (B) aromatic ring (C) acetal (D) amide

PQ-12. Which structure contains amide, ketone, ester, and ether functional groups?

(A) H_2N (B) H_2N

(C) H_2N (D)

PQ-13. Which functional group is NOT in this molecule?

(A) ether (B) amide (C) amine (D) alcohol

PQ-14. Which functional groups are in this molecule?

(A) aromatic ring, amine, ether, ketone

(B) aromatic ring, amide, ester

(C) aromatic ring, amine, ester

(D) alkene, amide, ketone, ether, ester

PQ-15. A tertiary carbon atom is present in which compounds?

| I | II | III | IV | V |

(A) III, IV, V (B) I, II, III, V (C) I, II, III, IV, V (D) III, IV

 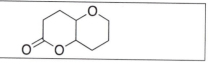
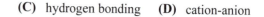

PQ-16. Which forces are the strongest?

    (A) dipole-dipole   **(B)** dispersion forces   **(C)** hydrogen bonding   **(D)** cation-anion

PQ-17. Which intermolecular force(s) is/are NOT present between molecules of this compound?

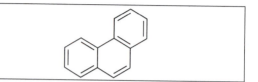

    (A) hydrogen bonding   **(B)** hydrogen bonding and dipole-dipole

    (C) dipole-dipole   **(D)** dipole-dipole and dispersion forces

PQ-18. Which intermolecular force(s) CANNOT be exhibited by this compound?

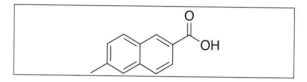

    (A) only hydrogen bonding   **(B)** only dipole-dipole

    (C) hydrogen bonding and dipole-dipole   **(D)** dipole-dipole and dispersion forces

PQ-19. What intermolecular force(s) can be exhibited by this compound?

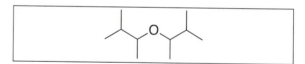

    (A) only dipole-dipole

    (B) dipole-dipole and dispersion forces

    (C) hydrogen bonding and dispersion forces

    (D) hydrogen bonding, dipole-dipole, dispersion forces

PQ-20. What intermolecular force(s) can be exhibited by this compound?

    (A) dipole-dipole and dispersion forces

    (B) hydrogen bonding and dipole-dipole

    (C) hydrogen bonding and dispersion forces

    (D) hydrogen bonding, dipole-dipole, dispersion forces

PQ-21. Which compound has the highest boiling point?

    (A) 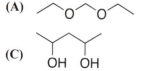   **(B)**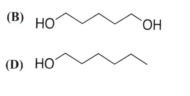

    (C)    **(D)**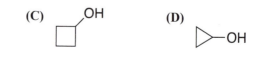

PQ-22. Which compound has the lowest boiling point?

    (A)   **(B)**   **(C)**   **(D)**

PQ-23. Rank these compounds from lowest to highest boiling point.

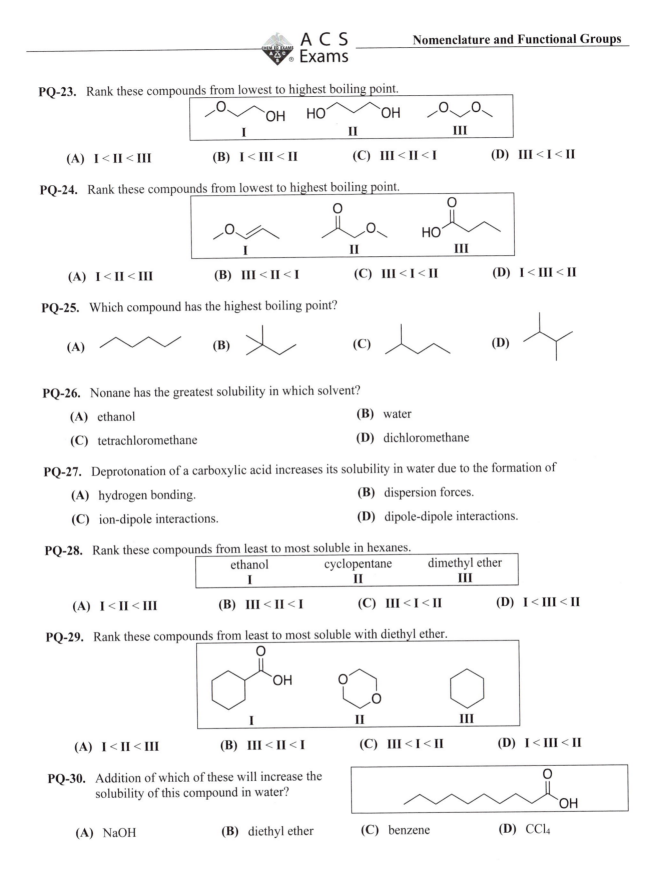

(A) I < II < III   (B) I < III < II   (C) III < II < I   (D) III < I < II

PQ-24. Rank these compounds from lowest to highest boiling point.

(A) I < II < III   (B) III < II < I   (C) III < I < II   (D) I < III < II

PQ-25. Which compound has the highest boiling point?

(A)   (B)   (C)   (D)

PQ-26. Nonane has the greatest solubility in which solvent?

(A) ethanol   (B) water

(C) tetrachloromethane   (D) dichloromethane

PQ-27. Deprotonation of a carboxylic acid increases its solubility in water due to the formation of

(A) hydrogen bonding.   (B) dispersion forces.

(C) ion-dipole interactions.   (D) dipole-dipole interactions.

PQ-28. Rank these compounds from least to most soluble in hexanes.

ethanol	cyclopentane	dimethyl ether
I	II	III

(A) I < II < III   (B) III < II < I   (C) III < I < II   (D) I < III < II

PQ-29. Rank these compounds from least to most soluble with diethyl ether.

(A) I < II < III   (B) III < II < I   (C) III < I < II   (D) I < III < II

PQ-30. Addition of which of these will increase the solubility of this compound in water?

(A) NaOH   (B) diethyl ether   (C) benzene   (D) CCl_4

Answers to Study Questions

SQ-1.	D	SQ-3.	D	SQ-5.	C
SQ-2.	C	SQ-4.	B	SQ-6.	A

Answers to Practice Questions

PQ-1.	C	PQ-11.	D	PQ-21.	B
PQ-2.	D	PQ-12.	B	PQ-22.	D
PQ-3.	B	PQ-13.	C	PQ-23.	D
PQ-4.	A	PQ-14.	C	PQ-24.	A
PQ-5.	C	PQ-15.	A	PQ-25.	A
PQ-6.	A	PQ-16.	D	PQ-26.	C
PQ-7.	A	PQ-17.	A	PQ-27.	C
PQ-8.	B	PQ-18.	C	PQ-28.	D
PQ-9.	A	PQ-19.	D	PQ-29.	B
PQ-10.	C	PQ-20.	A	PQ-30.	A

Chapter 3 – Structure: Constitutional, Stereochemical, & Conformational Isomers

Chapter Summary:

This chapter will focus on structural isomers including constitutional, stereochemical, and conformational isomers. This chapter will include components of molecular representations, structural relationships, nomenclature, physical properties, and energetics.

Specific topics covered in this chapter are:
- Newman projections
- Fischer projections
- Chair conformations
- Strain – ring, torsional, and steric
- Stereochemistry – chirality, optical activity, *cis/trans* relationships, *R/S*, *E/Z*, meso compounds
- Constitutional isomers
- Enantiomers and diastereomers

Previous material that is relevant to your understanding of questions in this chapter include:
- Bond-line structures (***Chapter 1***)
- Nomenclature (***Chapter 2***)

Where to find this in your textbook:

The material in this chapter typically aligns to "Molecular Representations", "Stereochemistry", and "Alkanes and Cycloalkanes" in your textbook. The names of your chapter may vary.

Practice exam:

There may be practice exam questions aligned to the material in this chapter. Because there are a limited number of questions on the practice exam, a review of the breadth of the material in this chapter is advised in preparation for your exam.

How this fits to the big picture:

The material in this chapter aligns to the Big Idea of "Bonding" (II) and "Structure and Function" (III) as listed on page 13 of this study guide.

Study Questions (SQ)

SQ-1.	What are the stereochemical assignments for carbon-**2** and carbon-**3** in this molecule?	

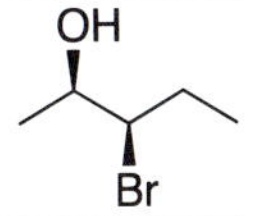

(A) (2*R*,3*R*)	(B) (2*R*,3*S*)	(C) (2*S*,3*R*)	(D) (2*S*,3*S*)

Knowledge Required: (1) Translation of wedge-dash representations to three-dimensional structures. (2) Cahn-Ingold-Prelog rules for assigning priority to substituents. (3) Rules for assigning (*R*) or (*S*) to a stereocenter (absolute configuration).

Thinking it Through: You have been asked to determine the stereochemical assignments of two carbons in the provided molecule. To complete this task, you need to recall the three-dimensional shape of carbons in a wedge-dash molecular representation, how to assign substituent priority based on the Cahn-Ingold-Prelog rules, and how to determine (*R*) or (*S*) configuration.

You begin by considering carbon-**2**. You note that there is an additional hydrogen atom on carbon-**2** that is not explicitly shown per wedge-dash conventions. After you draw this as part of the representation, you have:

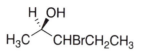

Next, you use the Cahn-Ingold-Prelog rules to assign priority. The atoms directly attached carbon-**2** are hydrogen, oxygen, carbon, and carbon. You recall that the lowest priority is assigned to the atom with the lowest atomic number, and the highest priority is assigned to the atom with the highest atomic number. Therefore, the –OH substituent has a priority of "1" and the –H substituent has a priority of "4". The two carbons, by definition, have the same atomic number; therefore, you have to consider what is attached to those carbons before assigning priority. One carbon has three hydrogens attached to it; the other carbon has a hydrogen, a bromine, and a carbon attached to it. Of these, the bromine has the highest atomic number and therefore the substituent that includes it has higher priority over the other. Thus, –CHBrCH$_2$CH$_3$ has a priority of "2" and –CH$_3$ has a priority of "3". You label the representation with these numbers:

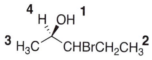

In order to determine (*R*) or (*S*) you have to consider the orientation of the three highest priority substituents with the lowest priority substituent pointed away from you. The structure, as drawn, has the lowest priority substituent pointed away from you. To make the stereochemical assignment, you consider the clockwise or counter-clockwise orientation of the three highest priority substituents in descending order of priority:

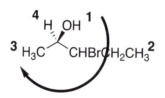

This is a clockwise orientation and thus you assign an (*R*) configuration to carbon-**2**.

You repeat the process for carbon-**3** noting the implicit hydrogen, priority of the four substituents, and orientation of the three highest priority substituents with the lowest priority substituent away from you:

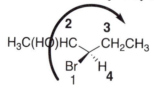

You determine that carbon-**3** has an (*R*) configuration. With both carbon-**2** and carbon-**3** having an (*R*) configuration, you determine that choice (**A**) is correct.

Choice (**B**) is not correct because it has the wrong stereochemical assignment for carbon-**3**. Choice (**C**) is not correct because it has the wrong stereochemical assignment for carbon-**2**. Choice (**D**) is not correct because it has the wrong stereochemical assignment for both carbon-**2** and **3**.

Practice Problems: PQ-1, PQ-2, PQ-3, PQ-4 and PQ-5

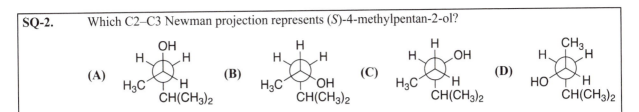
SQ-2. Which C2–C3 Newman projection represents (*S*)-4-methylpentan-2-ol?

(A)   (B)   (C)   (D)

Knowledge Required: (1) How to determine a structure from an IUPAC name. (2) How to translate between wedge-dash and Newman projection.

Thinking it Through: You are asked to determine the Newman projection of a molecule given its IUPAC name. You note that there are two ways to solve this problem: first, determine the wedge-dash formula for the given IUPAC name and then convert that structure to a Newman projection; or determine the IUPAC name for each of the answer options; you note that the lowest priority group on carbon-2 is not pointed away from you in any of the answer options, and thus choose to pursue the first method.

To draw the wedge-dash formula for the IUPAC name, you first draw the parent chain, substituents on the designated carbons, and confirm that the correct stereochemical assignment, (*S*), is drawn:

In the prompt, you are told that the Newman projection is drawn down the C2–C3 bond. For carbon-2, you note that it has three substituents besides carbon-3 attached to it: –OH, –H, and –CH₃. Considering the molecule from down the C2–C3 bond, you represent the three substituents on carbon-3 that you have yet to determine using "?":

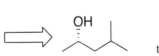   translates to

Next, you identify the three substituents on carbon-3: –H, –H, –CH(CH₃)₂. You include these in your Newman projection:

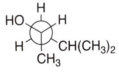

The Newman projection you have drawn does not immediately match any of the answer options. You recall that you can freely rotate the front and back carbons. After rotating the drawing by 60°, you determine that choice **(A)** is correct.

Choice **(B)** and **(D)** are not correct because the substituents on carbon-2 are incorrectly oriented. Choice **(C)** is not correct because the –OH substituent is on the wrong carbon.

You also recall that interpreting the energetics of Newman projections relative to each other is a common question. Staggered conformations are always lower in energy than eclipsed conformations. Fewer gauche interactions are lower in energy as is fewer eclipsing interactions of two non-hydrogen atoms. Finally you recall the larger the substituent the higher energy the gauche or eclipsing interaction will be.

Practice Problems: **PQ-6**, **PQ-7** and **PQ-8**

**A C S
Exams**

SQ-3. What is the IUPAC name of this molecule?

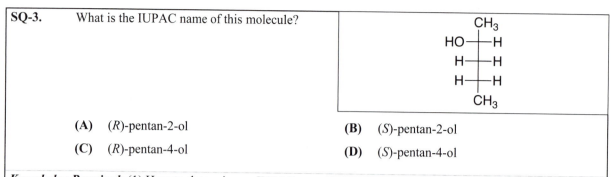

(A) (*R*)-pentan-2-ol	**(B)** (*S*)-pentan-2-ol
(C) (*R*)-pentan-4-ol	**(D)** (*S*)-pentan-4-ol

Knowledge Required: (1) How to determine an IUPAC name from a structure. (2) How to translate between Fischer projection and wedge-dash.

Thinking it Through: You are asked to determine the IUPAC name of a structure shown in a Fischer projection. You note that there are two ways to solve this problem: first, determine the wedge-dash formula for the given Fischer projection and then convert the wedge-dash formula to the IUPAC name; or, determine the IUPAC name directly from the Fischer projection. However, you note that carbon-2 is a stereocenter and thus assigning (*R*) and (*S*) can be difficult using the second method, you choose to pursue the first method.

To draw the wedge-dash formula from the Fischer projection, you first consider how the Fischer projection conveys the direction in which the substituents are pointed:

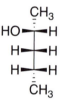

Next, you redraw the structure with the carbon backbone on the plane of the page followed by rotating the carbon-carbon single bonds into the zigzag shape:

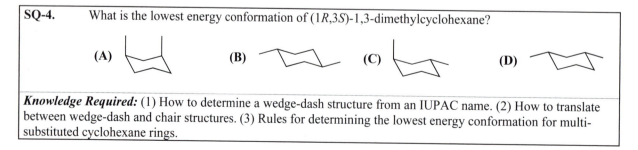

bonds rotated into

Finally, you determine the IUPAC name by noting the parent chain (pentane), the presence of an alcohol (-ol suffix on the parent chain, pentanol), the location of the alcohol on carbon-**2** (the lowest possible number for the substituent, pentan-2-ol), and the stereochemical configuration of carbon-**2** (*R*). The correct name is (*R*)-pentan-2-ol, which is choice **(A)**.

Choice **(B)** is not correct because carbon-2 is not in the (*S*) configuration. Choice **(C)** is not correct because the substituent has to have the lowest possible number. Choice **(D)** is not correct because carbon-2 is not in the (*S*) configuration and the substituent has to have the lowest possible number.

Practice Problems: **PQ-9**, and **PQ-10**

SQ-4. What is the lowest energy conformation of (1*R*,3*S*)-1,3-dimethylcyclohexane?

(A) **(B)** **(C)** **(D)**

Knowledge Required: (1) How to determine a wedge-dash structure from an IUPAC name. (2) How to translate between wedge-dash and chair structures. (3) Rules for determining the lowest energy conformation for multi-substituted cyclohexane rings.

Thinking it Through: You are asked in the prompt to determine the lowest energy conformation for a molecule for which you are provided the name only. You determine that the best strategy is to convert the name first to a wedge-dash structure, after which you will convert the wedge-dash structure into a chair structure, and lastly consider the two possible chair conformations to determine the lowest energy conformations.

You begin by drawing the structure in wedge-dash with the two methyl groups pointed towards you:

This choice ensures that the lowest priority group on both stereocenters is pointed away from you. You utilize the Cahn-Ingold-Prelog priority and (*R*)-(*S*) assignment rules to confirm that you have the correct structure. Had you determined that you did not have the correct stereochemical configuration drawn for each stereocenter, you would have changed the methyl group from wedge to dash, to the desired configuration.

Next, you convert the wedge-dash structure to a chair structure. You choose to make the methyl groups pointed up in the wedge-dash structure as being axial on the chair structure. Per convention, you determine that the methyl group on carbon-3 is also pointed axial due to the *cis* relationship between the two substituents:

 Choice **(A)**

Another possible chair conformation for the dash-wedge structure (when flipped horizontally) would be choice **(D)**:

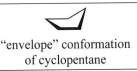 Choice **(D)**

You recall that the lowest energy conformation has the largest group(s) in the equatorial position(s). The structure in choice **(D)** has both methyl groups pointed equatorial, thus this is the lowest energy conformation, and choice **(D)** is the correct answer.

Choice **(A)** is not correct because both methyl groups are axial, a higher energy conformation. Choice **(B)** is not correct because the methyl groups are incorrectly at the 1,4 positions. Choice **(C)** is not correct because the methyl groups do not have the correct stereochemical configuration.

Practice Problems: **PQ-11, PQ-12, PQ-13** and **PQ-14**

SQ-5.	Cyclopentane adopts a conformation described as an "envelope" or "twist" rather than being flat (i.e., having all five carbons in the same plane). What reason best articulates the observed conformations?

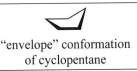
"envelope" conformation
of cyclopentane

(A) The observed conformation minimizes torsional strain arising from eclipsed hydrogens.

(B) The observed conformation maximizes torsional strain arising from eclipsed –CH$_2$– groups.

(C) The observed conformation minimizes ring strain arising from non-ideal H-C-H bond angles.

(D) The observed conformation maximizes ring strain arising from non-ideal C-C-C bond angles.

Knowledge Required: (1) Rings adopt conformations that reduce strain and overall energy. (2) Definitions of torsional strain and ring strain.

Thinking it Through: You are asked in the problem to provide a reason for the observed conformations of cyclopentane. In particular, you are asked to choose a reason related to strain (i.e., torsional or ring strain). You recall that conformations are adopted by a molecule to reduce overall energy; a valid rationale for a particular observed conformation should focus on minimizing strain and thus minimizing overall energy.

You also recall that torsional strain arises when atoms within three σ bonds of each other are eclipsed. You note that if cyclopentane is flat, that the hydrogens on each carbon are eclipsed. You sketch out a cyclopentane ring as if seeing it from the side and include the hydrogens on two adjacent carbons to confirm that the hydrogens would be eclipsed:

You additionally recall that ring strain arises from bond angles that are non-ideal (e.g., ~109.5° for sp^3 hybridized atoms). If cyclopentane were flat, the internal angles of the structure would be 108°, i.e. less than the ideal angles of the five sp^3 hybridized carbon atoms. Molecules with higher strain are higher in energy.

Based on your understanding of torsional strain and ring strain, you consider the answer options.

Choice **(A)** is correct because it identifies the torsional strain of cyclopentane that arises from eclipsed hydrogens of adjacent carbons.

Choice **(B)** is not correct because molecules do not adopt conformations by maximizing strain. Choice **(C)** is not correct because ring strain is associated with bond angles internal to the ring. The H–C–H bond angles are external to the ring and have a minor effect overall. Choice **(D)** is not correct because molecules do not adopt conformations by maximizing strain.

Practice Problems: **PQ-15**, **PQ-16** and **PQ-17**

SQ-6.	Which compounds are optically active?	

     I   II   III

  (A) I and III   **(B)** I and II   **(C)** II and III   **(D)** I, II, and III

Knowledge Required: (1) Definition of optical activity. (2) How to identify a chiral compound.

Thinking it Through: You have been asked to determine which of three molecules are optically active. You recall that optically active compounds are those compounds that are chiral. A chiral compound is a compound that is non-superimposable on its mirror image; or stated from a different perspective, lack symmetry. Molecules that contain a single stereogenic center are chiral and thus optically active.

You begin by evaluating each structure based on the definition of chirality. For **I**, you note that there is an internal mirror plane (i.e., a symmetry element).

Next, you evaluate **II** and **III**, noting that both molecules contain a stereogenic center (*) and lack an internal mirror plane.

Thus, you conclude that **I** is NOT optically active, while **II** and **III** are optically active, choice **(C)**.

You also recall that if a molecule had multiple stereogenic centers, you would need to evaluate whether the molecule had an internal mirror plane. If it did, this would result in the molecule being optically inactive. You know that molecules with two or more stereocenters that have a mirror plane are achiral and are termed meso compounds.

Choice **(C)** is the correct answer.

Choices **(A)**, **(B)**, and **(D)** are not correct because **I** is not chiral and thus is not optically active.

Practice Problems: **PQ-18, PQ-19**, and **PQ-20**

SQ-7.	What is the IUPAC name for this molecule?	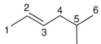

    (A)   (*E*)-5-methylhex-2-ene   **(B)**   (*Z*)-5-methylhex-2-ene

    (C)   (*E*)-2-methylhex-4-ene   **(D)**   (*Z*)-2-methylhex-4-ene

---

Knowledge Required: (1) Nomenclature of alkenes. (2) Cahn-Ingold-Prelog rules for assigning priority to substituents. (3) Rules for assigning (*E*) or (*Z*) to an asymmetric alkene.

Thinking it Through: You have been asked to determine the IUPAC name for a given structure. The first rule of nomenclature is to determine the longest chain; because this structure includes an alkene, a higher priority group than alkanes, the longest chain must include the alkene. Additionally, the longest chain should be numbered such that the alkene is located on the lowest numbered carbon possible. You number the longest chain, a six-membered chain accordingly:

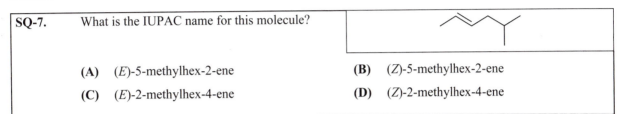

At present, the name of the structure includes "hex-2-ene", as the alkene begins on carbon-**2** and the chain is six carbons long, i.e. "hex".

Next, you note that there is one substituent on the chain that is not yet named: a methyl group on carbon-**5**. Thus, you add "5-methyl" to the name to make: 5-methylhex-2-ene.

Finally, you note that the alkene is asymmetric and thus requires an *(E)* or *(Z)* stereochemical designation. You draw a dashed line through the alkene such that you can determine the highest priority group on each side and the relationship between those two high priority groups. The Cahn-Ingold-Prelog rules for assigning priority note that the atom attached to the alkene with the highest atomic number is the higher priority group. For the left side of the alkene, this is carbon versus hydrogen; therefore, the "carbon" is the highest priority and you circle the methyl group. For the right side of the alkene, this is carbon versus hydrogen, again; therefore, the "carbon" is the highest priority and you circle the alkyl group.

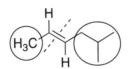

These highest priority groups are *trans* to each other and thus are designated with *(E)*. Thus, the IUPAC name for this compound is: *(E)*-5-methylhex-2-ene, choice **(A)**.

Choice **(B)** is not correct because the highest priority groups are not *cis* to each other, i.e. *(Z)*. Choice **(C)** is not correct because the alkene does not have the lowest number possible. Choice **(D)** is not correct because the highest priority groups are not *(Z)* and the alkene does not have the lowest possible number.

Practice Problems: **PQ-21, PQ-22, PQ-23**, and **PQ-24**

SQ-8.	What is the stereochemical relationship between these compounds?	

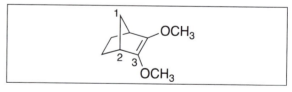

(A)	constitutional isomers	(B)	conformational isomers
(C)	enantiomers	(D)	diastereomers

Knowledge Required: (1) Definitions of constitutional isomers, conformational isomers, enantiomers, and diastereomers.

Thinking it Through: You are asked to determine the stereochemical relationships between two given compounds. Each answer choice is a different relationship.

You recall that constitutional isomers, choice **(A)**, have the same molecular formulas, but are not connected in the same way. You note that the two given compounds have the same molecular formula, but are connected in the same way, i.e., a six-membered ring that includes an alkene and has a methyl group at carbon-**3** and carbon-**6**.

You recall that conformational isomers, choice **(B)**, have the same molecular formula, are connected in the same absolute way, but differ in rotation of single bonds. You note that for the two given compounds, one methyl group differs in its absolute connectivity.

You recall that enantiomers, choice **(C)**, are non-superimposable, mirror-images of each other. You note that the two given compounds are not mirror images of each other.

You recall that diastereomers, choice **(D)**, are non-superimposable, non-mirror-images of each other. You note that the two given compounds match this definition. Therefore, choice **(D)** is the correct answer.

Practice Problems: **PQ-25**, **PQ-26**, **PQ-27**, **PQ-28**, **PQ-29** and **PQ-30**

Practice Questions (PQ)

PQ-1. How many stereocenters are present in this molecule?

(A) 1	(B) 2	(C) 3	(D) 4

PQ-2. Which of the numbered carbons in this compound are stereocenters?

(A) 1, 2, and 3	(B) 1 and 3	(C) 2 only	(D) 2 and 3

PQ-3. What are the absolute configurations of these two molecules?

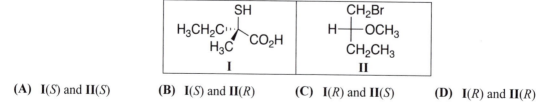

(A) **I**(S) and **II**(S)	(B) **I**(S) and **II**(R)	(C) **I**(R) and **II**(S)	(D) **I**(R) and **II**(R)

PQ-4. Which molecule has the (*R*) configuration?

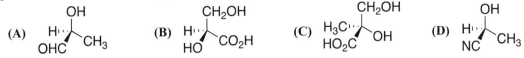

PQ-5. What is the molecular formula for an unsubstituted alkane of smallest molar mass which possesses a stereogenic center?

(A) C_5H_{12} (B) C_6H_{14} (C) C_7H_{16} (D) C_8H_{18}

PQ-6. Which Newman projection best depicts a gauche interaction between two bromine atoms?

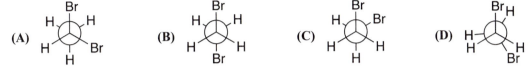

PQ-7. Which Newman projection represents the most stable conformation of 3-methylpentane when viewed down the 2-3 carbon-carbon bond?

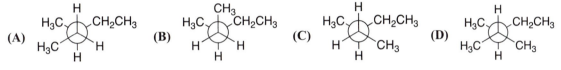

PQ-8. Rank these conformations from least to most stable.

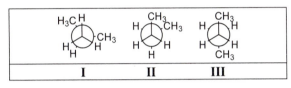

I	II	III

(A) I < II < III   (B) III < II < I   (C) II < III < I   (D) II < I < III

PQ-9. What is the name for this compound?

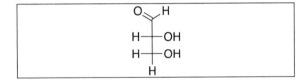

(A) (*S*)-1,2-dihydroxypropanal   (B) (*R*)-2,3-dihydroxypropanal

(C) (*S*)-2,3-dihydroxypropanal   (D) (2*R*,3*R*)-2,3-dihydroxypropanal

PQ-10. What are the configurations of the two stereocenters in this Fischer projection?

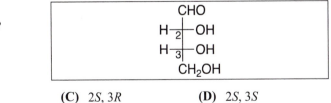

(A) 2*R*, 3*R*   (B) 2*R*, 3*S*   (C) 2*S*, 3*R*   (D) 2*S*, 3*S*

PQ-11. Rank these compounds from lowest to highest energy.

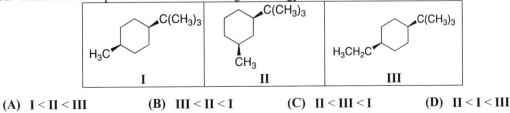

I	II	III

(A) I < II < III   (B) III < II < I   (C) II < III < I   (D) II < I < III

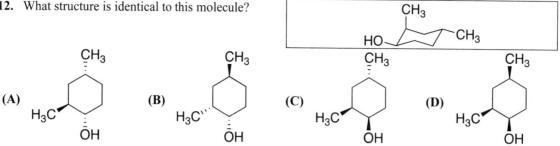

PQ-12. What structure is identical to this molecule?

(A)

(B)

(C)

(D)

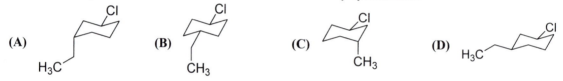

PQ-13. What best describes the most stable conformation of *trans*-1-isopropyl-3-methylcyclohexane?

(A) The isopropyl group is equatorial, and the methyl group is axial.

(B) The isopropyl group is axial, and the methyl group is equatorial.

(C) Both the isopropyl and methyl groups are equatorial.

(D) Both the isopropyl and methyl groups are axial.

PQ-14. Which compound has the IUPAC name *trans*-1-chloro-3-ethylcyclohexane?

(A)

(B)

(C)

(D)

PQ-15. What factor is responsible for a greater heat of combustion per CH_2 for cyclopropane than the heat of combustion per CH_2 for cyclohexane.

(A) Cyclohexane has a different hydrogen-to-carbon atom ratio than cyclopropane.

(B) Cyclohexane has greater ring strain than cyclopropane.

(C) Cyclopropane is a strained ring relative to cyclohexane.

(D) Cyclohexane has more carbon atoms than cyclopropane.

PQ-16. Which value is closest to the internal C–C–C bond angle in cyclohexane?

(A) 90°   **(B)** 100°   **(C)** 110°   **(D)** 120°

PQ-17. Which molecules would have the highest heat of combustion, or release most energy when burned to produce CO_2 and H_2O?

(A)   **(B)**   **(C)**   **(D)**

PQ-18. Which is/are optically inactive?

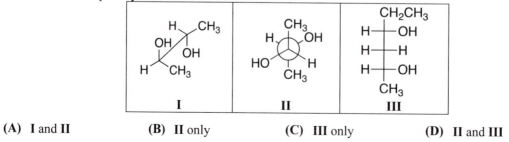

(A) I and II   **(B)** II only   **(C)** III only   **(D)** II and III

PQ-19. Which molecule is NOT optically active?

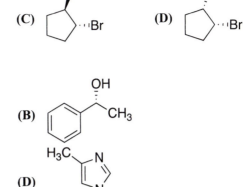

(A) (B) (C) (D)

PQ-20. Which compound is optically active?

(A) 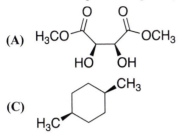 (B)

(C) (D)

PQ-21. What is the IUPAC name for this compound?

(A) (*Z*)-3-chloro-1-fluoro-2-hexene (B) (*E*)-3-chloro-1-fluoro-2-hexene

(C) (*Z*)-4-chloro-6-fluoro-4-hexene (D) (*E*)-4-chloro-6-fluoro-4-hexene

PQ-22. Which compound is (*E*)-1,2-dichloro-2-pentene?

(A) H_3CH_2C CH_2Cl
      H   Cl

(B) H_3CH_2C Cl
      H CH_2Cl

(C) H_3C H
      H $CHCH_2Cl$
           Cl

(D) Cl
    H_3C $CHCH_2Cl$
      H   H

PQ-23. What is the IUPAC name for this compound?

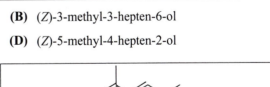
H_3CH_2C OH
         CH_2CHCH_3
    H_3C H

(A) (*Z*)-5-ethyl-4-hexen-2-ol (B) (*Z*)-3-methyl-3-hepten-6-ol

(C) (*E*)-5-methyl-4-hepten-2-ol (D) (*Z*)-5-methyl-4-hepten-2-ol

PQ-24. What is the IUPAC name for this compound?

(A) (*E*)-2,5-dimethylhexa-1,3-diene (B) (1*E*,3*E*)-2,5-dimethylhexa-1,3-diene

(C) (*Z*)-2,5-dimethylhexa-1,3-diene (D) (1*Z*,3*E*)-2,5-dimethylhexa-1,3-diene

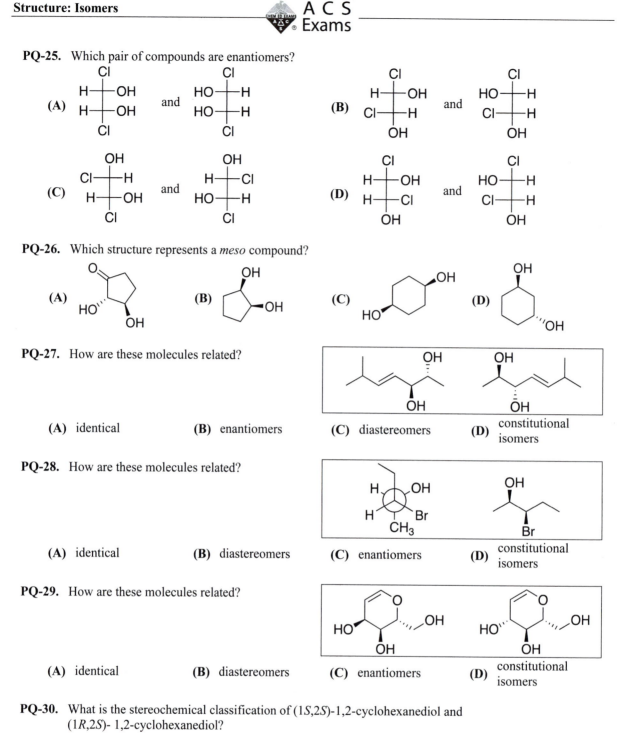

PQ-25. Which pair of compounds are enantiomers?

PQ-26. Which structure represents a *meso* compound?

PQ-27. How are these molecules related?

(A) identical   (B) enantiomers   (C) diastereomers   (D) constitutional isomers

PQ-28. How are these molecules related?

(A) identical   (B) diastereomers   (C) enantiomers   (D) constitutional isomers

PQ-29. How are these molecules related?

(A) identical   (B) diastereomers   (C) enantiomers   (D) constitutional isomers

PQ-30. What is the stereochemical classification of (1*S*,2*S*)-1,2-cyclohexanediol and (1*R*,2*S*)- 1,2-cyclohexanediol?

(A) enantiomers   (B) diastereomers   (C) meso compounds   (D) racemates

Answers to Study Questions

SQ-1.	A	SQ-4.	D	SQ-7.	A
SQ-2.	A	SQ-5.	A	SQ-8.	D
SQ-3.	A	SQ-6.	C		

Answers to Practice Questions

PQ-1.	B	PQ-11.	D	PQ-21.	A
PQ-2.	C	PQ-12.	C	PQ-22.	A
PQ-3.	B	PQ-13.	A	PQ-23.	D
PQ-4.	C	PQ-14.	A	PQ-24.	A
PQ-5.	C	PQ-15.	C	PQ-25.	D
PQ-6.	C	PQ-16.	C	PQ-26.	B
PQ-7.	A	PQ-17.	D	PQ-27.	A
PQ-8.	A	PQ-18.	B	PQ-28.	C
PQ-9.	B	PQ-19.	A	PQ-29.	B
PQ-10.	A	PQ-20.	B	PQ-30.	B

Chapter 4 – Acids and Bases

Chapter Summary:
　This chapter will focus on organic molecules as acids and bases. Included in this chapter are reactions of acids and bases and the qualitative arguments for strengths of acids and bases.

　Specific topics covered in this chapter are:
- Brønsted-Lowry acids and bases
- Lewis acids and bases
- Nucleophiles and electrophiles
- pK_a and its use in organic chemistry
- Qualitative predictions of acid and base strength: periodic trends, resonance, hybridization, and induction.
- Introduction to mechanisms and arrows

　Previous material that is relevant to your understanding of questions in this chapter include:
- pK_a (***Toolbox***)
- Molecular structure (***Chapter 1***)

　Where you might see related material in upcoming Study Guide chapters:
- Nucleophilic substitution reactions (***Chapter 5***)
- Aromatics (***Chapter 11***)

Where to find this in your textbook:
　The material in this chapter typically aligns to "Acids and Bases". The name of your chapter may vary.

Practice exam:
　There may be practice exam questions aligned to the material in this chapter. Because there are a limited number of questions on the practice exam, a review of the breadth of the material in this chapter is advised in preparation for your exam.

How this fits to the big picture:
　The material in this chapter aligns to the Big Idea of Structure and Function (III), Chemical Reactions (V), and Equilibrium (VIII) as listed on page 13 of this study guide.

Study Questions (SQ)

SQ-1. Which compound(s) act(s) as a Brønsted acid?

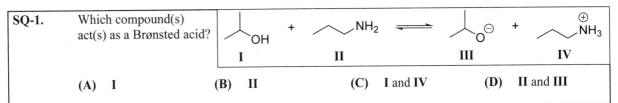

I　　　　II　　　　III　　　　IV

(A) I　　　(B) II　　　(C) I and IV　　　(D) II and III

Knowledge Required: (1) Definition of Brønsted-Lowry acid/base. (2) Understanding of acid/base equilibrium.

Thinking it Through: The first thing you recall when approaching this problem is that these reactions occur under equilibrium conditions. Thus, you know that there is an acid and a base on each side of the equation (i.e., acid/base on the left and conjugate acid/conjugate base on the right). You are asked which molecule is acting as a Brønsted acid, and thus you must identify one compound on each side of the equation. Finally, you recall that the Brønsted definition of an acid is a proton (H^+) donor, while a base is a proton acceptor.

Choice **(C)** is correct. The alcohol on the left donates a proton to the amine to become an alkoxide anion, while the ammonium ion on the right would donate a proton to the alkoxide (RO⁻) and become a neutral amine.

Choices **(A)** and **(B)** are not correct because a species must be identified on both sides of the chemical equation. Choice **(D)** is not correct because the identified species are Brønsted bases.

Practice Problems: **PQ-1**, **PQ-2**, **PQ-3**, and **PQ-4**

SQ-2.   Which species can act as a Lewis acid?

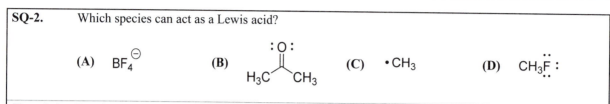

Knowledge Required: (1) Definition of Lewis acid/base. (2) Rules for drawing Lewis structures. (3) Minor resonance structures of molecules.

Thinking it Through: To solve this problem you recall the definition of a Lewis acid, i.e. that the molecule must be capable of accepting a lone pair of electrons (and a Lewis base is an electron pair donor). Apart from this, you also realize that you will need to draw out the full Lewis structures of these molecules and then assess which can accept a pair of electrons. You notice that all of the atoms in the molecules in this problem are in the second row of the periodic table, and thus none can have expanded octets. If the valence shell of a molecule is full in all possible resonance structures, it cannot act as a Lewis acid.

Choice **(B)** is correct. Although all atoms have a full octet, you recall that the carbon and oxygen atoms are sp^2 hybridized, and thus a resonance (minor) form of the molecule can be drawn in which the carbon atom can act as a Lewis acid:

Choice **(A)** is not correct because both boron and fluorine are sp^3-hybridized with full valence shells:

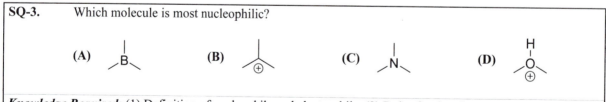

Choice **(C)** is not correct because the carbon with a radical cannot accept an electron pair.
Choice **(D)** is not correct because no atom is capable of accepting an electron pair.

Practice Problems: **PQ-5**, **PQ-6**, **PQ-7**, and **PQ-8**

SQ-3.   Which molecule is most nucleophilic?

(A)   B   (B)   ⊕   (C)   N   (D)   H O ⊕

Knowledge Required: (1) Definition of nucleophile and electrophile. (2) Rules for drawing Lewis structures.

Thinking it Through: To begin this problem, you recall that a nucleophile is electron-rich and capable of donating an electron pair to form a bond, and an electrophile is a species that can accept an electron pair forming a bond. Therefore, you are looking for the molecule most capable of donating an electron pair (either through a lone pair or π bond), thus, the strongest Lewis base.

Choice **(C)** is correct. The nitrogen contains a lone pair of electrons that is nucleophilic.

Choice **(A)** is not correct because boron only has 3 valence electrons and all of those electrons are making σ bonds. There is an empty p orbital, and boron is content with only 6 electrons in its valence shell. There is no lone pair of electrons to make this molecule nucleophilic.

Choice **(B)** is not correct because a carbocation is a carbon atom with 3 σ bonds and an empty p orbital. There is no lone pair of electrons to make this molecule nucleophilic.

Choice **(D)** is not correct because the oxygen is positively charged, making it more electrophilic than nucleophilic. Though there is still one lone pair of electrons on oxygen, this molecule is less nucleophilic than the amine in choice **(C)**.

Practice Problems: **PQ-9, PQ-10**, and **PQ-11**

SQ-4. If an amino acid is dissolved in water and the pH of the solution is adjusted to 12, which compound is the major species present?

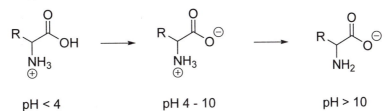

Knowledge Required: (1) Approximate pK_a values of carboxylic acids and the ammonium ion. (2) How relative species concentrations are determined by values for pH and pK_a in biochemical applications.

Thinking it Through: You notice that the question is asking about a pH of 12 for a biological molecule. Because you know the approximate pK_a of a carboxylic acid is about 4, at a basic pH of 12, the carboxylic acid would be deprotonated. At a pH of 12 the amine would also be neutral not protonated; you know this because the amine would be protonated at a pH of 10 or lower (ammonium's pK_a is approximately 10):

$$\text{R}\!-\!\underset{\underset{\oplus}{\text{NH}_3}}{\text{C}}\!-\!\overset{\text{O}}{\text{C}}\!-\!\text{OH} \quad \longrightarrow \quad \text{R}\!-\!\underset{\underset{\oplus}{\text{NH}_3}}{\text{C}}\!-\!\overset{\text{O}}{\text{C}}\!-\!\text{O}^{\ominus} \quad \longrightarrow \quad \text{R}\!-\!\underset{\text{NH}_2}{\text{C}}\!-\!\overset{\text{O}}{\text{C}}\!-\!\text{O}^{\ominus}$$

$$\text{pH} < 4 \qquad\qquad\qquad \text{pH } 4 - 10 \qquad\qquad\qquad \text{pH} > 10$$

In general, when thinking about pK_a, you recall that a lower pK_a corresponds to a stronger acid.

Choice **(D)** is correct. It has a neutral amine and a deprotonated carboxylic acid (carboxylate anion).

Choice **(A)** is not correct because the carboxylic acid should be deprotonated at a pH of 12. Choices **(B)** and **(C)** are not correct because the amine should be neutral and not protonated at a pH of 12.

Practice Problems: **PQ-12, PQ-13**, and **PQ-14**

SQ-5. Rank these molecules from weakest to strongest acid.

$H_3C\!-\!OH$	$H_3C\!-\!\overset{\oplus}{O}H_2$	$H_3C\!-\!NH_2$	$H_3C\!-\!\overset{\oplus}{N}H_3$
I	**II**	**III**	**IV**

(A) III < I < IV < II   **(B)** II < IV < I < III   **(C)** IV < II < III < I   **(D)** I < III < II < IV

Knowledge Required: (1) Qualitatively determining acid/base strength based on periodic trends. (2) Definition of strong and weak acid/base pairs and their conjugate relationships. (3) Acid strength of charged versus neutral species.

Thinking it Through: You recognize that to solve this problem you must determine the relative acid strength of the compounds listed. You quickly notice that there are two factors in play: (1) charged (positive) versus neutral species and (2) the atom bearing the acidic H is different, either bonding with oxygen or nitrogen.

First off, you know that positively charged species are typically stronger acids than neutral species (and negatively charged species are usually stronger bases than neutral species).

Secondly, you recall that when comparing two different atoms, one of two periodic trend arguments will be used to determine acid/base strength, either electronegativity or size of the atom. Because oxygen and nitrogen are in the same period of the periodic table, you know to use the electronegativity argument. If the atoms had been in the same column of the periodic table, you would use the size (or polarizability) argument.

To assess the strength of an acid, consider the stability of its conjugate base. To do this, you consider whether a lone pair of electrons on oxygen or nitrogen would be more stable. Because oxygen is more electronegative, the lone pair of electrons is more stable on oxygen, making the conjugate base (noted CB below) of compound **I** a weaker base than the conjugate base of compound **III**:

$$H_3C-\overset{..}{\underset{..}{O}}:{}^{\ominus} \qquad\qquad H_3C-\overset{\ominus}{\underset{..}{N}}\overset{H}{:}$$

CB of **I**   CB of **III**

Thus, compound **I** is more acidic than compound **III**, and, similarly, compound **II** is more acidic than compound **IV** because weaker bases have stronger conjugate acids and vice versa.

Choice **(A)** is correct. Neutral species are weaker acids than the positively charged species, and compound **I** is a stronger acid than compound **III**, while compound **II** is a stronger acid than compound **IV**.

Choice **(B)** is not correct because the order is backwards. Choice **(C)** is not correct because the order has the neutral compounds as stronger acids. Choice **(D)** is not correct because the order has the amines as a stronger acid than the alcohols.

Practice Problems: **PQ-15**, **PQ-16**, **PQ-17**, and **PQ-18**

SQ-6.	Identify the weaker base and correct relative value for the equilibrium constant (K).	

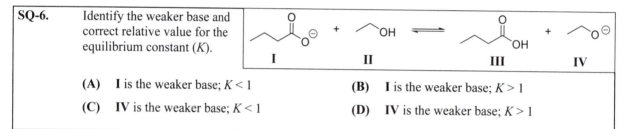

I   **II**   **III**   **IV**

   (A)   **I** is the weaker base; $K < 1$ **(B)**   **I** is the weaker base; $K > 1$

   (C)   **IV** is the weaker base; $K < 1$ **(D)**   **IV** is the weaker base; $K > 1$

Knowledge Required: (1) Qualitatively determining acid/base strength based on resonance stability of the base or conjugate base. (2) Definition of strong and weak acid/base pairs and their conjugate relationships.

Thinking it Through: You realize that first you must identify the weaker base between molecules **I** and **IV** because they are the two basic species in the equilibrium reaction. You must also be able to use qualitative arguments to explain whether the equilibrium will favor the "reactants" or the "products" because pK_a values are not given. The qualitative arguments you could potentially invoke are either periodic trends (when the atom bonded to the acidic hydrogen varies), resonance, induction, and/or hybridization.

You realize that the atom with the negative charge in both cases is oxygen, so periodic trends will not predict acid/base strength. You also notice that molecule **I**'s conjugate base can be resonance delocalized, stabilizing the base:

You know a more stable conjugate base is a weaker base, and thus molecule **I** is the weaker base. You further recall that an equilibrium equation would always prefer the side of the weaker acid/base, thus the 'reactant side' of the prompt. Because the equilibrium constant K is a ratio of products/reactants, the denominator in this case is larger, and therefore $K < 1$. Therefore, choice **(A)** is correct. It identifies the correct weak base and the correct K value.

Choice **(B)** is not correct because it has the correct base, but the wrong value for K. Choices **(C)** and **(D)** are not correct because they identify the wrong weak base.

Practice Problems: **PQ-19**, **PQ-20**, and **PQ-21**

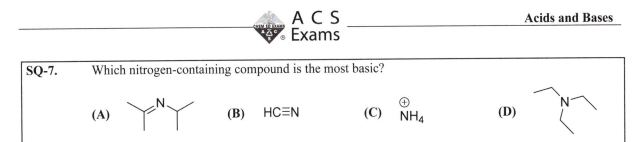

SQ-7. Which nitrogen-containing compound is the most basic?

(A) (B) $HC \equiv N$ (C) $\overset{\oplus}{NH_4}$ (D)

Knowledge Required: (1) Qualitatively determining acid/base strength based on hybridization. (2) Definition of strong and weak acid/base pairs and their conjugate relationships. (3) Base strength of charged and neutral species.

Thinking it Through: First, you identify that the source of the electrons for the base in each molecule is the nitrogen atom. Because the atom is the same element, there are no periodic trends to consider. You realize there are then two arguments you must use to determine the strongest base: 1) Neutral molecules are more basic than positively charged compounds (though negatively charged compounds would be even stronger bases had there been an answer option with a negatively charged species) and 2) Hybridization state of the basic electron pair will determine the relative strength of the base.

You recall that for hybridization, the more "s character" the hybridized orbital contains, the more stable it is, making the electrons in that orbital a weaker base. Base strength based on hybridized orbitals: $sp < sp^2 < sp^3$.

Choice **(D)** is correct. This is a neutral amine with the lone pair of electrons in an sp^3 orbital.

Choice **(A)** is not correct because though neutral, the lone pair of electrons is in an sp^2 orbital. Choice **(B)** is not correct. Though neutral, the lone pair of electrons is in an sp orbital. Choice **(C)** is not correct. This molecule is a cation and has no lone pair of electrons.

Practice Problems: **PQ-22**, **PQ-23**, and **PQ-24**

SQ-8. Rank these compounds from weakest to strongest acid.

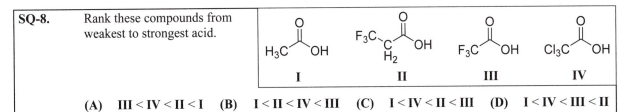

I II III IV

(A) III < IV < II < I (B) I < II < IV < III (C) I < IV < II < III (D) I < IV < III < II

Knowledge Required: (1) Qualitatively determining acid/base strength based on induction. (2) Definition of strong and weak acid/base pairs and their conjugate relationships.

Thinking it Through: You look at this problem and realize you will need to consider the conjugate bases of the given acids to make a qualitative determination. You draw the conjugate bases to each of the acids in the prompt:

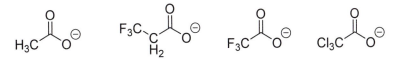

You now realize that the atom bearing the negative charge in all the conjugate bases is oxygen, thus a periodic trend will not help you. You also realize that the resonance stability of the carboxylate ion is present in the four conjugate bases. Finally, you notice that the only difference is the presence or absence of a halide substituent and the identity of that substituent. You recall that halides withdraw electron density by induction and there are two factors to consider:

(1) The number of bonds between halide and anion: the closer the halide, the larger the inductive effect.
(2) The electronegativity of the halide: the more electronegative, the stronger the inductive effect.

Finally, you recall that if a conjugate base is weak (due in this case to having the highest inductive effect) the acid will be strong. Thus, the molecule that experiences the most induction will be the strongest acid, and the one that experiences the least induction is the weakest acid.

Choice **(B)** is correct. Molecule **I** has no inductive effect, thus is the weakest acid. Molecule **II** has an inductive effect two carbon atoms away from the acid, so a lower inductive effect. Molecule **III** and **IV** both have

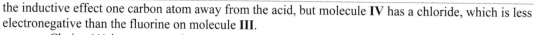

the inductive effect one carbon atom away from the acid, but molecule **IV** has a chloride, which is less electronegative than the fluorine on molecule **III**.

Choice (**A**) is not correct because it is the reverse order. Choice (**C**) is not correct because having the halide closer to the acidic site has a larger effect than the halide being more electronegative. Choice (**D**) is not correct because the answer assumes that fluoride is more inductive than chlorine at any position and has the molecule with the fluorine further away as being more inductive. Neither of these are correct.

Practice Problems: **PQ-25**, **PQ-26**, and **PQ-27**

SQ-9.   Which structure is formed by these electron-pushing arrows?

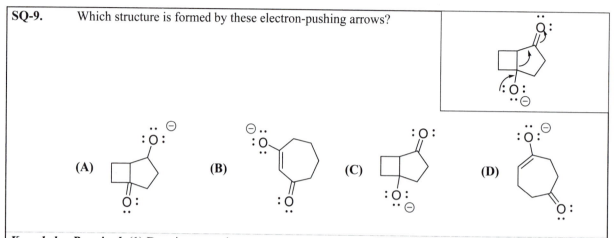

(A)   (B)   (C)   (D)

Knowledge Required: (1) Drawing curved arrows. (2) Mechanism basics: following curved arrows.

Thinking it Through: You realize that this problem wants you to follow the flow of electrons indicated with the curved arrows. Three curved arrows will mean a total of six electrons have moved (three pairs of two electrons each). At the bottom of the compound you realize that the lone pair of electrons on the oxygen has become a carbonyl. The σ bond between the two rings has been broken forming a carbon-carbon π bond. You also note that the breaking of this bond also breaks the bicyclic and makes a one-ringed structure. Finally, you see that the carbonyl is being opened to form an anionic oxygen.

To determine the correct configuration of the final ring, you recall that atom mapping can be helpful, and you therefore number the carbon atoms in the starting material helping you to then draw the final product:

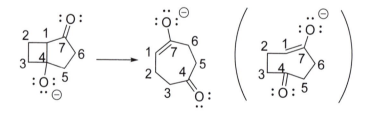

Choice (**D**) is correct. As shown above, this is the correct configuration of the final ring.

Choice (**A**) and (**C**) are not correct because they still contain the bicyclic structure. Choice (**A**) also has a pentavalent carbon. Choice (**B**) is not correct because the spacing of the oxygen atoms is not correct. From the numbering, there should be three carbon atoms between the two C-O bonds on one side of the ring, and two carbon atoms between them on the other side of the ring, not one and four carbon atoms, respectfully.

Practice Problems: **PQ-28**, **PQ-29**, and **PQ-30**

Practice Questions (PQ)

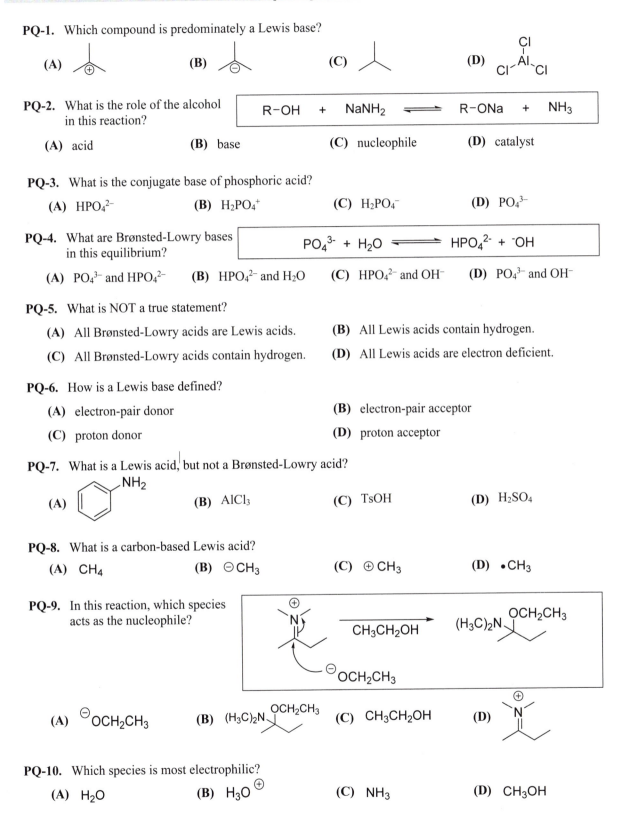

PQ-1. Which compound is predominately a Lewis base?

(A) (B) (C) (D)

PQ-2. What is the role of the alcohol in this reaction?

$$R-OH \ + \ NaNH_2 \ \rightleftharpoons \ R-ONa \ + \ NH_3$$

(A) acid (B) base (C) nucleophile (D) catalyst

PQ-3. What is the conjugate base of phosphoric acid?

(A) HPO_4^{2-} (B) $H_2PO_4^+$ (C) $H_2PO_4^-$ (D) PO_4^{3-}

PQ-4. What are Brønsted-Lowry bases in this equilibrium?

$$PO_4^{3-} \ + \ H_2O \ \rightleftharpoons \ HPO_4^{2-} \ + \ ^-OH$$

(A) PO_4^{3-} and HPO_4^{2-} (B) HPO_4^{2-} and H_2O (C) HPO_4^{2-} and OH^- (D) PO_4^{3-} and OH^-

PQ-5. What is NOT a true statement?

(A) All Brønsted-Lowry acids are Lewis acids. (B) All Lewis acids contain hydrogen.

(C) All Brønsted-Lowry acids contain hydrogen. (D) All Lewis acids are electron deficient.

PQ-6. How is a Lewis base defined?

(A) electron-pair donor (B) electron-pair acceptor

(C) proton donor (D) proton acceptor

PQ-7. What is a Lewis acid, but not a Brønsted-Lowry acid?

(A) (B) $AlCl_3$ (C) TsOH (D) H_2SO_4

PQ-8. What is a carbon-based Lewis acid?

(A) CH_4 (B) $^-CH_3$ (C) $^+CH_3$ (D) $\cdot CH_3$

PQ-9. In this reaction, which species acts as the nucleophile?

(A) $^-OCH_2CH_3$ (B) $(H_3C)_2N\text{-}OCH_2CH_3$ (C) CH_3CH_2OH (D)

PQ-10. Which species is most electrophilic?

(A) H_2O (B) H_3O^+ (C) NH_3 (D) CH_3OH

PQ-11. What MUST be an electrophile?

(A) a Brønsted-Lowry acid

(B) a Brønsted-Lowry base

(C) a Lewis acid

(D) a Lewis base

PQ-12. Which compound is the strongest acid?

(A) propane, C_3H_8, $pK_a = 43$

(B) ethyne, C_2H_2, $pK_a = 25$

(C) water, H_2O, $pK_a = 15.7$

(D) benzoic acid, $C_7O_2H_6$, $pK_a = 4.2$

PQ-13. Which hydrogen atom is most likely to be abstracted when this molecule is reacted with NaH?

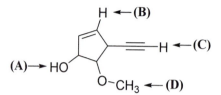

PQ-14. Which proton would be most acidic?

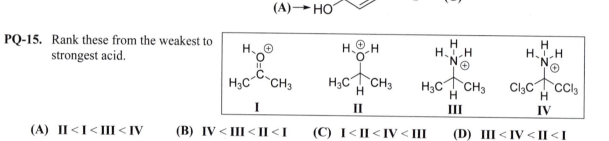

PQ-15. Rank these from the weakest to strongest acid.

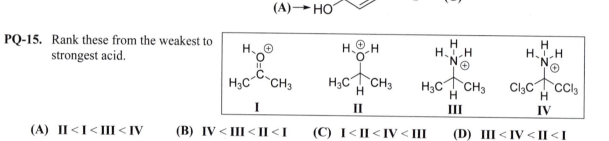

(A) II < I < III < IV

(B) IV < III < II < I

(C) I < II < IV < III

(D) III < IV < II < I

PQ-16. Assuming equimolar quantities of reactants, which compound will react to the greatest extent with boron trifluoride (BF_3) in a Lewis acid/base reaction and why?

(A) $\overset{..}{N}$ due to the periodic property of electronegativity

(B) $\overset{..}{O}:$ due to the periodic property of electronegativity

(C) $\overset{..}{N}$ due to the periodic property of atomic size

(D) $\overset{..}{O}:$ due to the periodic property of atomic size

PQ-17. Which molecule has the highest pK_a value?

(A) HF

(B) HCl

(C) HBr

(D) HI

PQ-18. Rank these from the weakest to strongest acid.

(A) $CH_3CO_2H < CH_3OH < CH_3NH_2$

(B) $CH_3CO_2H < CH_3NH_2 < CH_3OH$

(C) $CH_3OH < CH_3NH_2 < CH_3CO_2H$

(D) $CH_3NH_2 < CH_3OH < CH_3CO_2H$

PQ-19. What indicated hydrogen atom is most acidic?

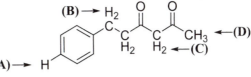

PQ-20. What reason best explains why $K > 1$ for this reaction?

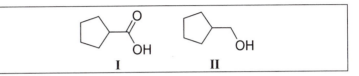

(A) The conjugate base of 2-butyne is a weaker base due to resonance.

(B) The conjugate base of 2-butyne is a stronger base due to resonance.

(C) The conjugate base of 2-butyne is a weaker base due to hybridization.

(D) The conjugate base of 2-butyne is a stronger base due to hybridization.

PQ-21. Which statement is true?

(A) Compound **I** is the stronger acid because its conjugate base is resonance stabilized.

(B) Compound **II** is the stronger acid because its conjugate base is resonance stabilized.

(C) Compound **I** is the stronger acid because its O-H bond is shorter.

(D) Compound **II** is the stronger acid because its O-H bond is shorter.

PQ-22. Rank from the least to most acidic.

(A) **III** < **I** < **II**   (B) **I** < **II** < **III**   (C) **II** < **I** < **III**   (D) **II** < **III** < **I**

PQ-23. Which indicated proton would have the smallest pK_a value?

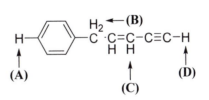

PQ-24.

Why is ‸N≈ a weaker base than ‸N‸ ?
    I   **II**

(A) Because molecule **II** is more stable than molecule **I**.

(B) Because molecule **I** is less sterically hindered.

(C) Because the nitrogen atom in **I** is sp^2 hybridized while the nitrogen atom in **II** is sp^3 hybridized.

(D) Because molecule **II** has more R-groups attached to the nitrogen atom.

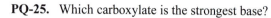

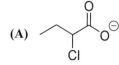

A C S
Exams

PQ-25. Which carboxylate is the strongest base?

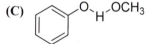

PQ-26. What is the weaker base and correct value for the equilibrium constant (*K*)?

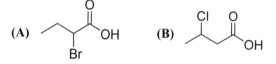

(A) **I** is the weaker base, $K < 1$

(C) **IV** is the weaker base, $K < 1$

(B) **I** is the weaker base, $K > 1$

(D) **IV** is the weaker base, $K > 1$

PQ-27. Which carboxylic acid has the highest pK_a?

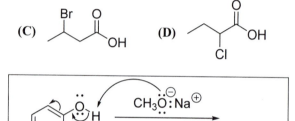

PQ-28. What is/are the product(s) of the acid/base reaction based on the arrows drawn?

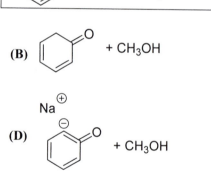

(A) ... + CH_3OH

(B) ... + CH_3OH

(C) ...

(D) ... + CH_3OH

PQ-29. What is the best description of the role of a curved arrow in a mechanism?

(A) It shows the movement of bonds and charges.

(B) It shows the movement of lone pairs of electrons and π–bonds.

(C) It represents the flow of electrons from the electrophile to the nucleophile.

(D) It represents the flow of electrons from the nucleophile to the electrophile.

PQ-30. What are the products of the acid/base reaction based on the arrows drawn?

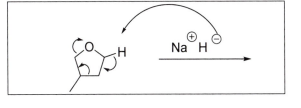

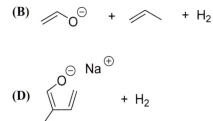

(A) 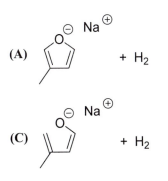 + H$_2$

(B) + + H$_2$

(C) + H$_2$

(D) + H$_2$

A C S
Exams

Answers to Study Questions

SQ-1.	C	SQ-4.	D	SQ-7.	D
SQ-2.	B	SQ-5.	A	SQ-8.	B
SQ-3.	C	SQ-6.	A	SQ-9.	D

Answers to Practice Questions

PQ-1.	B	PQ-11.	C	PQ-21.	A
PQ-2.	A	PQ-12.	D	PQ-22.	C
PQ-3.	C	PQ-13.	A	PQ-23.	D
PQ-4.	D	PQ-14.	D	PQ-24.	C
PQ-5.	B	PQ-15.	D	PQ-25.	B
PQ-6.	A	PQ-16.	A	PQ-26.	D
PQ-7.	B	PQ-17.	A	PQ-27.	C
PQ-8.	C	PQ-18.	D	PQ-28.	A
PQ-9.	A	PQ-19.	C	PQ-29.	D
PQ-10.	B	PQ-20.	A	PQ-30.	B

Chapter 5 – Nucleophilic Substitution Reactions

Chapter Summary:

This chapter will focus on how to recognize nucleophilic substitution reactions, where nucleophiles react as Lewis bases and displace leaving groups to form products. Also included in this chapter are questions related to unimolecular (S_N1) and bimolecular (S_N2) elimination pathways, mechanisms of these reactions, stereochemistry of the reactions, and carbocation formation.

Specific topics covered in this chapter are:
- Reactants and products of nucleophilic substitution reactions
- Unimolecular substitution pathways (S_N1)
- Bimolecular substitution pathways (S_N2)
- Mechanisms including stereochemistry of nucleophilic substitution reactions
- Carbocation formation in unimolecular pathways
- Solvent effects on the two mechanistic pathways
- Nucleophilic substitution reactions of alcohols

Previous material that is relevant to your understanding of questions in this chapter include:
- Constitutional and stereochemical isomers (***Chapter 3***)

Where you might see related material in upcoming Study Guide chapters:
- Elimination reactions (***Chapter 6***)
- Alcohols and ethers (***Chapter 8***)
- Chapters associated with the second semester organic chemistry course: Carbonyl chemistry (***Chapter 13***) and the cumulative full-year examination.

Where to find this in your textbook:

The material in this chapter typically aligns to "Nucleophilic Substitution Reactions" and "Alkyl Halides" in your textbook. The name of your chapter may vary.

Practice exam:

There may be practice exam questions aligned to the material in this chapter. Because there are a limited number of questions on the practice exam, a review of the breadth of the material in this chapter is advised in preparation for your exam.

How this fits to the big picture:

The material in this chapter aligns to the Big Ideas of Chemical Reactions (V) and Kinetics (VII) as listed on page 13 of this study guide.

Study Questions (SQ)

SQ-1. Examine the reaction of benzyl bromide ($PhCH_2Br$) with the azide ion (N_3^-). When the

$$PhCH_2Br + N_3^{\ominus} \longrightarrow PhCH_2N_3 + Br^{\ominus}$$

benzyl bromide concentration is constant and azide concentration doubles, the reaction rate is observed to increase by a factor of two. When the azide concentration is held constant and the benzylbromide concentration is doubled, the rate of the reaction doubles. What is the rate law for the reaction?

(A) Rate = $k[PhCH_2Br]^2[N_3^-]^2$ **(B)** Rate = $k[PhCH_2Br]^4[N_3^-]^2$

(C) Rate = $k[PhCH_2Br]^2[N_3^-]$ **(D)** Rate = $k[PhCH_2Br][N_3^-]$

Knowledge Required: (1) Definition of nucleophiles, Lewis bases, and leaving groups. (2) Reactants, products, and mechanisms of nucleophilic substitution reactions. (3) Kinetics of nucleophilic substitution reactions.

Thinking it Through: You are asked in the problem to determine the rate law for a given reaction and set of experimental data on how the change in concentration of species changes the overall reaction rate. You recognize that reaction rates in chemical reactions depend in some way on the concentration of some or all of the reactants. This makes sense because you know that all chemical reactions depend on how much reactant is present to react or how frequently the reactants collide with each other.

You decide to consider the exponent in the rate equation for azide ion. You reason that if the concentration of benzyl bromide is held constant, azide ion concentration doubling results in a doubling of the overall reaction rate. Because the cause and effect are the same, the exponent is one (1). The same can be said for the doubling of the concentration of the benzyl bromide when azide ion is held constant.

In addition, you recognize that this is a bimolecular substitution (S_N2) pathway, which means that the sum of the rate law exponents must be two (2), and that the rate-limiting-step in the mechanism involves both the substrate (the benzyl bromide) and the nucleophile (N_3^-). Had this reaction proceeded via a unimolecular substitution (S_N1), the rate would have only been affected by a change in the concentration of the substrate (benzyl bromide) and not the nucleophile (N_3^-).

Choice **(D)** is correct because both exponents in the rate law equations are one (1).

Choices **(A)**, **(B)**, and **(C)** are incorrect because one or both of the exponents are not one (1).

Practice Problems: PQ-1 and PQ-2

SQ-2.   What is the configuration of the product in the base-catalyzed hydrolysis of
(R)-1-chloro-1-deuteriobutane ($CH_3CH_2CH_2CHDCl$)?

(A)   (S)-1-deutero-1-butanol

(B)   (R)-1-deutero-1-butanol

(C)   *meso*-1-deutero-1-butanol

(D)   A racemic mixture of **(A)** and **(B)**

Knowledge Required: (1) Definition of nucleophiles, Lewis bases, and leaving groups. (2) Reactants, products, and mechanisms of nucleophilic substitution reactions. (3) Assignment of (R) and (S) absolute configurations. (4) Stereochemistry of bimolecular nucleophilic substitution (S_N2).

Thinking it Through: From the prompt, you realize you are performing a substitution reaction. You know that in a basic hydrolysis reaction, a leaving group (i.e., chloride in this case) is replaced by hydroxide forming a neutral alcohol. You also know that the chloride leaving group in the substrate of this reaction is on a primary carbon atom. Because you have identified the substrate as a primary alkyl halide, you know displacement of chloride by hydroxide will proceed by an S_N2 mechanism.

You know that an S_N2 mechanism proceeds via a "back-side" attack, meaning that as the hydroxide oxygen atom is forming a new bond it is 180° opposite to the leaving chloride ion. Bonds to the other three substituents (H, D, and $CH_2CH_2CH_3$) change to the opposite configuration as shown:

$$H_3CH_2CH_2C-\overset{H}{\underset{Cl}{\diagup}}D \quad \xrightarrow{\ominus OH} \quad H_3CH_2CH_2C-\overset{OH}{\underset{D}{\diagdown}}H \quad + \quad \ominus Cl$$

You know that the (R) configuration changes to (S) because the hydroxide and chloride both have the highest priority on the carbon stereocenter that is reacting. S_N2 reactions proceed with inversion of configuration of the stereocenter.

For other problems that are similar you recall that S_N2 reactions are fastest on methyl halides, followed by 1° alkyl halides and then 2° alkyl halides. S_N2 reactions do not proceed to any great extent on 3° alkyl halides, because the backside attack is sterically blocked. Finally, you recall that leaving group ability affects all substitution reactions; the best leaving group is the weakest base.

You also recall that had this reaction proceeded via an S_N1 mechanism, the stereochemical outcome would have been a racemic mix of the two stereoisomers. This is due to the carbocation intermediate formed in the rate-determining step of the S_N1 reaction. Once the carbocation forms, nucleophilic attack can occur at either lobe of the empty p orbital, giving rise to both stereoisomers.

Choice **(A)** is correct because the starting material must be the opposite stereochemistry of the product. Choice **(B)** is incorrect because it illustrates a retention of stereochemistry. Choice **(D)** is incorrect because it contains the structure from choice **(B)**. Choice **(D)** is the answer for an S_N1 mechanism.

Choice **(C)** is incorrect because *meso* compounds require at least two stereocenters and are achiral.

Practice Problems: **PQ-3, PQ-4, PQ-5, PQ-6**, and **PQ-7**

SQ-3.	From the data, what is the specific rotation of alcohol produced from a bimolecular nucleophilic substitution (S_N2) reaction?

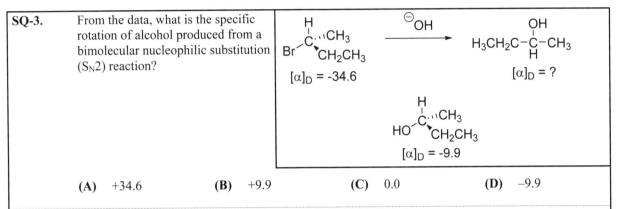

(A)	+34.6	**(B)**	+9.9	**(C)**	0.0	**(D)**	−9.9

Knowledge Required: (1) Stereochemistry of the S_N2 reaction. (2) Relationship between stereochemistry and optical rotation.

Thinking it Through: You know that because this is an S_N2 reaction, the reaction occurs with inversion of configuration at the chiral center. You also know this means optical activity value is retained but the sign of the rotation is inverted.

You realize that the optical rotation of 2-bromobutane is not related to the optical rotation of 2-butanol, but the values for the optical rotation of both of the (*R*)-stereocenters is given. The product's optical rotation will be related to the value of the (*R*)-2-butanol's given optical rotation.

Choice **(B)** is correct because the (*R*) starting material should result in an (*S*) product. Because the example given states that $[\alpha]_D = -9.9$ and this structure is (*R*), the product will have the opposite sign for its $[\alpha]_D$.

Choice **(A)** is incorrect. This is the optical rotation of (*S*)-2-bromobutane, which is not the product. Choice **(C)** is incorrect. This value (0.0) corresponds to a racemic mixture of products, and this would be the result of an S_N1 reaction mechanism, which is not correct. Alternatively, 0.0 could correspond to an achiral product, which is also incorrect in this case. Choice **(D)** is incorrect because the (*R*) starting material should result in an (*S*) product.

Practice Problems: **PQ-8**

SQ-4.	Rank these nucleophiles from slowest to fastest with respect to rate of reaction with propyl bromide.

$$CH_3CH_2CH_2Br \xrightarrow{\ Nu\ } CH_3CH_2CH_2Nu$$

$$Nu = CH_3OH, CH_3\overset{\ominus}{O}, CH_3NH_2$$

(A)	$CH_3O^- < CH_3NH_2 < CH_3OH$	**(B)**	$CH_3OH < CH_3O^- < CH_3NH_2$
(C)	$CH_3OH < CH_3NH_2 < CH_3O^-$	**(D)**	$CH_3NH_2 < CH_3OH < CH_3O^-$

Knowledge Required: (1) Definition of nucleophiles as Lewis bases (nucleophilicity).

Thinking it Through: You know that there are three generalizations concerning relative strengths of nucleophiles: (1) negatively-charged nucleophiles react faster than their neutral counterparts; (2) nucleophilic strength is in the same order as Brønsted-Lowry base strength when the nucleophilic atoms are in the same period of the periodic table; (3) nucleophilic strength increases with increasing atomic size when nucleophilic atoms are in the same family or group of the periodic table. You realize that the first and second criteria apply to this problem.

Specifically, you note that the negatively charged oxygen of the methoxide anion will be more nucleophilic than the neutral oxygen of the alcohol. It will also be more nucleophilic than the neutral amine. However, a neutral nitrogen is more basic than a neutral oxygen, so the amine will be a stronger nucleophile than the alcohol.

Choice **(C)** is correct because the negatively charged nucleophile is the fastest and methylamine is faster than methanol.

Choices **(A)** and **(B)** are incorrect because the methoxide anion is not listed as the fastest. Choice **(D)** is incorrect because methanol is listed as faster than methylamine.

Practice Problems: **PQ-9, PQ-10, PQ-11 and PQ-12**

SQ-5. Which alkyl halide would you expect to undergo an S_N1 reaction most rapidly?

(A) $(CH_3)_3CI$ (B) $(CH_3)_3CBr$ (C) $(CH_3)_3CCl$ (D) $(CH_3)_3CF$

Knowledge Required: (1) Mechanism of the S_N1 reaction. (2) Carbocation generation. (3) Leaving group ability.

Thinking it Through: Given that the prompt tells you the reaction type, you recall that the speed of an S_N1 reaction depends upon the ability of the substrate to form a carbocation. You note that from the options given in the question, the rate-determining step of this S_N1 reaction is the generation of the same tertiary carbocation by the displacement of a halide leaving group (X^-):

$$(CH_3)_3C{-}X \longrightarrow (CH_3)_3\overset{\oplus}{C} + \overset{\ominus}{X}$$

You know that leaving group ability increases with decreasing Brønsted-Lowry base strength or increasing strength of the leaving group's conjugate acid. For the halogens, iodide is the weakest base, while fluoride is the strongest base. The weaker base is always the better leaving group.

For other similar questions, you recall that carbocation stability decreases in the following order: $3°\ C^+ > 2°\ C^+ \gg 1°\ C^+$. This is due to the fact that electron-donating groups stabilize the carbocation, and alkyl (R) groups are mildly electron donating.

Choice **(A)** is correct because iodide is the weakest Brønsted-Lowry base of the halides and HI is the strongest conjugate acid of the halides.

Choices **(B)**, **(C)**, and **(D)** all contain stronger halide bases (and thus weaker conjugate acids than HI).

Practice Problems: **PQ-13, PQ-14, PQ-15, PQ-16, PQ-17 and PQ-18**

SQ-6. Which bromide will undergo a solvolysis reaction the fastest?

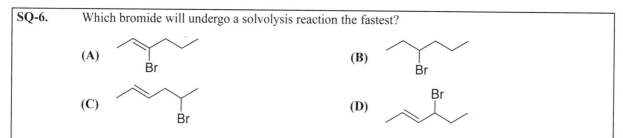

Knowledge Required: (1) Substitution of alkyl halides. (2) Effects of steric and electronic factors in the substrate on S_N1 reactions.

Thinking it Through: You know that the rate of an S_N1 reaction is a function of the stability of the carbocation that forms in the rate-determining first step of the mechanism. Further in this question you must recall the stability of allylic carbocations (and also recall that benzylic carbocations behave similarly).

Allylic and benzylic carbocations are resonance-stabilized by delocalizing the carbocation through the π-system. For allylic or benzylic stability, you are looking for a leaving group to be on the carbon adjacent to the π-bond.

Choice **(D)** is correct because it forms a secondary allylic carbocation that is resonance stabilized.

Choice **(A)** is not correct because it forms a vinylic carbocation, which is far less stable than an alkyl (or allylic) carbocation. Placing the carbocation on a carbon of the double bond is NOT favored. Choices **(B)** and **(C)** are not correct because they form carbocations that are secondary, but not resonance-stabilized (allylic).

Practice Problems: **PQ-19, PQ-20, PQ-21, PQ-22, PQ-23** and **PQ-24**

SQ-7	What is the major substitution product of the reaction?

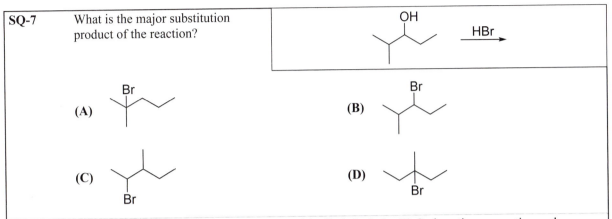

Knowledge Required: (1) Mechanism of HX reaction with alkyl alcohols. (2) Carbocation generation and rearrangement in S_N1 reactions.

Thinking it Through: You know that secondary and tertiary alcohols react with hydrogen halides through the S_N1 mechanism. You know that rearrangements can occur (hydride, alkyl, or carbon backbone) when a more stable carbocation can be formed from the initial carbocation. You see that the initial carbocation that forms, after the protonation of the hydroxyl and loss of a water molecule, is secondary. You recall that after rearrangement by way of 1,2-hydride shift, this initial carbocation can form a tertiary carbocation:

After the formation of the stable tertiary carbocation, a bromide ion will attack and form the final product. This attack can happen from either the top or bottom face of the trigonal planar carbocation. If this carbon were a stereocenter a racemic mix of products would occur.

Choice **(A)** is correct because this structure is the result of bromide nucleophile attacking the carbocation that forms after the initial carbocation undergoes a 1,2-hydride shift.

Choice **(B)** is not correct because although it appears the initial carbocation was formed, no rearrangement has taken place with the initial secondary carbocation. Choice **(C)** is not correct because although a 1,2-methyl shift has taken place, the resulting carbocation that reacted with the bromide nucleophile was not more stable than the initial carbocation. Choice **(D)** is not correct because it corresponds to the product of a 1,2-methyl shift without rearrangement of the initial carbocation.

Practice Problems: **PQ-25 and PQ-26**

SQ-8.	What reagent is needed to complete the reaction?

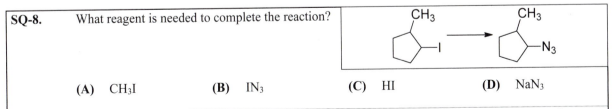

(A) CH_3I **(B)** IN_3 **(C)** HI **(D)** NaN_3

Knowledge Required: (1) Definition of nucleophiles, Lewis bases, and leaving groups. (2) Reactants, products, and mechanisms of nucleophilic substitution reactions.

Thinking it Through: You know that the switching of one functional group for another is the definition of a substitution reaction. You also know that halides, such as the given iodide, are good leaving groups for nucleophilic substitution reactions. The appearance of the azide (N_3^-) group in the product indicates it needs to be added to the reaction mixture to form this specific product. You recall that nucleophiles are often delivered to reaction mixtures as ionic salts including appropriate spectator counter-cations.

Choice **(D)** is correct because it both includes the azide nucleophile and an appropriate counterion, sodium cation.

Choice **(B)** is not correct because iodine and nitrogen do not make an ionic bond, and therefore cannot supply the needed azide anion.

Choices **(A)** and **(C)** are not correct because they would not supply azide anion to the reaction mixture.

Practice Problems: **PQ-27**

SQ-9.   Which structure best depicts the transition state for the reaction of CH_3Br with CH_3OK in CH_3OH?

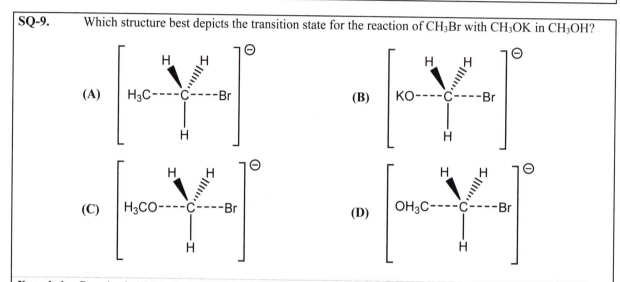

Knowledge Required: (1) Mechanism of the S_N2 reaction. (2) How to draw transition states.

Thinking it Through: You know that the reaction of methyl bromide (CH_3Br) with potassium methoxide (CH_3OK) is a bimolecular nucleophilic substitution (S_N2) reaction. You also know that the mechanism of S_N2 reactions proceeds through a concerted mechanism where the bond to the nucleophile is partially formed, and the bond to the leaving group is partially broken.

In addition, you know that the S_N2 mechanism occurs by the nucleophile attacking from the "backside" of the alkyl halide, meaning the nucleophile must approach at an angle 180° away from the leaving group. You also know that on methoxide, it is the oxygen atom that is nucleophilic and not the carbon atom.

In general, for reaction diagrams you recall that there is a transition state between each reactant-intermediate and product, so in order to identify transition states you must first draw the mechanism of the reaction. You know a transition state will occur between each isolatable species in your mechanism:

Choice **(C)** is correct because it shows the bond to the nucleophile (methoxide) partially formed and the bond to the leaving group (bromide) partially broken. The new bond is forming from the nucleophile's oxygen atom.

Choice **(A)** is not correct because the attacking nucleophile is not a methyl carbanion. Choice **(B)** is not correct because the attacking nucleophile is not an oxygen/potassium salt. In addition, this oxygen atom would carry a –2 charge. Choice **(D)** is not correct because although it shows a bond forming from the nucleophile, the atom forming the bond is a carbon, not the nucleophilic oxygen.

Practice Problems: **PQ-28** and **PQ-29**

SQ-10.	Which solvent best promotes a unimolecular (S$_N$1) mechanistic pathway?

    (A)   acetone (H$_3$CCOCH$_3$)   **(B)**   methylene chloride (CH$_2$Cl$_2$)

    (C)   ethanol (H$_3$CCH$_2$OH)   **(D)**   *n*-hexane (H$_3$C(CH$_2$)$_4$CH$_3$)

Knowledge Required: (1) Mechanism of unimolecular substitution (S$_N$1) pathways. (2) Solvent effects on nucleophilic substitution pathways.

Thinking it Through: You know that solvents can play a role in the kinetics of nucleophilic substitution reactions. You recall that nonpolar solvents do not allow S$_N$1 reactions to occur because they cannot stabilize the ionic intermediates, but polar solvents do. You also know that polar protic solvents, like water and alcohols, tend to assist with leaving group dissociation. They also solvate the ionic intermediates, so they are known to speed up unimolecular pathways like S$_N$1.

        You recall that most organic reactions require a polar solvent to dissolve the reactants: S$_N$1 reactions occur in polar protic solvents and S$_N$2 reactions occur in polar aprotic solvents. You know that in this case you do not want the solvent to interact too strongly with the nucleophile, as the nucleophile is involved in the rate-determining-step, thus a solvent with a lower dielectric constant, while still capable of dissolving the molecules, is preferred.

        Choice **(C)** is correct because ethanol is a polar protic solvent, preferred in an S$_N$1 reaction.

        Choices **(A)** and **(B)** are not correct because although they are polar solvents, they are aprotic. Choice **(D)** is not correct because hexanes are a nonpolar solvent.

Practice Problems: **PQ-30**

Practice Questions (PQ)

PQ-1. The effect of doubling the concentration of bromomethane for the reaction would be to multiply the reaction rate by a factor of

$$CH_3Br + {}^{\ominus}OH \longrightarrow CH_3OH + {}^{\ominus}Br$$

    (A) ¼.   **(B)** ½.   **(C)** 2.   **(D)** 4.

PQ-2. Consider the reaction of 2-chloro-2-methylpentane with sodium iodide. Assuming no other changes, how would it affect the rate if one simultaneously doubled the concentration of 2-chloro-2-methylpentane and sodium iodide?

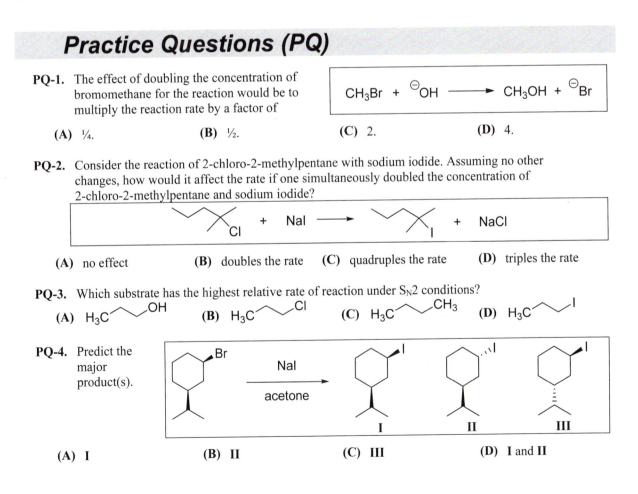

    (A) no effect   **(B)** doubles the rate   **(C)** quadruples the rate   **(D)** triples the rate

PQ-3. Which substrate has the highest relative rate of reaction under S$_N$2 conditions?

    (A) H$_3$C⌒⌒OH   **(B)** H$_3$C⌒⌒Cl   **(C)** H$_3$C⌒⌒CH$_3$ **(D)** H$_3$C⌒⌒I

PQ-4. Predict the major product(s).

    (A) I   **(B)** II   **(C)** III   **(D)** I and II

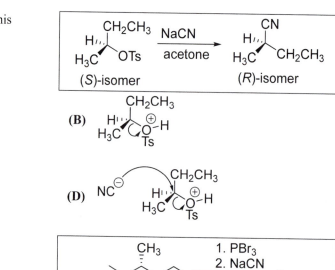

PQ-5. A bimolecular nucleophilic substitution (S_N2) is

    (A) a two-step process in which a bond is broken, then a new bond is formed and there is inversion of configuration.

    (B) a two-step process in which a bond is broken, then a new bond is formed and there is retention of configuration.

    (C) a one-step process with inversion of configuration.

    (D) a one-step process with retention of configuration.

PQ-6. What is the rate determining step of this reaction?

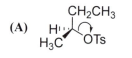

    (A)

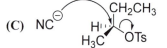

    (B)

    (C)

    (D)

PQ-7. What is the major product?

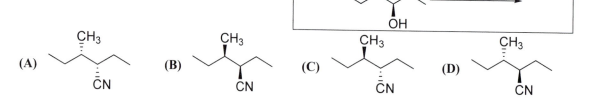

    (A)   **(B)**   **(C)**   **(D)**

PQ-8. Consider the substitution reaction that takes place when (*R*)-3-bromo-3-methylhexane is treated with methanol. What would be true?

    (A) The reaction would take place <u>only</u> with inversion of configuration at the stereogenic center.

    (B) The reaction would take place <u>only</u> with retention of configuration at the stereogenic center.

    (C) The reaction would take place with racemization.

    (D) The alkyl halide does not possess a stereogenic center.

PQ-9. What is the *weakest* nucleophile?

    (A)   **(B)**   **(C)**   **(D)**

PQ-10. What is the strongest nucleophile when dimethyl sulfoxide (DMSO) is used as a solvent in an S_N2 reaction?

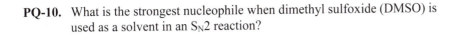

(A) F^- (B) Cl^- (C) Br^- (D) I^-

PQ-11. Which reaction would proceed the fastest?

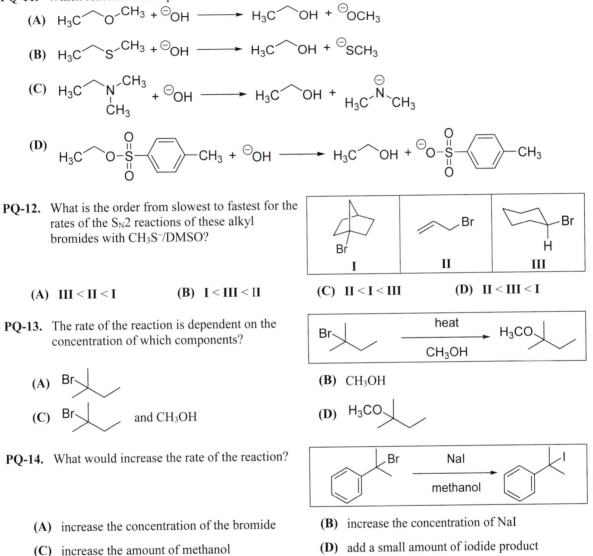

PQ-12. What is the order from slowest to fastest for the rates of the S_N2 reactions of these alkyl bromides with CH_3S^-/DMSO?

(A) $III < II < I$ (B) $I < III < II$ (C) $II < I < III$ (D) $II < III < I$

PQ-13. The rate of the reaction is dependent on the concentration of which components?

(A) (structure)   (B) CH_3OH

(C) (structure) and CH_3OH (D) (structure)

PQ-14. What would increase the rate of the reaction?

(A) increase the concentration of the bromide   (B) increase the concentration of NaI

(C) increase the amount of methanol   (D) add a small amount of iodide product

PQ-15. Which statement(s) is/are true regarding leaving groups?

I.	Weak bases make good leaving groups.
II.	Large, polarizable anions make good leaving groups.
III.	Alkyl groups make good leaving groups.
IV.	Leaving group ability is only important for S_N2 reactions.

(A) I only   (B) I and II   (C) I, II, and III   (D) I, II, and IV

PQ-16. What would not act as a leaving group?

(A) $Br^\ominus$ (B) $TsO^\ominus$ (C) H_2O (D) $^\ominus NH_2$

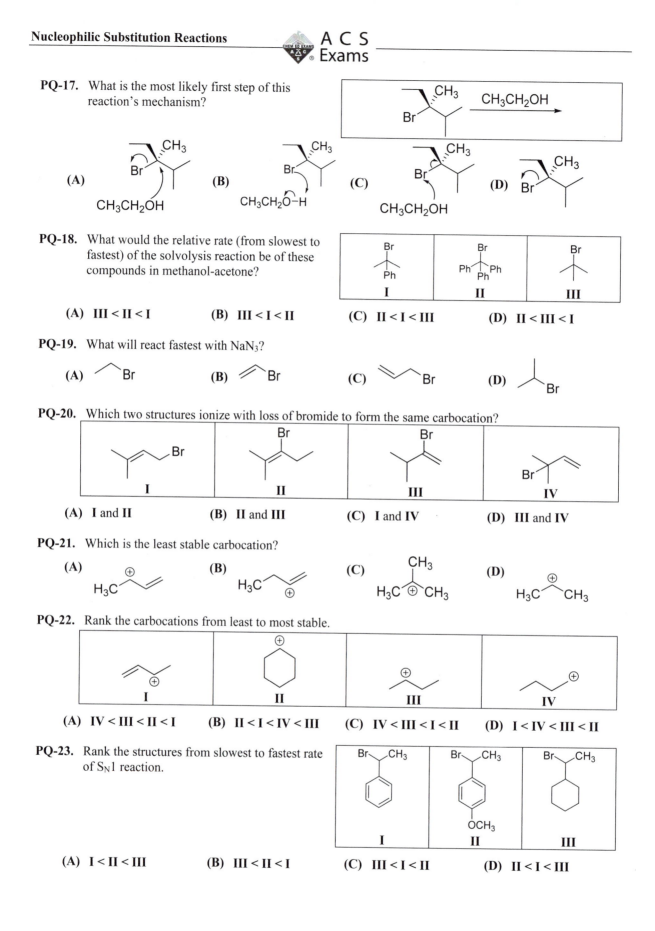

PQ-17. What is the most likely first step of this reaction's mechanism?

PQ-18. What would the relative rate (from slowest to fastest) of the solvolysis reaction be of these compounds in methanol-acetone?

(A) III < II < I   (B) III < I < II   (C) II < I < III   (D) II < III < I

PQ-19. What will react fastest with NaN_3?

PQ-20. Which two structures ionize with loss of bromide to form the same carbocation?

(A) I and II   (B) II and III   (C) I and IV   (D) III and IV

PQ-21. Which is the least stable carbocation?

PQ-22. Rank the carbocations from least to most stable.

(A) IV < III < II < I   (B) II < I < IV < III   (C) IV < III < I < II   (D) I < IV < III < II

PQ-23. Rank the structures from slowest to fastest rate of S_N1 reaction.

(A) I < II < III   (B) III < II < I   (C) III < I < II   (D) II < I < III

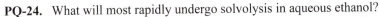 
PQ-24. What will most rapidly undergo solvolysis in aqueous ethanol?

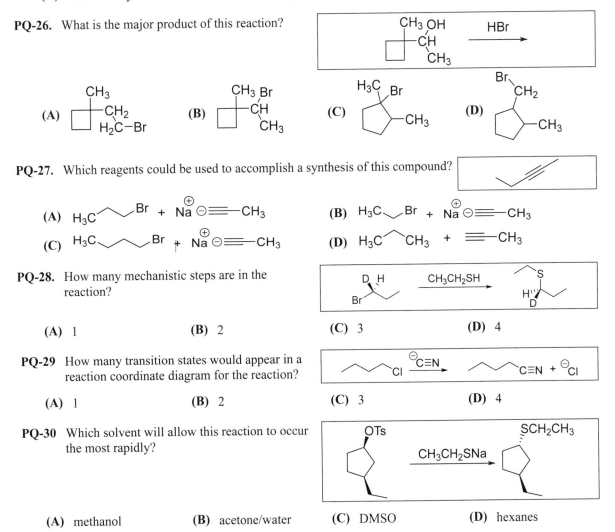

(A) **(B)** **(C)** **(D)**

PQ-25. Why must a secondary alcohol react with a haloacid to form an alkyl halide instead of just reacting with the halide nucleophile in a polar aprotic solvent?

(A) Halides are not strong enough nucleophiles to force this reaction.

(B) The acid must protonate the hydroxyl group to form a reasonable leaving group.

(C) Halides won't dissolve in polar aprotic solvents.

(D) A secondary alcohol is less reactive than a primary alcohol in an S_N1-like reaction.

PQ-26. What is the major product of this reaction?

(A) **(B)** **(C)** **(D)**

PQ-27. Which reagents could be used to accomplish a synthesis of this compound?

(A) **(B)**

(C) **(D)**

PQ-28. How many mechanistic steps are in the reaction?

(A) 1 **(B)** 2 **(C)** 3 **(D)** 4

PQ-29 How many transition states would appear in a reaction coordinate diagram for the reaction?

(A) 1 **(B)** 2 **(C)** 3 **(D)** 4

PQ-30 Which solvent will allow this reaction to occur the most rapidly?

(A) methanol **(B)** acetone/water **(C)** DMSO **(D)** hexanes

Answers to Study Questions

SQ-1.	D	SQ-5.	A	SQ-9.	C
SQ-2.	A	SQ-6.	D	SQ-10.	C
SQ-3.	B	SQ-7.	A		
SQ-4.	C	SQ-8.	D		

Answers to Practice Questions

PQ-1.	C	PQ-11.	D	PQ-21.	B
PQ-2.	B	PQ-12.	B	PQ-22.	A
PQ-3.	D	PQ-13.	A	PQ-23.	C
PQ-4.	B	PQ-14.	A	PQ-24.	A
PQ-5.	C	PQ-15.	B	PQ-25.	B
PQ-6.	C	PQ-16.	D	PQ-26.	C
PQ-7.	D	PQ-17.	D	PQ-27.	B
PQ-8.	C	PQ-18.	B	PQ-28.	B
PQ-9	A	PQ-19.	C	PQ-29.	A
PQ-10.	A	PQ-20.	C	PQ-30.	C

Chapter 6 – Elimination Reactions

Chapter Summary:

This chapter will focus on how to recognize elimination reactions, where nucleophiles react as Brønsted-Lowry bases with the acidic protons of alkyl substrates to form alkene products after loss of a leaving group. Also included in this chapter are questions related to unimolecular (E1) and bimolecular (E2) elimination pathways, mechanisms of these reactions, regioselective and stereospecific reactions, and carbocation rearrangements. In addition, questions related to competition between elimination and nucleophilic substitution reactions are covered.

Specific topics covered in this chapter are:
- Reactants and products of elimination reactions
- Unimolecular elimination pathway (E1)
- Bimolecular elimination pathway (E2)
- Mechanisms including regioselectivity and stereospecificity of elimination reactions
- Carbocation rearrangements in dehydration reactions of alcohols
- Competition between elimination and nucleophilic substitution reactions

Previous material that is relevant to your understanding of questions in this chapter include:
- Constitutional and Stereochemical Isomers *(Chapter 3)*
- Acids and Bases *(Chapter 4)*
- Nucleophilic Substitution *(Chapter 5)*

Where you might see related material in upcoming Study Guide chapters:
- Chapters associated with the second semester organic chemistry course: Conjugated Systems and Aromaticity *(Chapter 11)* and the cumulative full-year examination.

Where to find this in your textbook:

The material in this chapter typically aligns to "Elimination Reactions" and "Alkenes" in your textbook. The name of your chapter may vary.

Practice exam:

There may be practice exam questions aligned to the material in this chapter. Because there are a limited number of questions on the practice exam, a review of the breadth of the material in this chapter is advised in preparation for your exam.

How this fits to the big picture:

The material in this chapter aligns to the Big Ideas of Chemical Reactions (V) and Kinetics (VII) as listed on page 13 of this study guide.

Study Questions (SQ)

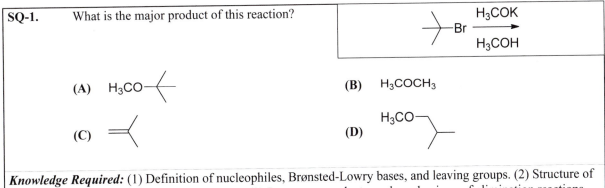

SQ-1.   What is the major product of this reaction?

(A) H_3CO—

(B) H_3COCH_3

(C)

(D) H_3CO—

Knowledge Required: (1) Definition of nucleophiles, Brønsted-Lowry bases, and leaving groups. (2) Structure of primary, secondary, and tertiary alkyl groups. (3) Reactants, products, and mechanisms of elimination reactions. (4) Factors that control elimination versus substitution pathways.

Thinking it Through: You observe that this is a reaction of a tertiary alkyl halide with a strong unhindered base (methoxide anion) in methanol solvent. You recall that this combination of base/nucleophile and solvent may favor either a bimolecular elimination (E2) or substitution (S_N1) pathway, and that these differing pathways result in the formation of different products.

You recall that tertiary alkyl halides will prefer to go via an elimination pathway, as the alkene formed will be stable, and substitution on a hindered carbon atom is difficult. Thus, to complete this problem, you simply need to eliminate a β hydrogen and the bromide leaving group and introduce a π bond. You note that there is only one type of β hydrogen available for this molecule and thus no further considerations need to be given.

Choice (C) is the correct answer. It is the only elimination product.

Choice (A) is not correct because it is the substitution product, unfavorable given the reagents. Choices (B) and (D) are not correct because they are not viable major or minor products for this reaction.

Practice Problems: **PQ-1** and **PQ-2**

SQ-2. Which reactant would yield these two products?

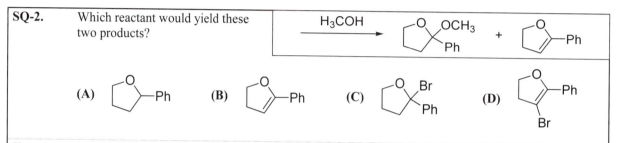

Knowledge Required: (1) Definition of nucleophiles, Brønsted-Lowry bases, and leaving groups. (2) Reactants, products, and mechanisms of elimination and substitution reactions.

Thinking it Through: Upon reading the prompt, you note that two products are formed. In this case both a substitution and an elimination product have formed. The second product containing the π bond you recognize as an elimination product, while the first product is formed via a substitution, where the methanol solvent has added, followed by a deprotonation.

You realize that the substitution product tells you the carbon-atom on which the leaving group was located prior to the reaction. Thus, you will need a reactant with a reasonable leaving group on the carbon attached to the oxygen in the ring, which also holds the phenyl group, as long as rearrangements do not occur. You also note that this carbon in the starting material will thus be a 3° carbon atom, and thus there will be no rearrangement.

You know that tertiary carbon atoms in the absence of a good nucleophile (methanol is a poor nucleophile) will undergo S_N1 reactions, with accompanying E1 minor products.

Choice (C) is correct because it contains a leaving group (–Br) connected to the correct carbon atom.

Choices (A), (B), and (D) are not correct because they do not contain leaving groups attached to the correct carbon atom.

Practice Problems: **PQ-1** and **PQ-2**

SQ-3. What is the major product of this reaction?

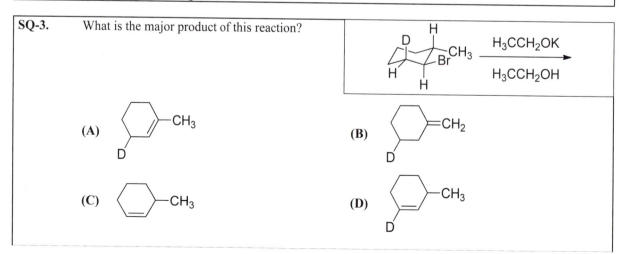

Knowledge Required: (1) Stereochemical requirements for β eliminations that proceed by the E2 pathway. (2) Conformational changes for cyclohexanes.

Thinking it Through: You recognize in the prompt that you are reacting a 2° alkyl halide with a strong unhindered base (ethoxide, $CH_3CH_2O^-$), these conditions favor the E2 reaction pathway as the major product. You recognize that you will therefore be looking for a β hydrogen atom to eliminate along with the bromide leaving group.

      You further recall that E2 reactions require a transition state in which the β hydrogen atom and the leaving group lie in the same plane and are often in the *anti*-conformation. You know that when an elimination occurs in a cyclohexane ring, anti-periplanar requirement means the –H atom and the leaving group are related as *trans*- and diaxial. You notice that in the given chair conformation, the bromide is equatorial; therefore, the ring must flip to the other conformation before an elimination reaction can occur:

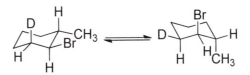

      You inspect the new conformation, which reveals that there is only one β hydrogen that is both axial and *trans*- to the bromide leaving group. Thus, the hydrogen on that carbon that also holds the deuterium will be eliminated, not what may appear to be the more stable choice, the hydrogen attached to the carbon with the methyl group. This is a very common error, as usually the more substituted alkene is preferred, but when an E2 reaction occurs on a ring, the mechanistic requirement of periplanar atoms supersedes the formation of a stable alkene. This anti-periplanar requirement also effects E2 reactions on planar molecules and can affect whether the *E* or *Z* alkene is formed.

      Choice **(D)** is correct because it is the only alkene that can be produced.

      Choices **(A)** and **(C)** are not correct because they would be formed by a *syn* elimination. Choice **(B)** is not possible because the removed hydrogen atom and bromide leaving group are not on adjacent carbon atoms.

Practice Problems: **PQ-3, PQ-4, PQ-5, PQ-6, PQ-7** and **PQ-8**

SQ-4.   What is the major product of this reaction?

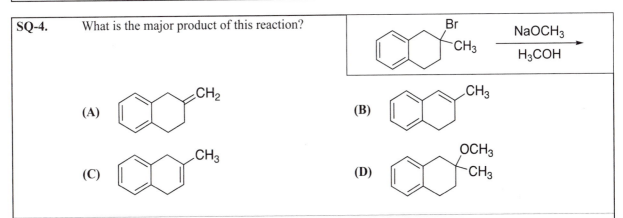

Knowledge Required: (1) Factors that control regiochemistry of β elimination.

      Thinking it Through: You recognize that the starting material is a 3° alkyl halide that is reacting with a strong unhindered base (methoxide, CH_3O^-), and you identify that this reaction will proceed via an E2 elimination pathway. You know that when more than one set of β hydrogen atoms is present in an alkyl halide, electronic and steric factors control which β hydrogen is preferentially abstracted by a base in an elimination reaction.

      You recognize that when the alkyl halide and base are sterically unhindered, electronic factors dominate. You recall that the transition state for an E2 mechanism has double bond formation character; therefore, alkene stability affects transition state energy. In other words, when using an unhindered base (Zaitsev base), you know that the base removes the –H atom which will lead to the most thermodynamically stable alkene, you also refer to this as the Zaitsev product. You notice that the alkyl halide reactant contains three types of β hydrogen atoms (shown below) and thus there are three possible products:

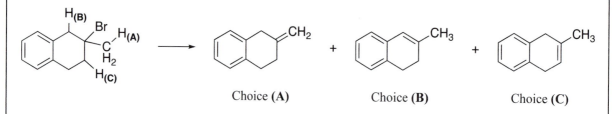

Choice (**A**)   Choice (**B**)   Choice (**C**)

Alkene stability in this reaction has two components. First, the more substituted alkene (more –R groups on the double bond) is always more stable. Two of the possible products in this example would have three –R groups attached, while the third product would have only two –R groups. To decide between the two more substituted products, you notice that one possibility would be conjugated to the aromatic ring, while the other would not. Conjugation is preferred.

Choice (**B**) is the correct answer because it is the most thermodynamically stable product due to three –R groups on the alkene and conjugation to the aromatic ring.

Choice (**A**) is not correct because it is the least thermodynamically stable possible product. It would form by the reaction of the starting material with a strong hindered base (known as a Hoffman base).

Choice (**C**) is not correct because though the alkene has three –R group substituents, it is not conjugated.

Choice (**D**) is not correct because it is produced through a substitution mechanism which is not favored based on the substrate, reactant, and solvent conditions.

Practice Problems: **PQ-9, PQ-10, PQ-11, PQ-12, PQ-13** and **PQ-14**

SQ-5. Which alkene is likely to be formed in the largest quantity if the alcohol is dehydrated?

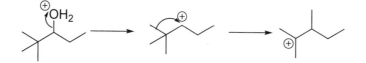

(A)   (B)   (C)   (D)

Knowledge Required: (1) Dehydration of alcohols with strong acid to form leaving groups. (2) Elimination reactions. (3) Carbocation rearrangements.

Thinking it Through: You recognize the reaction in the prompt as a dehydration of an alcohol, proceeding via an E1 reaction pathway. You know that the addition of strong acids like sulfuric acid (H_2SO_4) to alkyl alcohols protonates their hydroxyl groups to form water. You also know that dehydration reactions involve the loss of a water molecule as a leaving group. When the OH group in the given starting material is protonated by the sulfuric acid, a secondary carbocation will form. However, you know that carbocations can rearrange by shifting an alkyl group or hydride, if the resulting carbocation will be more stable. You note that in this reaction, a methyl shift would generate a more stable tertiary carbocation:

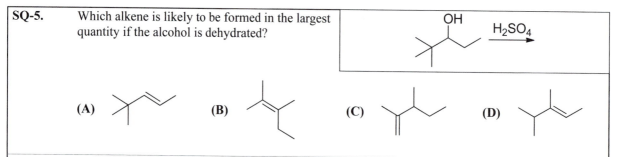

You recall that next deprotonation of the β hydrogen relative to the carbocation takes place, and you recognize that there are 2 different sources of β hydrogen atoms. The removal of the β-hydrogen atom that leads to the more stable alkene (more highly substituted) is thermodynamically preferred.

Choice (**B**) is correct. It comes from the correct carbocation and is most thermodynamically stable.

Choice **(A)** is not correct. The carbocation rearrangement did not occur. Choice **(C)** is not correct. It arises from the β deprotonation of a methyl group, resulting in a less stable alkene. Choice **(D)** is not correct. It could arise from multiple, successive carbocation rearrangements (beyond the one illustrated), but these mechanistic steps are very fast and tend to generate the most stable alkene product in the fewest possible steps.

Practice Problems: **PQ-15, PQ-16, PQ-17, PQ-18,** and **PQ-19**

SQ-6. What is the proper representation of the flow of electrons in the E2 elimination mechanism?

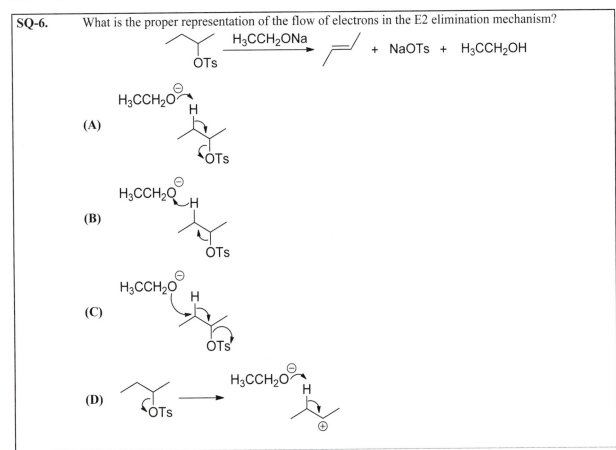

Knowledge Required: (1) Mechanisms of E2 and E1 elimination reactions.

Thinking it Through: You know that the E2 elimination reaction is described by a concerted, bimolecular mechanism where deprotonation of a H atom beta to a leaving group (in this case tosylate, –OTs) leads to dissociation of the leaving group and generation of a new alkene. You recall that the flow of electrons starts at the Brønsted-Lowry base, moves toward the β hydrogen, then toward the new alkene, then finally to the leaving group. All of these atoms must lie in the same plane, often referred to as an anti-periplanar arrangement of atoms in the starting material.

Choice **(A)** is correct. It shows the arrows flowing in the correct direction and would lead to the product.

Choice **(B)** is not correct because the "flow" of electrons begins at the leaving group and moving ultimately toward the attacking Brønsted-Lowry base. Choice **(C)** is not correct because the base is attacking a carbon atom instead of a β hydrogen and the electrons are not flowing toward the heteroatom in the leaving group. Choice **(D)** is not correct because this is a two-step mechanism involving the generation of an intermediate carbocation. This is an E1 pathway.

Practice Problems: **PQ-20, PQ-21 and PQ-22**

SQ-7. Which compound would give only one alkene product when treated with sodium methoxide and heat?

(A) 1-bromo-2,3-dimethylpentane

(B) 2-bromo-2,3-dimethylpentane

(C) 3-bromo-2,3-dimethylpentane

(D) 2-bromo-3,4-dimethylpentane

Knowledge Required: (1) Nomenclature of alkyl halides. (2) Elimination reaction products.

Thinking it Through: You know that strong bases such as sodium methoxide, when reacted with alkyl halides in the presence of heat give alkene functional group products through elimination pathways. Because the choices are all given as their IUPAC names, you know to translate these into structures.

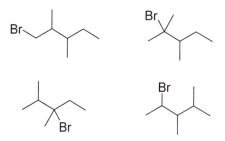

You know that bimolecular elimination pathways (E2 reactions) proceed with strong Brønsted-Lowry bases removing a hydrogen atom beta, or two carbons away, from the bromide leaving group. You realize that this question is not asking for the major product, which would be governed by whether the base was hindered or unhindered, but instead is looking for a starting material that will produce only one product. You realize that you are therefore looking for a starting material with only ONE source of β-hydrogen atoms.

Choice (A) is the correct response because the removal of the β hydrogen and bromide leaving group generates only one possible alkene product.

Choices (B) and (D) are not correct because there are two unique sets of hydrogen atoms beta to the bromide leaving group in each. Choice (C) is not correct because there are three unique sets of hydrogen atoms beta to the bromide leaving group.

Practice Problems: **PQ-23** and **PQ-24**

SQ-8. Each condition would promote an elimination pathway with this reaction EXCEPT one. What is the EXCEPTION?

(A) increase in temperature

(B) dissolution in nonpolar solvent

(C) addition of a base which is also a poor nucleophile

(D) addition of a strong base

Knowledge Required: (1) Conditions and mechanism for elimination mechanistic pathways.

Thinking it Through: You recall that elimination reactions take place when alkyl halides are added to conditions which remove hydrogen atoms and lose halide leaving groups. Both unimolecular (E1) and bimolecular (E2) mechanism pathways are possible, usually determined by the strength of the added Brønsted-Lowry base. You also know that temperature variations have the ability to effect elimination reactions, higher temperatures will drive elimination pathways in preference to the substitution alternatives.

Choice (B) is the correct. Dissolution of alkyl halide in non-polar solvents does not favor an elimination.

Choices (C) and (D) are not correct. They involve the addition of bases where deprotonation and loss of a leaving group is possible (dehydrohalogenation), resulting in elimination products. Choice (A) is not correct. It involves the addition of heat, which can increase the likelihood of elimination reactions due to increasing the entropy of the reaction, making ΔG more negative for elimination.

Practice Problems: **PQ-25** and **PQ-26**

SQ-9. What is the product of this reaction?

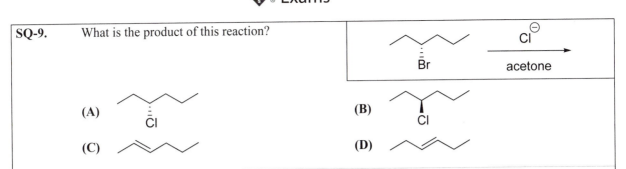

(A) $\overset{..}{Cl}$

(B) Cl

(C)

(D)

Knowledge Required: (1) Deciding on the mechanistic pathway between S_N1, S_N2, E1 and E2 reactions.

Thinking it Through: As you complete the review of substitution and elimination reactions, a key step to any of these questions is to correctly identify which of the four potential mechanisms will produce the major product. Though heat and solvent choice can certainly vary the outcome, it is good to have a guide to the most common outcomes of these reactions.

You recall that both the nature of substrate (1°, 2°, or 3°) will play a role as will the nature and strength of the nucleophile/base. The table below provides a good guide for general outcomes of these reactions in absence of changes in heat and solvents:

Type of alkyl halide	Poor Nu; Weak base	Good Nu; Weak base	Good Nu; Moderate base	Good Nu; strong unhindered base	Poor Nu; strong hindered base
1° unbranched	S_N2	S_N2	S_N2	S_N2	E2
1° branched	S_N2	S_N2	S_N2	E2	E2
2°	S_N1	S_N2	S_N2	E2	E2
3°	S_N1	S_N1	E2	E2	E2
Example Nu/Bases	water or alcohol	halides	^-CN, $^-N_3$, ^-SH	unhindered alkoxides, hydroxide	LDA and t-BuO$^-$

You note that in this prompt, the reaction is that of a secondary alkyl halide with a weak base/good nucleophile (i.e., Cl⁻) and thus will proceed via an S_N2 pathway as the major project.

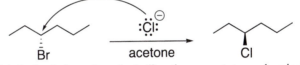

Choice **(B)** is correct. This is the S_N2 product, including the correct stereochemical outcome.

Choice **(A)** is not correct. Though this appears to be a substitution product, the stereochemistry is incorrect.

Choices **(C)** and **(D)** are not correct. These are the elimination products, which would be minor products.

Practice Problems: **PQ-27, PQ-28, PQ-29** and **PQ-30**

Practice Questions (PQ)

PQ-1. What is the product of this reaction?

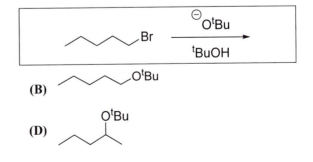

(A)

(B) O^tBu

(C)

(D) O^tBu

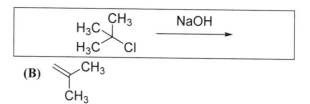

PQ-2. What is the product of this reaction?

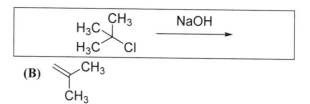

(A)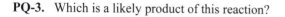

(B)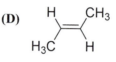

(C)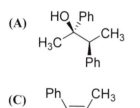

(D)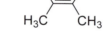

PQ-3. Which is a likely product of this reaction?

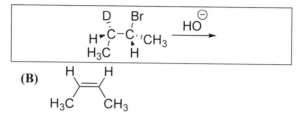

(A)

(B)

(C)

(D)

PQ-4. What is the major product of this reaction?

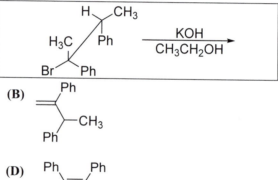

(A)

(B)

(C)

(D)

PQ-5. What is/are the possible product(s) of dehydrohalogenation of *cis*-1-bromo-2-methylcyclohexane?

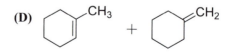

(A)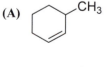

(B)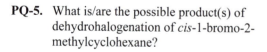

(C)

(D)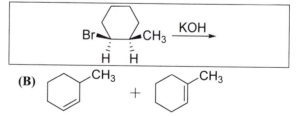

PQ-6. What is/are the possible product(s) of dehydrohalogenation of *trans*-1-bromo-2-methylcyclohexane?

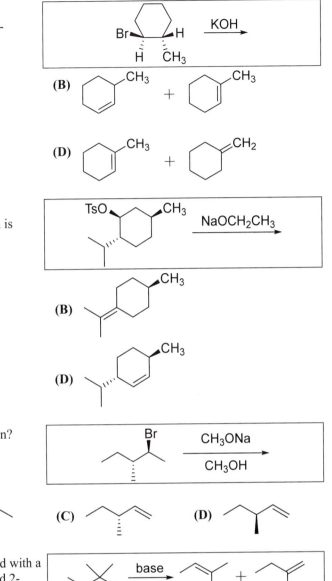

(A)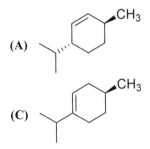

(B)

(C)

(D)

PQ-7. Which product would suggest that a bimolecular elimination (E2) mechanism is occurring?

(A)

(B)

(C)

(D)

PQ-8. What is the major product of this reaction?

(A)   (B)   (C)   (D)

PQ-9. When 2-bromo-2-methylbutane is treated with a base, a mixture of 2-methyl-2-butene and 2-methyl-1-butene is produced; when potassium hydroxide is the base, 2-methyl-1-butene accounts for 45% of the product mixture. However, when potassium *tert*-butoxide is the base, 2-methyl-1-butene accounts for 70% of the product mixture. What percent of 2-methyl-1-butene would be in the mixture if potassium propoxide were the base?

(A) Less than 45%

(B) 45%

(C) Between 45% and 70%

(D) More than 70%

PQ-10. What would be the major product of the dehydrohalogenation of 2-chloropentane by KOH?

(A)

(B)

(C)

(D)

PQ-11. Zaitsev's rule states that

 (A) the order of reactivity of alcohols in dehydration reactions is 3° > 2° > 1°.

 (B) an equatorial substituent in cyclohexane results in a more stable conformation than if that substituent were axial.

 (C) E2 reactions occur only if the β hydrogen and leaving group can assume an anti-periplanar arrangement.

 (D) when a reaction forms an alkene, and several possibilities exist, the more (or most) stable isomer is the one which predominates.

PQ-12. What would be the major product of the dehydrohalogenation of 3-chloropentane by KOH?

 (A)

 (B)

 (C)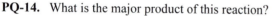

 (D)

PQ-13. In the dehydrohalogenation of 2-bromo-2-methylbutane with potassium hydroxide, which hydrogen atom is preferentially abstracted?

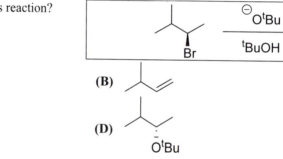

 (A) I   (B) II   (C) III   (D) I or II

PQ-14. What is the major product of this reaction?

 (A)   (B)

 (C)   (D)

PQ-15. What would be the first step in the dehydration reaction of cyclohexanol in sulfuric acid?

 (A) loss of hydroxide   (B) loss of proton by the alcohol

 (C) formation of a sulfite ester   (D) protonation of the alcohol

PQ-16. Which molecule is dehydrated fastest in concentrated H_2SO_4?

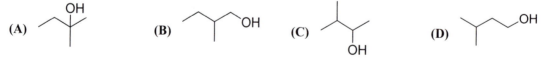

 (A)   (B)   (C)   (D)

PQ-17. Which step is NOT reasonable in the mechanism to describe the formation of 2-methyl-1-butene by dehydration of 3-methyl-2-butanol?

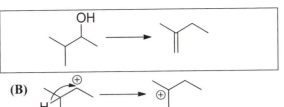

(A)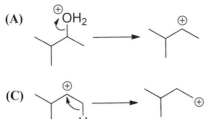

(B)

(C)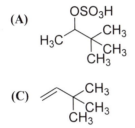

(D)

PQ-18. What is the major product of this dehydration reaction?

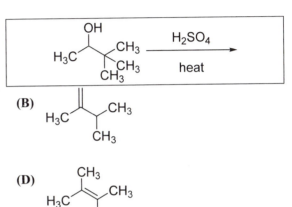

(A)

(B)

(C)

(D)

PQ-19. Why would concentrated hydrobromic acid be an inappropriate catalyst for the dehydration of alcohols?

(A) HBr is too weakly acidic to protonate the alcohol.

(B) The conjugate base, Br⁻, is a good nucleophile, and it would attack the carbocation to form an alkyl bromide.

(C) HBr is strongly acidic, so the water molecule would not be a good leaving group after protonation of the alcohol.

(D) HBr would be more likely to promote rearrangement of the carbocation intermediate.

PQ-20. What effect will reducing the volume of H_2O by half have on the reaction rate?

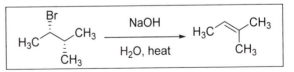

(A) reaction rate will double

(B) reaction rate will reduce by half

(C) reaction rate will quadruple

(D) no effect on the rate of this reaction

PQ-21. What is an example of a mechanistic step involved in an E2 reaction?

(A)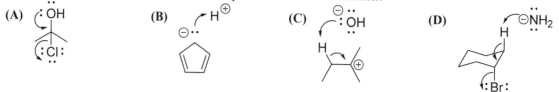

(B)

(C)

(D)

PQ-22. In a unimolecular elimination (E1) reaction, the correct order of mechanistic steps is

(A) dissociation of the leaving group, then deprotonation at the β position

(B) simultaneous dissociation of the leaving group and deprotonation of the β position

(C) association of the nucleophile/base, then dissociation of the leaving group

(D) deprotonation at the β position, then dissociation of the leaving group

PQ-23. How many alkene products, including *E/Z* isomers, can form from the E2 elimination of the compound?

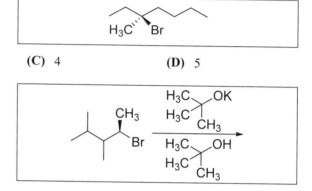

(A) 2   **(B)** 3   **(C)** 4   **(D)** 5

PQ-24. What is the major product of this reaction?

(A) 2,3-dimethyl-2-pentene   **(B)** 3,4-dimethyl-1-pentene

(C) *E*-3,4-dimethyl-2-pentene   **(D)** *Z*-3,4-dimethyl-2-pentene

PQ-25. Which reagents best accomplish this transformation?

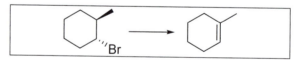

(A) CH₃ONa   **(B)** CH₃OH, heat

(C) POCl₃, pyridine   **(D)** H₃C–C(CH₃)₂–OK

PQ-26. What solvent results in the fastest rate for this reaction?

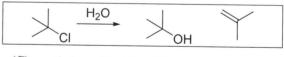

(A) hexanes   **(B)** acetone   **(C)** methylene chloride   **(D)** water

PQ-27. What is the product of this reaction?

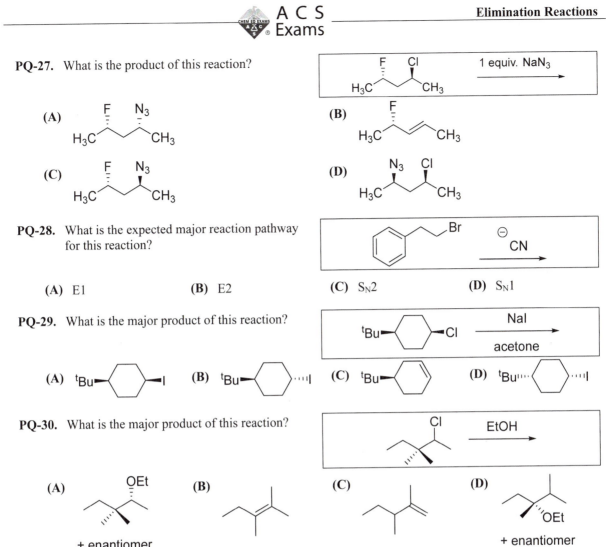

(A)

(B)

(C)

(D)

PQ-28. What is the expected major reaction pathway for this reaction?

(A) E1   (B) E2   (C) S_N2 (D) S_N1

PQ-29. What is the major product of this reaction?

(A) ^tBu (B) ^tBu (C) ^tBu (D) ^tBu

PQ-30. What is the major product of this reaction?

(A)

+ enantiomer

(B)

(C)

(D)

+ enantiomer

Answers to Study Questions

SQ-1.	C	SQ-4.	B	SQ-7.	A
SQ-2.	C	SQ-5.	B	SQ-8.	B
SQ-3.	D	SQ-6.	A	SQ-9.	B

Answers to Practice Questions

PQ-1.	A	PQ-11.	D	PQ-21.	D
PQ-2.	B	PQ-12.	D	PQ-22.	A
PQ-3.	D	PQ-13.	C	PQ-23.	D
PQ-4.	C	PQ-14.	B	PQ-24.	B
PQ-5.	B	PQ-15.	D	PQ-25.	B
PQ-6.	A	PQ-16.	A	PQ-26	D
PQ-7.	A	PQ-17.	C	PQ-27	A
PQ-8.	A	PQ-18	D	PQ-28	C
PQ-9	C	PQ-19.	B	PQ-29	B
PQ-10.	B	PQ-20.	C	PQ-30	D

Chapter 7 – Addition Reactions to Alkenes and Alkynes

Chapter Summary:

   This chapter will focus on addition reactions to alkenes and alkynes including Markovnikov's rule and *syn/anti*-addition reactions, hydration and hydrogenation reactions, and oxidation reactions.

Specific topics covered in this chapter are:
- Markovnikov's rule
- *Syn* and *anti*-addition
- Addition reactions utilizing HX and H_2O/H^+
- Hydration of alkenes involving oxymercuration/demercuration and hydroboration/oxidation
- Hydration of alkynes including tautomerization
- Oxidation of alkenes to form *syn*-diols
- Oxidation resulting in molecular cleavage
- Addition reactions utilizing X_2
- Hydrogenation reactions

Previous material that is relevant to your understanding of questions in this chapter include:
- Carbocation stability *(Chapter 1)*
- Carbocation rearrangements *(Chapter 5)*
- Energy diagrams including transition states and intermediates *(Chapter 5)*
- Regioselective reactions *(Chapter 6)*
- Stereospecific reactions *(Chapter 6)*

Where you might see this material in upcoming Study Guide chapters:
- Epoxide formation and reactions *(Chapter 8)*
- Anti-Markovnikov addition *(Chapter 10)*
- Enol tautomerization *(Chapter 14)*
- Application to Multi-step Synthesis *(Chapter 15)*

Where to find this in your textbook:

   The material in this chapter typically aligns to "Alkenes and Alkynes" or "Addition Reactions" in your textbook. The name of your chapter may vary.

Practice exam:

   There may be practice exam questions aligned to the material in this chapter. Because there are a limited number of questions on the practice exam, a review of the breadth of the material in this chapter is advised in preparation for your exam.

How this fits to the big picture:

   The material in this chapter aligns to the Big Ideas of Structure and Function (III) and Chemical Reactions (V) as listed on page 13 of this study guide.

Study Questions (SQ)

SQ-1. Which structure is the most likely intermediate for this reaction?

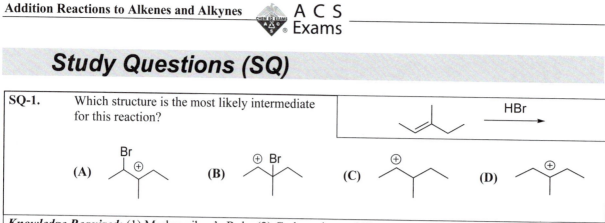

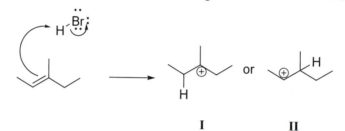

(A)   (B)   (C)   (D)

Knowledge Required: (1) Markovnikov's Rule. (2) Carbocation stability.

Thinking it Through: In solving this problem, you recall the mechanism for the addition of HBr to an alkene follows Markovnikov's rule, that the proton adds to the side of the alkene with the most H atoms. In this situation, the electron rich double bond acts as a nucleophile and attacks the partially positive H atom on HBr. Theoretically, the hydrogen may add to either side of the double bond, creating a carbocation on the other carbon.

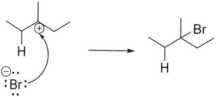

I   II

You recognize that intermediate **I**, which results from a Markovnikov addition, is a tertiary carbocation. You also recognize that intermediate **II** is a secondary carbocation. You remember that a tertiary carbocation is more stable than a secondary carbocation, so the transition state leading to it will also be lower in energy. This makes choice **(D)** the most favorable intermediate.

The reaction proceeds with the nucleophilic bromide attacking the carbocation, which completes the Markovnikov addition:

Choice **(D)** is correct because it is the only answer that leads to the correct product.

Choice **(A)** is not correct because the proton should add to the double bond first. Choice **(B)** is not correct because the proton should add to the double bond first and a less stable carbocation would result. Choice **(C)** is not correct because this intermediate forms the less stable carbocation after the protonation of the alkene.

Practice Problems: **PQ-1, PQ-2, PQ-3,** and **PQ-4**

SQ-2.	Which is the energy diagram for this reaction?	H_2O/H^+

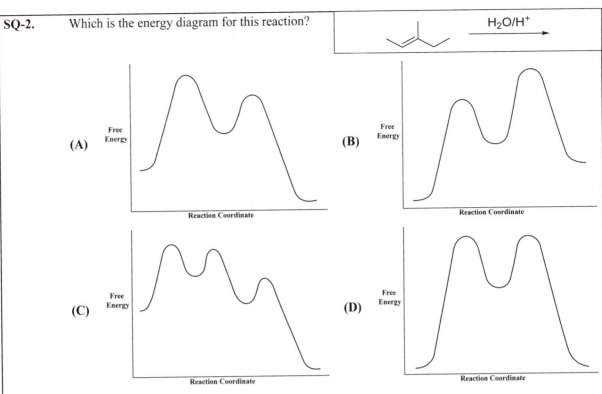

(A) Free Energy Reaction Coordinate

(B) Free Energy Reaction Coordinate

(C) Free Energy Reaction Coordinate

(D) Free Energy Reaction Coordinate

Knowledge Required: (1) Markovnikov's Rule. (2) Energy diagrams including transition states and intermediates.

Thinking it Through: You recognize that this reaction follows Markovnikov's rule and recall that it follows this mechanism:

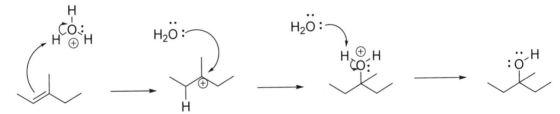

You recall that each reaction step has its own transition state. Because there are three reaction steps in this mechanism, there are three transition states, so that eliminates choices **(A)**, **(B)**, and **(D)**. You also remember that the formation of a carbocation intermediate takes a lot of energy and is endergonic. Because the formation of the carbocation occurs in the first step, this must be the rate determining step.

Choice **(C)** is the correct answer.

Choice **(A)** is not correct because it only has two transition states. (Note that this is the energy diagram for the mechanism in **SQ1**). Choices **(B)** and **(D)** are not correct because they only have two transition states.

Practice Problems: PQ-5, PQ-6 and PQ-7

| **SQ-3.** | What are the best reagents to complete this transformation? | 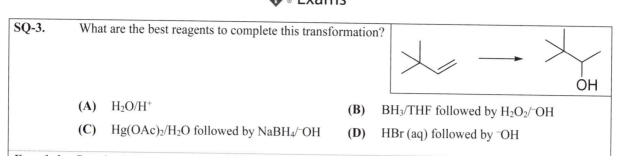 |

(A) H₂O/H⁺   **(B)** BH₃/THF followed by H₂O₂/⁻OH

(C) Hg(OAc)₂/H₂O followed by NaBH₄/⁻OH   **(D)** HBr (aq) followed by ⁻OH

Knowledge Required: (1) Markovnikov's Rule. (2) Hydration of alkenes involving oxymercuration/demercuration and hydroboration/oxidation. (3) Carbocation rearrangements. (4) Regioselective reactions.

Thinking it Through: In solving this problem, you first identify what atoms add to the alkene to yield the final product. In this reaction, you note that –H and –OH add. Next, you consider what regioselectivity the reaction follows and that this addition reaction yields a Markovnikov product, i.e. where the –H adds to the side of the alkene with the most hydrogens.

       Given the choice of reagents in the answer options, you recall that while the reagents in choices **(A)**, **(B)**, and **(C)** all yield alcohols, only choices **(A)** and **(C)** lead to Markovnikov additions. To consider which of these two choices is preferred, you notice the high level of branching on carbon-3, (i.e. the carbon next to the alkene). The addition reaction of H₂O/H⁺ to an alkene involves a carbocation intermediate. For choice **(A)**, the intermediate will undergo a 1,2-methyl shift resulting in a rearrangement, forming a more stable carbocation and a different product:

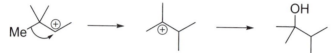

       Choice **(C)** is correct because it is the only answer that leads to the correct product. Oxymercuration gives a Markovnikov product but does not involve carbocation formation and therefore no rearrangement will occur.

       Choice **(A)** is not correct because after a 1,2-methyl shift, a different product forms. Choice **(B)** is not correct because hydroboration/oxidation results in an *anti*-Markovnikov product. Choice **(D)** is not correct because the reagents will produce a mixture of substitution and elimination products.

Practice Problems: **PQ-8, PQ-9, PQ-10,** and **PQ-11**

| **SQ-4.** | Predict the major product(s) of this reaction. | |

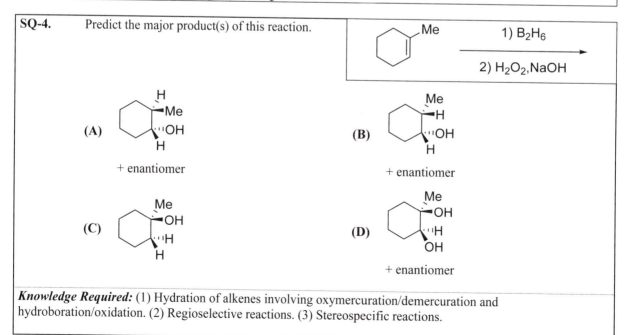

Knowledge Required: (1) Hydration of alkenes involving oxymercuration/demercuration and hydroboration/oxidation. (2) Regioselective reactions. (3) Stereospecific reactions.

Thinking it Through: In solving this problem, you first identify BH_3/THF followed by $H_2O_2/^-OH$ as reagents that react with alkenes in the hydroboration/oxidation reaction. You know that this reaction results in an *anti-Markovnikov* addition of –H and –OH to the alkene, where the –H adds to the side of the alkene with the fewest hydrogens. You note that only choices **(A)** and **(B)** lead to *anti*-Markovnikov addition. To consider which of these two choices is preferred, you recall that hydroboration/oxidation may be a stereospecific reaction where the –H and –OH add *syn* to the double bond.

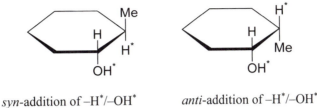

syn-addition of –H*/–OH*   *anti*-addition of –H*/–OH*

Choice **(A)** is correct because the products demonstrate both the correct regioselectivity (i.e., *anti*-Markovnikov addition) and stereospecificity (i.e., *syn* addition).

Choice **(B)** is not correct because these products result from *anti*-addition. Choice **(C)** is not correct because these products result from a Markovnikov addition. Choice **(D)** is not correct because these products result from *syn*-addition of two –OH groups.

Practice Problems: **PQ-12** and **PQ-13**

SQ-5. What is the major product of this reaction?

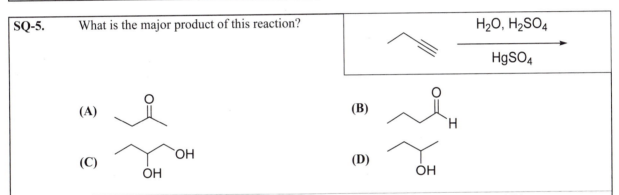

Knowledge Required: (1) Hydration of alkynes including tautomerization. (2) Markovnikov addition.

Thinking it Through: In solving this problem, you first identify that these reagents react with the alkyne resulting in Markovnikov addition; here the electrophile adds to the side with the most hydrogens, while water adds to the more substituted side. You recall that after the water is deprotonated, an enol forms which tautomerizes to its keto form.

enol   keto

Choice **(A)** is the correct answer because the ketone results from the Markovnikov addition followed by tautomerization.

Choice **(B)** is not correct because the aldehyde results from the *anti*-Markovnikov addition followed by tautomerization. Choices **(C)** and **(D)** are incorrect because neither are the enol or keto form of an addition product. Choice **(C)** is an example of a vicinal diol, typically produced from 1-butene and OsO_4/NMO. If the starting molecule was 1-butene and it reacted through a Markovnikov hydration reaction, choice **(D)** would be the product of that Markovnikov addition.

Practice Problems: **PQ-14**

SQ-6.   Which reagents will yield these products?

(A)   KMnO₄/⁻OH followed by an acid wash with heat

(B)   KMnO₄/⁻OH followed by a water wash, keep reaction cold

(C)   O₃/Me₂S

(D)   OsO₄/NMO/Δ

Knowledge Required: (1) Oxidation of alkenes to form *syn*-diols. (2) Oxidation resulting in molecular cleavage.

Thinking it Through: In solving this problem, you first note that each of these reagents oxidize alkenes. To figure out which reagent is used, you recall the favored products for each set of reagents. When the reagents in choices **(B)** and **(D)** react with alkenes, both form *syn*-diols. Given the reagents in choices **(A)** versus **(C)**, you recall that ozonolysis (O₃/Me₂S) of alkenes results in the formation of ketones and aldehydes; whereas, with heat, KMnO₄ will oxidize alkenes to ketones and carboxylic acids.

     Choice **(C)** is the correct answer because ozonolysis results in ketone and aldehyde products.

     Choices **(B)** and **(D)** are not correct because these reagents yield *syn*-diols. Choice **(A)** is not correct because with heat, the oxidative products are ketones and carboxylic acids.

Practice Problems: **PQ-15, PQ-16,** and **PQ-17**

SQ-7.   Which is an intermediate for this reaction?

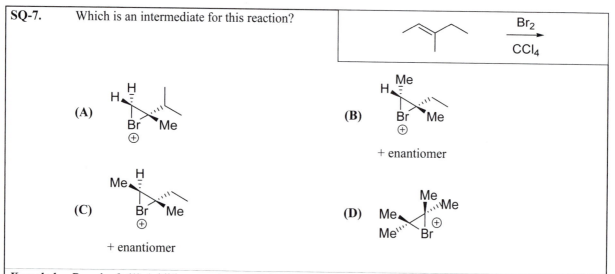

Knowledge Required: (1) Addition reactions utilizing X₂. (2) Stereospecific reactions.

Thinking it Through: In solving this problem, you recall that the reaction of an alkene with Br₂ forms a bromonium ion as an intermediate. All of the possible answers show a bromonium ion. Next you identify differences among the answers and note that choices **(B)** and **(C)** each show the bromine adding to the carbons involved in the double bond of the starting material. You recall that the bromonium ion forms by adding to the carbons in the double bond. You remember that this reaction involves a stereospecific addition where the bridge forms *syn*. Only choice **(C)** retains the stereochemistry from the alkene with the two methyl groups remaining *cis*.

     Therefore, choice **(C)** is correct.

     Choices **(A)** and **(D)** are not correct because they would involve a rearrangement of the molecule. Choice **(B)** is not correct because it would require a change in stereochemistry of the alkene substituents.

Practice Problems: **PQ-18,** and **PQ-19**

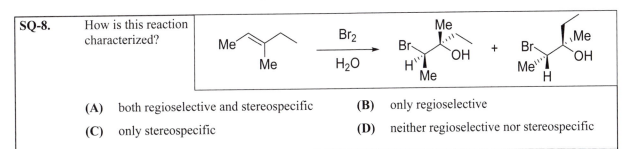

SQ-8.	How is this reaction characterized?

(A) both regioselective and stereospecific

(B) only regioselective

(C) only stereospecific

(D) neither regioselective nor stereospecific

Knowledge Required: (1) Addition reactions of diatomic halogens to alkenes. (2) Regioselective reactions. (3) Stereospecific reactions.

Thinking it Through: To solve this problem, you focus on differences between the reactants and the products. In the product, you note that –Br and –OH added to the alkene. Because the –OH added exclusively to the more substituted carbon, yielding only one constitutional isomer, this reaction is regioselective. Additionally, you notice that the reaction begins with a specific stereoisomer (*E*-alkene), and the product has two stereocenters. You recall that when you have two stereocenters there are up to four possible stereoisomers. The reaction, however, yields two stereoisomers (i.e., a set of enantiomers); thus, this reaction is stereospecific.

Choice **(A)** is the correct answer because you identified that the reaction is both regioselective and stereospecific.

Choices **(B)**, **(C)** and **(D)** are not correct because each option ignores one reaction characteristic.

Practice Problems: PQ-20 and **PQ-21**

SQ-9.	What is the product of this reaction?

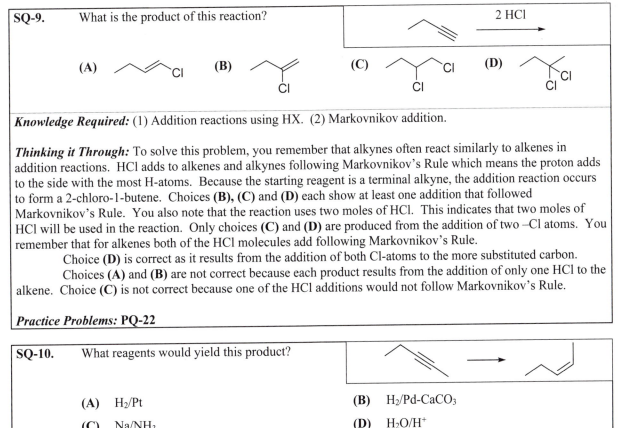

Knowledge Required: (1) Addition reactions using HX. (2) Markovnikov addition.

Thinking it Through: To solve this problem, you remember that alkynes often react similarly to alkenes in addition reactions. HCl adds to alkenes and alkynes following Markovnikov's Rule which means the proton adds to the side with the most H-atoms. Because the starting reagent is a terminal alkyne, the addition reaction occurs to form a 2-chloro-1-butene. Choices **(B)**, **(C)** and **(D)** each show at least one addition that followed Markovnikov's Rule. You also note that the reaction uses two moles of HCl. This indicates that two moles of HCl will be used in the reaction. Only choices **(C)** and **(D)** are produced from the addition of two –Cl atoms. You remember that for alkenes both of the HCl molecules add following Markovnikov's Rule.

Choice **(D)** is correct as it results from the addition of both Cl-atoms to the more substituted carbon.

Choices **(A)** and **(B)** are not correct because each product results from the addition of only one HCl to the alkene. Choice **(C)** is not correct because one of the HCl additions would not follow Markovnikov's Rule.

Practice Problems: PQ-22

SQ-10.	What reagents would yield this product?

(A) H_2/Pt

(B) H_2/Pd-CaCO$_3$

(C) Na/NH$_3$

(D) H_2O/H$^+$

Knowledge Required: (1) Hydrogenation of alkenes and alkynes. (2) *Syn-* and *anti-*addition. (3) Tautomerization.

Thinking it Through: As you approach this question, you recall the various reagents used for hydrogenation of alkenes and alkynes. You remember that choice **(A)**, H_2/Pt, hydrogenates alkenes and alkynes through *syn-*addition. However, the alkyne does not stop after a single addition to form the (*Z*)-2-pentene; it will completely hydrogenate the alkyne to form pentane. You identify choices **(B)** and **(D)** as reagents that hydrogenate alkynes stopping after an alkene forms. The presence of Lindlar's catalyst (Pd-$CaCO_3$) with the H_2 in choice **(B)**, results in a single *syn-*addition of hydrogen atoms. Using Na/NH_3 in choice **(C)**, results in *anti-*addition of hydrogen atoms. Choice **(D)** results in the addition of water across the triple bond and subsequent formation of a ketone through tautomerization.

     Choice **(B)** is the correct answer because a single *syn-*hydrogenation occurs yielding (*Z*)-2-pentene.

     Choice **(A)** is not correct because two *syn-*hydrogenations will occur resulting in pentane. Choice **(C)** is not correct because a single *anti-*hydrogenation occurs yielding (*E*)-2-pentene. Choice **(D)** is not correct because this results in the addition of water across the triple bond yielding a mixture of ketones after tautomerization.

Practice Problems: PQ-23, PQ-24, PQ-25, PQ-26, and PQ-27

SQ-11.   Identify the major product(s) for this synthesis:

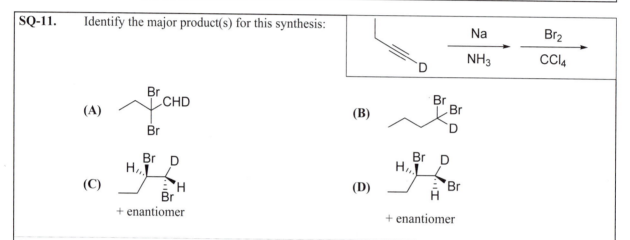

(A)

(B)

(C)

+ enantiomer

(D)

+ enantiomer

Knowledge Required: (1) Hydrogenation of alkenes and alkynes. (2) *syn-* and *anti-*addition. (3) Addition reactions utilizing X_2.

Thinking it Through: In thinking through this synthesis, you recall how each reagent transforms the reactant. You remember that Na/NH_3 reacts with alkynes to do an *anti-*hydrogenation producing an *E*-alkene.

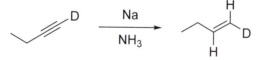

     Next you recall that Br_2/CCl_4 results in the *anti-*addition of two bromine atoms to the double bond, one on each carbon of the double bond (i.e., vicinal addition). You eliminate choices **(A)** and **(B)** because both indicate two bromine atoms adding to one carbon (i.e. geminal addition.) Next you determine that choice **(C)** results from the *anti-*addition of bromine atoms to the (*E*)-double bond. Choice **(D)** results from the *syn-*addition of the bromine atoms.

     Choice **(C)** is the correct answer because the product results from the *anti-*addition of the bromine atoms to an (*E*)-alkene.

     Choices **(A)** and **(B)** are not correct because the product results from the addition of the bromine atoms to the same carbon. Choice **(D)** is not correct because the product results from the *syn-*addition of the bromine atoms to an (*E*)-alkene.

Practice Problems: PQ-28, PQ-29, and PQ-30

Practice Questions (PQ)

PQ-1. What is the major product of this reaction?

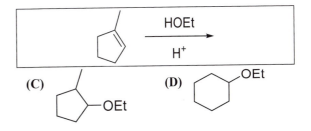

(A) 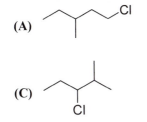 EtO

(B) 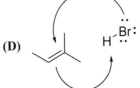 OEt

(C) 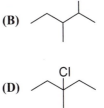 OEt

(D) 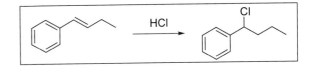 OEt

PQ-2. Why does this reaction selectively form this product?

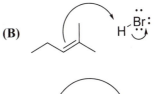

(A) The benzene ring sterically hinders the reaction.

(B) The chlorine has an electronic attraction for the benzene ring.

(C) The carbocation intermediate is stabilized through resonance

(D) The alternative product undergoes a rearrangement reaction.

PQ-3. What is a step in the mechanism of this reaction?

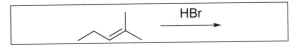

(A)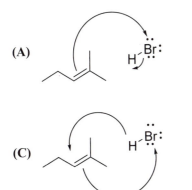

(B)

(C)

(D)

PQ-4. What is the major product of this reaction?

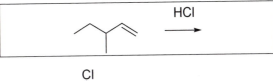

(A) ⟋⟍⟍Cl

(B) Cl

(C) Cl

(D) Cl

PQ-5. What characterizes the product(s) formed from this reaction?

(A) a mixture of enantiomers

(B) a racemic mixture

(C) an achiral molecule

(D) a mixture of diastereomers

PQ-6. Which energy diagram is consistent with this reaction?

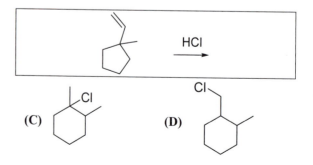

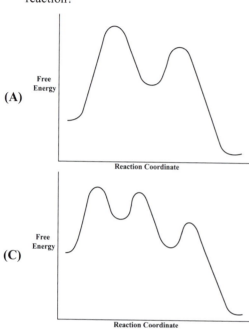

PQ-7. What is/are intermediate(s) for this reaction?

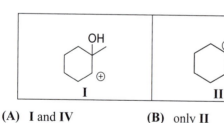

(A) I and **IV**

(B) only **II**

(C) II and **IV**

(D) only **III**

PQ-8. Which product results from this addition reaction?

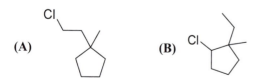

(A)

(B)

(C)

(D)

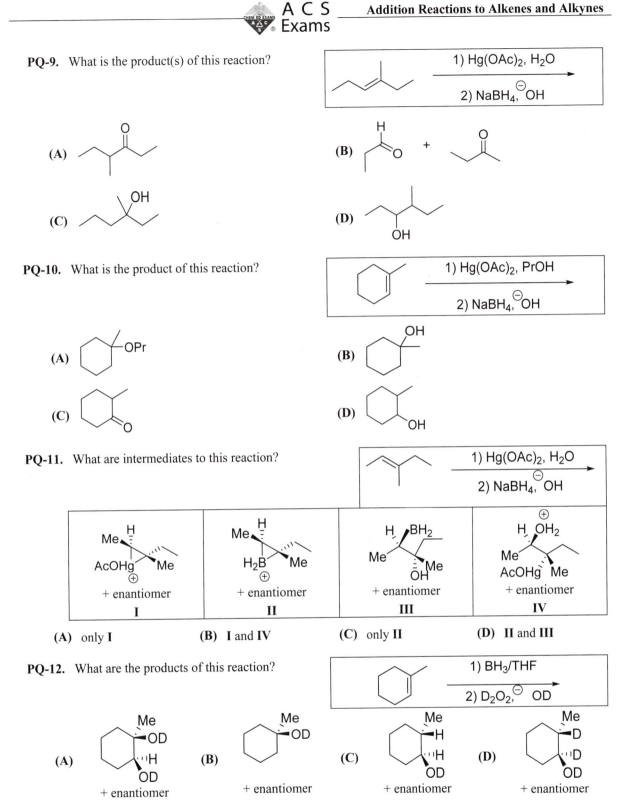

PQ-9. What is the product(s) of this reaction?

1) Hg(OAc)$_2$, H$_2$O

2) NaBH$_4$, $^{\ominus}$OH

(A)

(B)   +

(C)

(D)

PQ-10. What is the product of this reaction?

1) Hg(OAc)$_2$, PrOH

2) NaBH$_4$, $^{\ominus}$OH

(A) —OPr

(B) OH

(C)

(D) OH

PQ-11. What are intermediates to this reaction?

1) Hg(OAc)$_2$, H$_2$O

2) NaBH$_4$, $^{\ominus}$OH

I	II	III	IV
Me, H / AcOHg⊕ Me / + enantiomer	Me, H / H$_2$B⊕ Me / + enantiomer	H BH$_2$ / Me Me OH / + enantiomer	H OH$_2$⊕ / Me AcOHg Me / + enantiomer

(A) only **I**   (B) **I** and **IV**   (C) only **II**   (D) **II** and **III**

PQ-12. What are the products of this reaction?

1) BH$_3$/THF

2) D$_2$O$_2$, $^{\ominus}$OD

(A) Me OD / H / OD / + enantiomer

(B) Me OD / + enantiomer

(C) Me H / H / OD / + enantiomer

(D) Me D / D / OD / + enantiomer

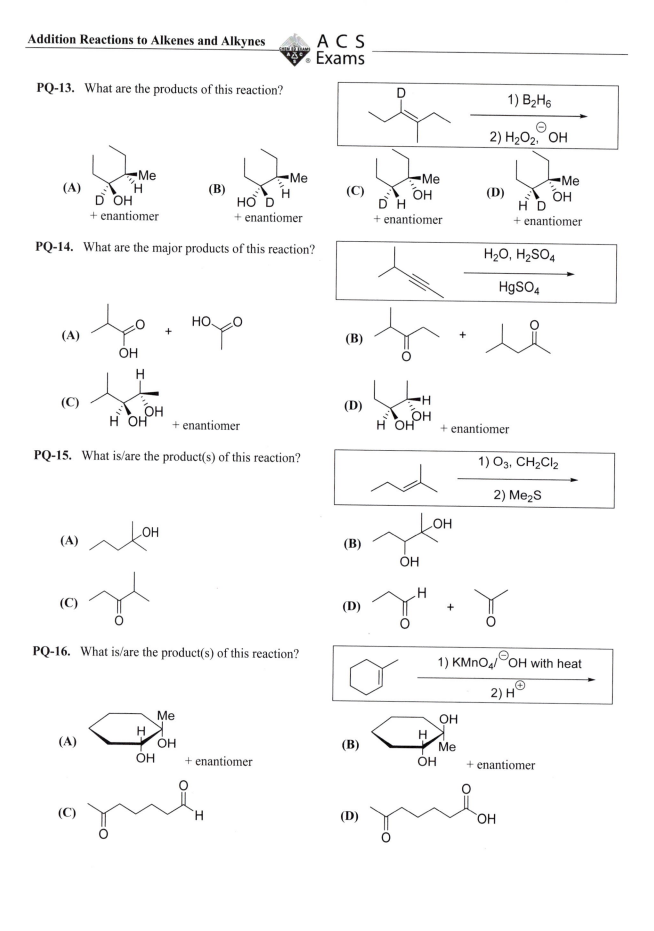

PQ-13. What are the products of this reaction?

(A) + enantiomer

(B) + enantiomer

(C) + enantiomer

(D) + enantiomer

PQ-14. What are the major products of this reaction?

(A)

(B)

(C) + enantiomer

(D) + enantiomer

PQ-15. What is/are the product(s) of this reaction?

(A)

(B)

(C)

(D)

PQ-16. What is/are the product(s) of this reaction?

(A) + enantiomer

(B) + enantiomer

(C)

(D)

PQ-17. How is this reaction characterized?

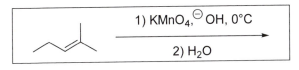

(A) only regioselective

(B) both regioselective and stereospecific

(C) only stereospecific

(D) neither regioselective nor stereospecific

PQ-18. Which reaction step occurs in this reaction mechanism?

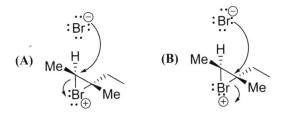

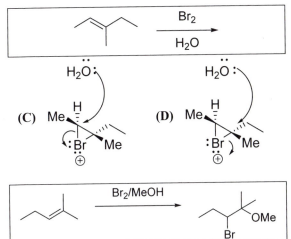

PQ-19. Why is the product shown the preferred constitutional isomer of this reaction?

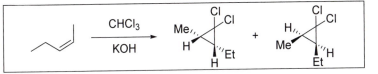

(A) The nucleophile attacks the more stable carbocation formed during a Markovnikov addition.

(B) The nucleophile attacks the carbon with the largest δ+ charge.

(C) Steric hindrance inhibits the nucleophile attack on the other carbon.

(D) The bromonium bridge forces an *anti*-addition of the nucleophile.

PQ-20. How is this reaction characterized?

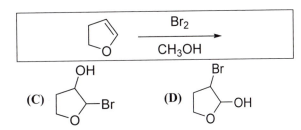

(A) both regioselective and stereospecific

(B) only regioselective

(C) only stereospecific

(D) neither regioselective nor stereospecific

PQ-21. What is the product of this reaction?

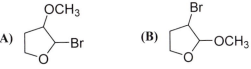

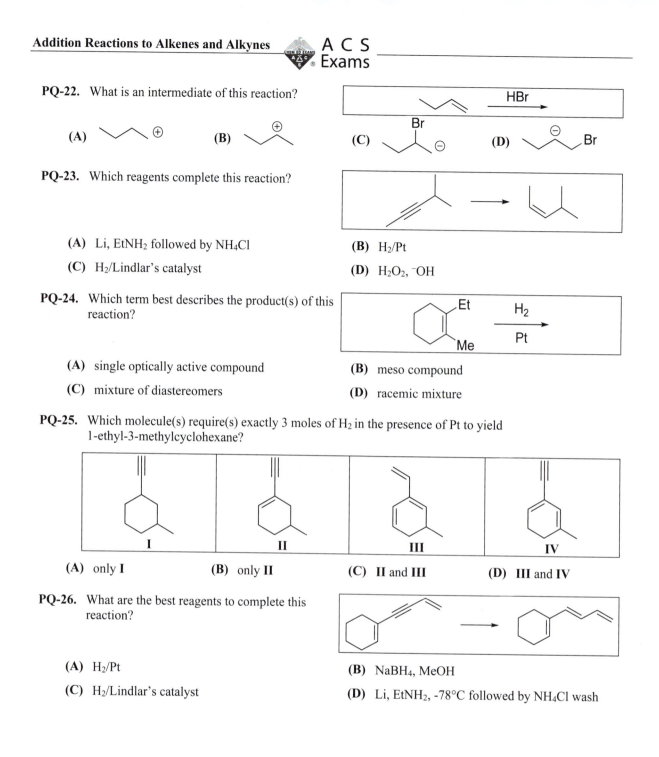

PQ-22. What is an intermediate of this reaction?

(A) ⊕   (B) ⊕   (C) Br ⊖   (D) ⊖ Br

PQ-23. Which reagents complete this reaction?

(A) Li, EtNH₂ followed by NH₄Cl

(B) H₂/Pt

(C) H₂/Lindlar's catalyst

(D) H₂O₂, ⁻OH

PQ-24. Which term best describes the product(s) of this reaction?

(A) single optically active compound

(B) meso compound

(C) mixture of diastereomers

(D) racemic mixture

PQ-25. Which molecule(s) require(s) exactly 3 moles of H₂ in the presence of Pt to yield 1-ethyl-3-methylcyclohexane?

| I | II | III | IV |

(A) only **I**   (B) only **II**   (C) **II** and **III**   (D) **III** and **IV**

PQ-26. What are the best reagents to complete this reaction?

(A) H₂/Pt

(B) NaBH₄, MeOH

(C) H₂/Lindlar's catalyst

(D) Li, EtNH₂, -78°C followed by NH₄Cl wash

PQ-27. What is the product of this reaction?

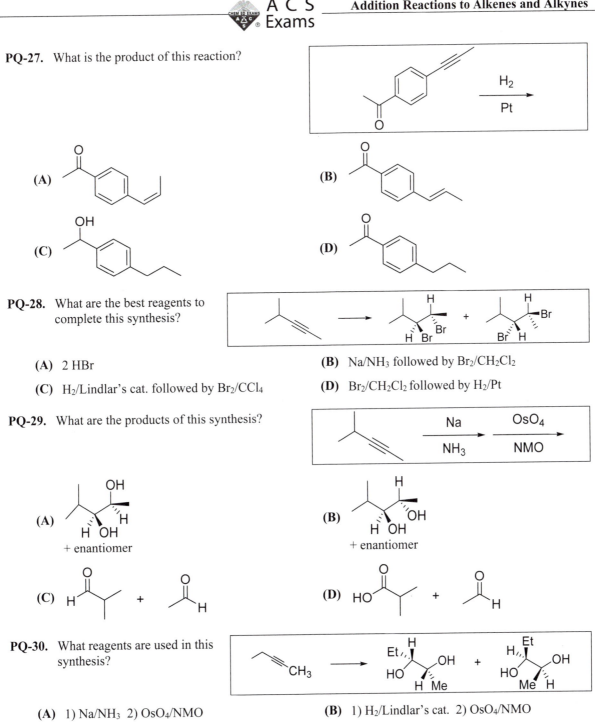

(A)

(B)

(C)

(D)

PQ-28. What are the best reagents to complete this synthesis?

(A) 2 HBr

(B) Na/NH₃ followed by Br₂/CH₂Cl₂

(C) H₂/Lindlar's cat. followed by Br₂/CCl₄

(D) Br₂/CH₂Cl₂ followed by H₂/Pt

PQ-29. What are the products of this synthesis?

(A)
+ enantiomer

(B)
+ enantiomer

(C)

(D)

PQ-30. What reagents are used in this synthesis?

(A) 1) Na/NH₃ 2) OsO₄/NMO

(B) 1) H₂/Lindlar's cat. 2) OsO₄/NMO

(C) 1) Na/NH₃ 2) O₃ followed by Me₂S

(D) 1) H₂/Lindlar's cat. 2) O₃ followed by Me₂S

Answers to Study Questions

SQ-1.	D	SQ-5.	A	SQ-9.	D		
SQ-2.	C	SQ-6.	C	SQ-10.	B		
SQ-3.	C	SQ-7.	C	SQ-11.	C		
SQ-4.	A	SQ-8.	A				

Answers to Practice Questions

PQ-1.	B	PQ-11.	A	PQ-21.	B
PQ-2.	C	PQ-12.	C	PQ-22.	B
PQ-3.	B	PQ-13.	A	PQ-23.	C
PQ-4.	D	PQ-14.	B	PQ-24.	D
PQ-5.	C	PQ-15.	D	PQ-25.	C
PQ-6.	A	PQ-16.	D	PQ-26.	D
PQ-7.	C	PQ-17.	C	PQ-27.	C
PQ-8.	C	PQ-18.	D	PQ-28.	B
PQ-9.	C	PQ-19.	B	PQ-29.	A
PQ-10.	A	PQ-20.	C	PQ-30.	A

Chapter 8 – Addition Reactions to Alcohols and Ethers

Chapter Summary:

This chapter will focus on addition reactions to alcohols and ethers. Included in this chapter are the oxidation of alcohols to form carbonyl functional groups and the reduction of carbonyl functional groups. This chapter also presents the conversion of alcohols into good leaving groups and the protection of alcohols. The formation of ethers, including epoxides, and addition reactions to epoxides are also included.

Specific topics covered in this chapter are:
- Oxidation reactions to form carbonyl functional groups
- Reduction reactions of carbonyl functional groups
- Converting alcohols into good leaving groups
- Alcohol protecting groups
- Synthesis of ethers
- Synthesis of epoxides
- Addition reactions of epoxides

Previous material that is relevant to your understanding of questions in this chapter include:
- Nucleophilic Substitution Reactions *(Chapter 5)*
- Elimination Reactions *(Chapter 6)*
- Regoiselective reactions *(Chapter 6)*
- Stereospecific reactions *(Chapter 6)*
- *Anti*-addition *(Chapter 7)*
- Hydrogenation of alkenes and alkynes *(Chapter 7)*

Where you might see this material in upcoming Study Guide chapters:
- Reactions of aldehydes and ketones *(Chapter 13)*
- Acetal and hemi-acetal formation *(Chapter 13)*
- Enol and enolate chemistry *(Chapter 14)*
- Application to Multi-step Synthesis *(Chapter 15)*

Where to find this in your textbook:

The material in this chapter typically aligns to "Alcohols and Ethers" or "Addition Reactions" in your textbook. The name of your chapter may vary.

Practice exam:

There may be practice exam questions aligned to the material in this chapter. Because there are a limited number of questions on the practice exam, a review of the breadth of the material in this chapter is advised in preparation for your exam.

How this fits to the big picture:

The material in this chapter aligns to the Big Idea of Structure and Function (III) and Chemical Reactions (V) as listed on page 13 of this study guide.

A C S
Exams
®

Study Questions (SQ)

SQ-1. What are the best reagents to complete this reaction?

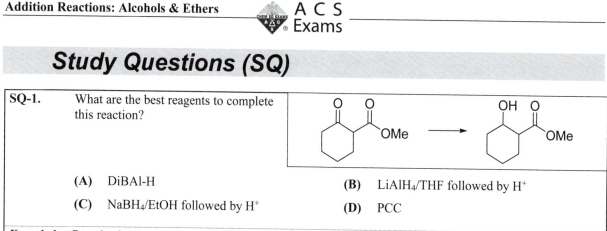

(A) DiBAl-H

(B) LiAlH₄/THF followed by H⁺

(C) NaBH₄/EtOH followed by H⁺

(D) PCC

Knowledge Required: (1) Reduction of carbonyl functional groups.

Thinking it Through: To solve this problem, you first consider the differences in the starting molecule's structure and in the product structure. The starting molecule contains both a ketone and an ester, while in the final product, the ketone is reduced to an alcohol and the ester is unchanged. Next, you look at the reagents in each answer option. You recall that PCC is a weak oxidizing agent that oxidizes alcohols to ketones or aldehydes; the transformation in the problem, however, is a reduction. Next, you note that choices **(A)**, **(B)**, and **(C)** are all reducing reagents. Choice **(A)**, DiBAl-H, when used stoichiometrically, reduces carboxylic acids and derivatives to aldehydes. LiAlH₄, choice **(B)**, is a strong reducing agent that reduces ketones, carboxylic acid and derivatives to alcohols. Choice **(C)** is a weak reducing agent that selectively reduces ketones and aldehydes and does not reduce carboxylic acids or derivative (such as esters).

Therefore, choice **(C)** is the correct answer because NaBH₄ selectively reduces ketones.

Choices **(A)** and **(B)** are not correct because they will reduce the ester as well. Choice **(D)** is not correct because PCC is an oxidizing agent.

Practice Problems: **PQ-1**, and **PQ-2**

SQ-2. What is the product of this reaction?

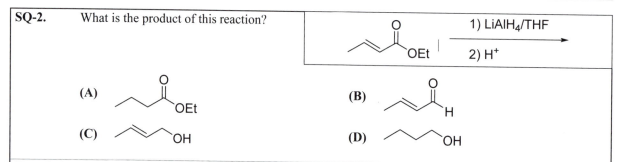

(A)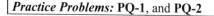

(B)

(C)

(D)

Knowledge Required: (1) Reduction of carbonyl compounds. (2) Hydrogenation of alkenes.

Thinking it Through: When solving this problem, you recall that LiAlH₄ is a strong reducing agent that reduces esters to alcohols. Therefore, choices **(A)** and **(B)** are not correct because for choice **(A)** the ester is not reduced, and for choice **(B)** the ester is reduced to an aldehyde. You also remember that LiAlH₄ does not hydrogenate alkenes, so choices **(A)** and **(D)** are not correct.

Choice **(C)** is the correct answer because the product is the result of the reduction of the ester to an alcohol while the alkene remains unhydrogenated.

Choice **(A)** is not correct because it is the product after hydrogenation of the alkene using H₂/Pt. Choice **(B)** is not correct because the needed reagents for the transformation would be LiAlH(O-ᵗBu)₃. Choice **(D)** is not correct because the transformation would result from two sets of reagents: (1) the reduction of the ester, and (2) hydrogenation.

Practice Problems: **PQ-3**, and **PQ-4**

| SQ-3. | What is/are the best reagent(s) to complete this reaction? | 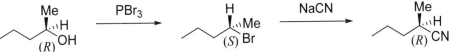 |

(A) $CrO_3/H_2SO_4/H_2O$

(B) $KMnO_4/{}^-OH$ followed by H^+

(C) OsO_4/NMO

(D) PCC

Knowledge Required: (1) Oxidation reactions of alcohols to form carbonyl functional groups.

Thinking it Through: To solve this problem, you first examine the structures of the starting molecule and the product of the reaction. You note that the 1° alcohol is oxidized to a carboxylic acid, but the double bond has not reacted. In looking at the answer options, you note that all the possible answers are oxidizing agents. You remember that choices (A) and (B) both oxidize 1° alcohols to a carboxylic acid. Choice (B), $KMnO_4$, also oxidizes double bonds as well as alcohols, and the oxidizing effect of $KMnO_4$ on alkenes is temperature dependent. At low temperatures, the oxidation product of an alkene with $KMnO_4$ is a *syn*-diol, and, at elevated temperatures, the reaction results in the cleavage of the double bond.

Choice (A) is the correct answer because $CrO_3/H_2SO_4/H_2O$ forms chromic acid which only oxidizes the 1° alcohol to a carboxylic acid.

Choice (B) is not correct because $KMnO_4$ oxidizes both the alkene and the alcohol. Choice (C) is not correct because OsO_4 oxidizes the alkene resulting in a *syn*-diol. Choice (D) is not correct because oxidation of the 1° alcohol by PCC yields an aldehyde.

Practice Problems: PQ-5, PQ-6, PQ-7, PQ-8, and **PQ-9**

| SQ-4. | What reagents best complete this synthesis? | 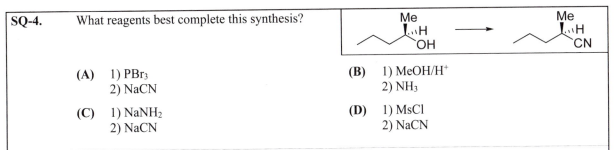 |

(A) 1) PBr_3
      2) NaCN

(B) 1) $MeOH/H^+$
      2) NH_3

(C) 1) $NaNH_2$
      2) NaCN

(D) 1) MsCl
      2) NaCN

Knowledge Required: (1) Converting alcohols into good leaving groups. (2) S_N2 reactions.

Thinking it Through: In your approach to this question, you note that there is a retention of the configuration from the starting molecule (R)-2-pentanol, to the final product, (R)-2-cyanopentane. Next, you recall that to become better leaving groups, alcohols are often converted to alkyl halides or alkyl mesylates. Choice (A), PBr_3, will convert an alcohol into 2-bromopentane. The mechanism of this addition occurs so that there is an inversion of configuration as (R)-2-pentanol becomes (S)-2-bromopentane. In the second step of the synthesis, the halide undergoes an S_N2 reaction with ^-CN, resulting in inversion of configuration. The net result will be an (R)-configuration:

You note that the $MeOH/H^+$ in choice (B) will form an ether, which acts as a protecting group, preventing further reactions at that site of the molecule. The sodium amide, $NaNH_2$, in choice (C) is a strong base and will extract the acidic hydrogen from the alcohol and will not result in a substitution product. Choice (D), MsCl, converts the alcohol into the corresponding alkyl mesylate ($R–OSO_2Me$). You recall that this reaction occurs with retention of configuration, so the product of the first step will have an (R)-configuration. After the S_N2 reaction with ^-CN, the final product stereochemistry is (S).

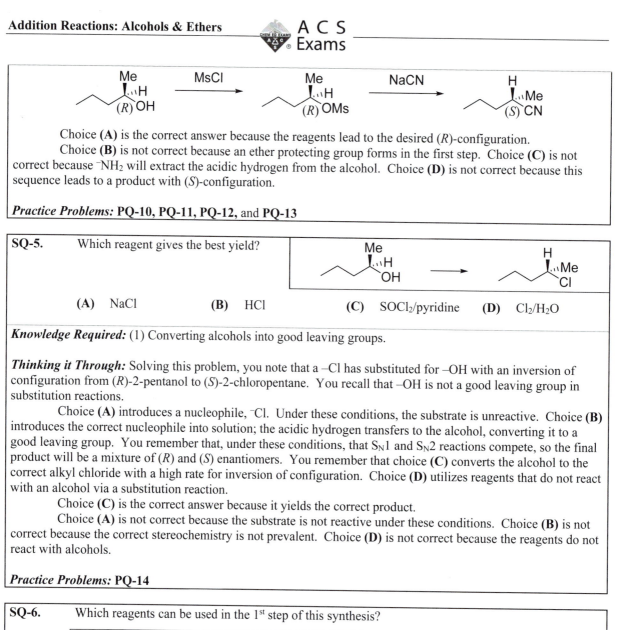

Choice (**A**) is the correct answer because the reagents lead to the desired (*R*)-configuration.

Choice (**B**) is not correct because an ether protecting group forms in the first step. Choice (**C**) is not correct because ⁻NH₂ will extract the acidic hydrogen from the alcohol. Choice (**D**) is not correct because this sequence leads to a product with (*S*)-configuration.

Practice Problems: **PQ-10, PQ-11, PQ-12,** and **PQ-13**

SQ-5. Which reagent gives the best yield?

(**A**) NaCl   (**B**) HCl   (**C**) SOCl₂/pyridine   (**D**) Cl₂/H₂O

Knowledge Required: (1) Converting alcohols into good leaving groups.

Thinking it Through: Solving this problem, you note that a –Cl has substituted for –OH with an inversion of configuration from (*R*)-2-pentanol to (*S*)-2-chloropentane. You recall that –OH is not a good leaving group in substitution reactions.

Choice (**A**) introduces a nucleophile, ⁻Cl. Under these conditions, the substrate is unreactive. Choice (**B**) introduces the correct nucleophile into solution; the acidic hydrogen transfers to the alcohol, converting it to a good leaving group. You remember that, under these conditions, that S_N1 and S_N2 reactions compete, so the final product will be a mixture of (*R*) and (*S*) enantiomers. You remember that choice (**C**) converts the alcohol to the correct alkyl chloride with a high rate for inversion of configuration. Choice (**D**) utilizes reagents that do not react with an alcohol via a substitution reaction.

Choice (**C**) is the correct answer because it yields the correct product.

Choice (**A**) is not correct because the substrate is not reactive under these conditions. Choice (**B**) is not correct because the correct stereochemistry is not prevalent. Choice (**D**) is not correct because the reagents do not react with alcohols.

Practice Problems: **PQ-14**

SQ-6. Which reagents can be used in the 1ˢᵗ step of this synthesis?

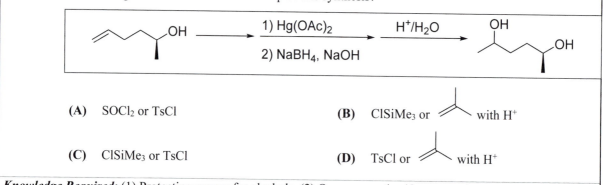

(**A**) SOCl₂ or TsCl

(**B**) ClSiMe₃ or ⟋⟍ with H⁺

(**C**) ClSiMe₃ or TsCl

(**D**) TsCl or ⟋⟍ with H⁺

Knowledge Required: (1) Protecting groups for alcohols. (2) Oxymercuration/demercuration.

Thinking it Through: When solving this question, you start by comparing the starting molecule and product, and note that, during the synthesis, the double bond undergoes a Markovnikov addition of –H and –OH; the other functional group, a 1° ROH, is unchanged. You suspect that the alcohol must be protected so that it does not react with the second set of reagents. Looking at the answer options, you identify choice (**B**) as two reagents that will convert the alcohol to ethers, making them unreactive. The protecting group is removed in the third step.

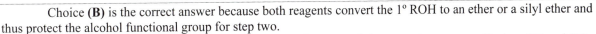

Choice **(B)** is the correct answer because both reagents convert the 1° ROH to an ether or a silyl ether and thus protect the alcohol functional group for step two.

Choice **(A)** is not correct because these reagents do not result in protecting groups. Choices **(C)** and **(D)** are not correct because TsCl results in an alkyl tosylate, which is not a protecting group.

Practice Problems: **PQ-15, PQ-16,** and **PQ-17**

SQ-7. What reagents yield this product in high yield?

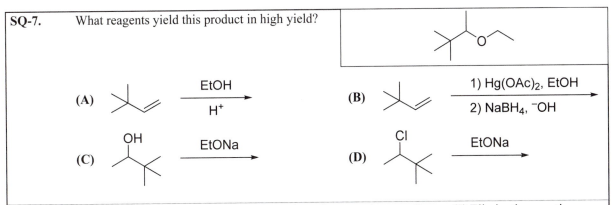

(A) $\xrightarrow[\text{H}^+]{\text{EtOH}}$

(B) $\xrightarrow[\text{2) NaBH}_4, \ ^-\text{OH}]{\text{1) Hg(OAc)}_2, \text{EtOH}}$

(C) $\xrightarrow{\text{EtONa}}$

(D) $\xrightarrow{\text{EtONa}}$

Knowledge Required: (1) Synthesis of ethers. (2) Markovnikov reactions to alkenes. (3) Elimination reactions. (4) Oxymercuration/demercuration.

Thinking it Through: To answer this question, you first look at the answer options and recall the transformations associated with each. You recognize that choices **(A)** and **(B)** both yield ethers. Choice **(A)** proceeds through a Markovnikov addition, creating a 2° carbocation. This intermediate undergoes a 1,2-methyl shift to create a more stable carbocation, such that the product is 2,3-dimethyl-2-ethoxybutane:

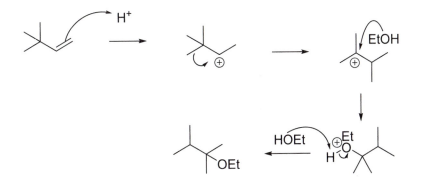

Choice **(B)** proceeds through an oxymercuration/demercuration mechanism which produces a Markovnikov addition of –H and –OEt without a carbocation intermediate.

The reagents in choice **(C)** proceed through an acid/base mechanism, where EtO⁻ extracts a hydrogen atom from the alcohol.

The reagents in choice **(D)**, a 2° RX and a strong base, primarily react through an E2 mechanism producing 3,3-dimethyl-1-butene.

Choice **(B)** is the correct answer because it produces the target molecule.

Choice **(A)** is not correct because the carbocation intermediate rearranges producing the wrong ether. Choice **(C)** is not correct because the reagents undergo an acid/base reaction. Choice **(D)** is not correct because the reagents react primarily through an E2 mechanism.

Practice Problems: **PQ-18, PQ-19,** and **PQ-20**

SQ-8. Which step occurs in the mechanism to produce this molecule?

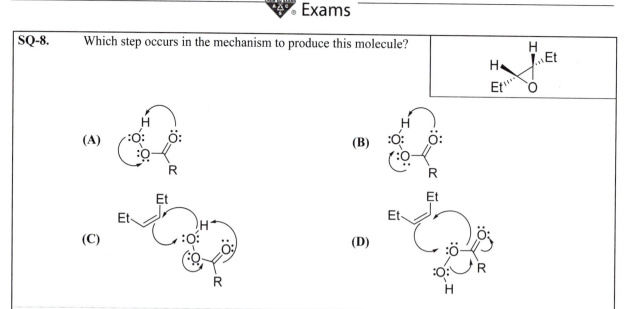

Knowledge Required: (1) Formation of epoxides.

Thinking it Through: To solve this problem, you recall several things about epoxidation reactions. First, it is a concerted mechanism that occurs through *syn*-addition. Therefore, choices **(A)** and **(B)** are not correct because they are part of stepwise mechanisms and do not show the addition of an oxygen atom to an alkene to form an epoxide functional group. Next, you recall that the indicated (*) oxygen atom adds to the alkene:

Choice **(C)** is the correct answer because the indicated oxygen atom adds to the alkene through a concerted, *syn*-addition mechanism.

Choices **(A)** and **(B)** are not correct because they do not show the formation of an epoxide. Choice **(D)** is not correct because the incorrect oxygen atom from the peroxide adds to the alkene.

Practice Problems: PQ-21, PQ-22, PQ-23, PQ-24, and PQ-25

SQ-9. Which is a step in the mechanism of this reaction?

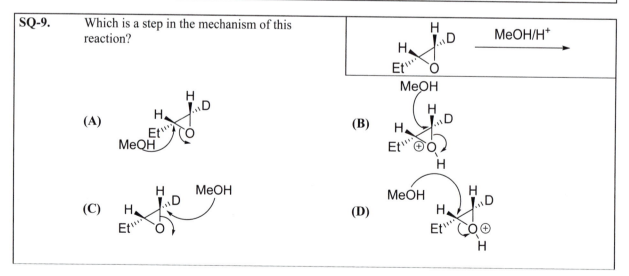

Knowledge Required: (1) Addition reactions of epoxides. (2) *Anti-* and *syn*-additions.

Thinking it Through: To solve this problem, you first remember that nucleophiles attack epoxides *anti* to the oxygen. Choices **(A)** and **(C)** are eliminated because both show *syn*-additions of the MeOH. Next, you recall that reaction conditions control the regiochemistry of epoxide reactions. In basic solution, the nucleophile attacks the less sterically hindered, less substituted side. In acidic solution, the oxygen atom on the epoxide protonates and the positive charge on the epoxide is delocalized. This creates δ^+ charges on the carbons in the epoxide ring. In this reaction, the more substituted side resembles a 2° carbocation and has a larger δ^+ than the less substituted side of the epoxide and the nucleophile attacks the more substituted side of the epoxide as shown in choice **(D)**.

       Choice **(D)** is the correct answer because the nucleophile attacks the more substituted side of the protonated epoxide in an *anti*-addition.

       Choices **(A)** and **(C)** are not correct because they are *syn*-additions, and the epoxide is NOT protonated. Choice **(B)** is not correct because the nucleophile is attacking the less substituted side of the protonated epoxide.

Practice Problems: **PQ-26, PQ-27, and PQ-28**

SQ-10.   What are the products of this reaction?

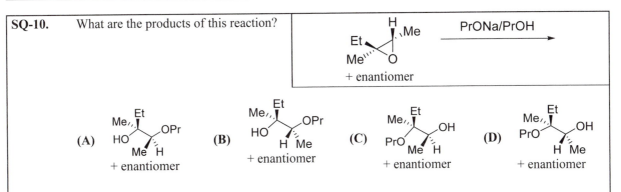

Knowledge Required: (1) Addition reactions of epoxides.

Thinking it Through: As you think about this reaction, you remember that in reactions with epoxides, nucleophiles attack *anti-* to the epoxide in a stereospecific manner. Examining the products, you note that choices **(B)** and **(D)** result from the *anti*-addition of the nucleophile to the epoxide.

       You also recall that the regiochemistry of an addition reaction to an epoxide is controlled by either acidic or basic conditions. In acidic conditions, the nucleophile attacks the more substituted carbon; under basic conditions, the nucleophile attacks the less substituted carbon. Because this reaction occurs under basic conditions, the ⁻OPr nucleophile attacks on the less substituted carbon of the epoxide, choice **(B)**.

       Therefore, choice **(B)** is the correct answer.

       Choices **(A)** and **(C)** are not correct because they result from a *syn*-addition of the nucleophile. Choice **(D)** is not correct because the nucleophile adds to the more substituted carbon of the epoxide.

Practice Problems: **PQ-29, and PQ-30**

Practice Questions (PQ)

PQ-1.   What is the product of this reaction?

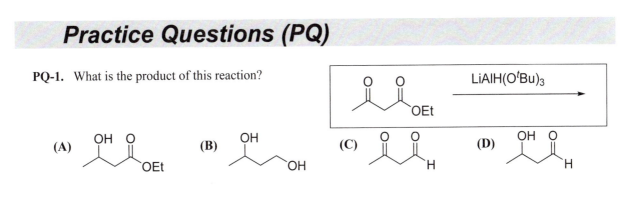

PQ-2. Which reagents complete this reaction?

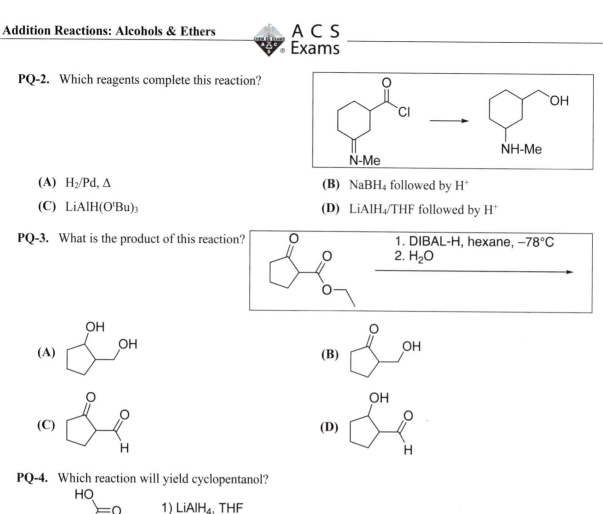

(A) H_2/Pd, Δ

(B) $NaBH_4$ followed by H^+

(C) $LiAlH(O^tBu)_3$

(D) $LiAlH_4$/THF followed by H^+

PQ-3. What is the product of this reaction?

1. DIBAL-H, hexane, −78°C
2. H_2O

(A) [structure]

(B) [structure]

(C) [structure]

(D) [structure]

PQ-4. Which reaction will yield cyclopentanol?

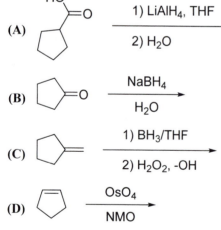

(A) 1) $LiAlH_4$, THF
2) H_2O

(B) $NaBH_4$ / H_2O

(C) 1) BH_3/THF
2) H_2O_2, -OH

(D) OsO_4 / NMO

PQ-5. Which reagent(s) yield this product?

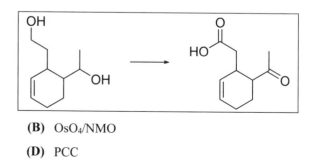

(A) $KMnO_4$/^-OH followed by H^+

(B) OsO_4/NMO

(C) H_2CrO_4

(D) PCC

PQ-6. What is/are the product(s) of this synthesis?

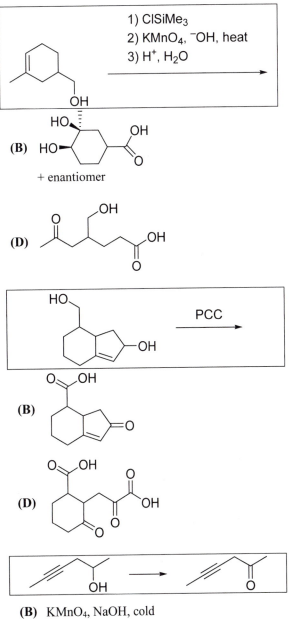

1) ClSiMe₃
2) KMnO₄, ⁻OH, heat
3) H⁺, H₂O

(A)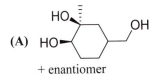

+ enantiomer

(B) HO, OH
+ enantiomer

(C)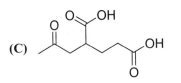

(D)

PQ-7. What is the product of this reaction?

PCC

(A)

(B)

(C)

(D)

PQ-8. Which reagents complete this reaction?

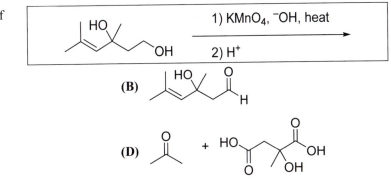

(A) OsO₄/NMO

(B) KMnO₄, NaOH, cold

(C) CrO₃/H₂SO₄/H₂O

(D) H⁺/H₂O

PQ-9. What is/are the product(s) of this reaction?

1) KMnO₄, ⁻OH, heat

2) H⁺

(A)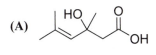

(B)

(C)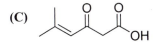

(D)

A C S
Exams

PQ-10. What is the major product of this reaction?

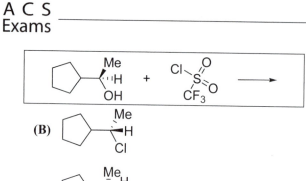

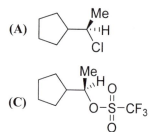

(A)

(B)

(C)

(D)

PQ-11. Which reagents can be used in the first step of this synthesis?

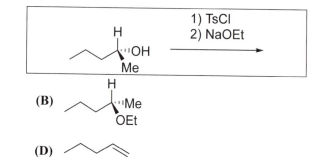

(A) TfCl or SOCl₂ or HCl/ZnCl₂

(B) TfCl or SOCl₂

(C) TfCl or HCl/ZnCl₂

(D) SOCl₂ or HCl/ZnCl₂

PQ-12. What is/are the most effective reagent(s) to complete this reaction?

(A) NaOMe

(B) HCl/HOMe

(C) (1) SOCl₂ (2) NaOMe

(D) (1) TsCl (2) NaOMe

PQ-13. What is the major product of this reaction?

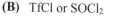

(A)

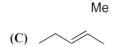

(B)

(C)

(D)

PQ-14. What is the best reagent to complete this synthesis?

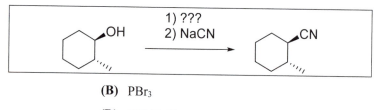

(A) TsCl

(B) PBr₃

(C) ClSiMe₃

(D) HCl/ZnCl₂

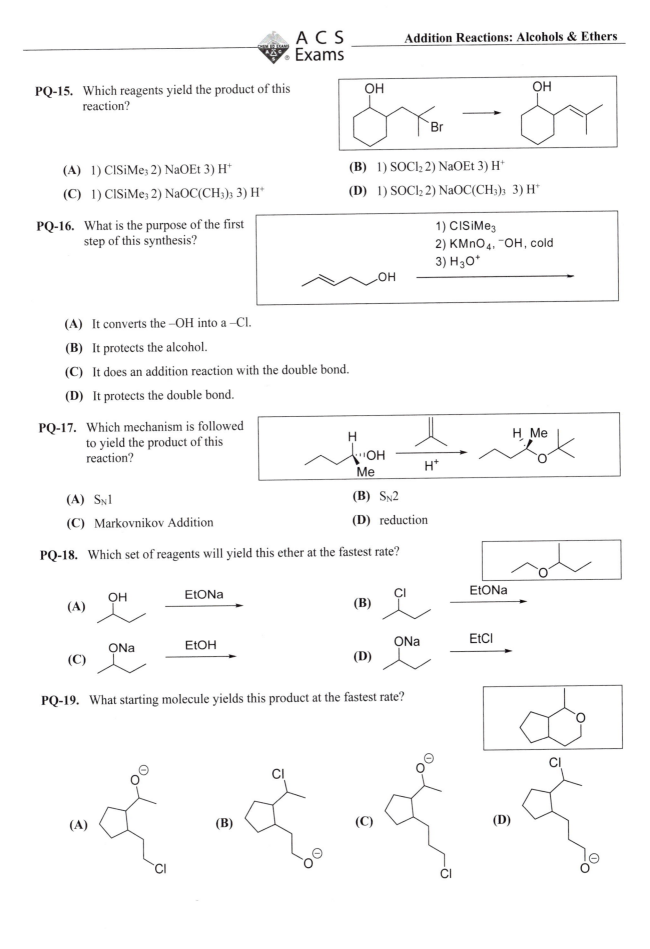

PQ-15. Which reagents yield the product of this reaction?

(A) 1) ClSiMe₃ 2) NaOEt 3) H⁺

(C) 1) ClSiMe₃ 2) NaOC(CH₃)₃ 3) H⁺

(B) 1) SOCl₂ 2) NaOEt 3) H⁺

(D) 1) SOCl₂ 2) NaOC(CH₃)₃ 3) H⁺

PQ-16. What is the purpose of the first step of this synthesis?

1) ClSiMe₃
2) KMnO₄, ⁻OH, cold
3) H₃O⁺

(A) It converts the –OH into a –Cl.

(B) It protects the alcohol.

(C) It does an addition reaction with the double bond.

(D) It protects the double bond.

PQ-17. Which mechanism is followed to yield the product of this reaction?

(A) S_N1

(B) S_N2

(C) Markovnikov Addition

(D) reduction

PQ-18. Which set of reagents will yield this ether at the fastest rate?

(A) [structure] EtONa

(B) [structure] EtONa

(C) [structure] EtOH

(D) [structure] EtCl

PQ-19. What starting molecule yields this product at the fastest rate?

(A) [structure]

(B) [structure]

(C) [structure]

(D) [structure]

PQ-20. What is the product of this reaction?

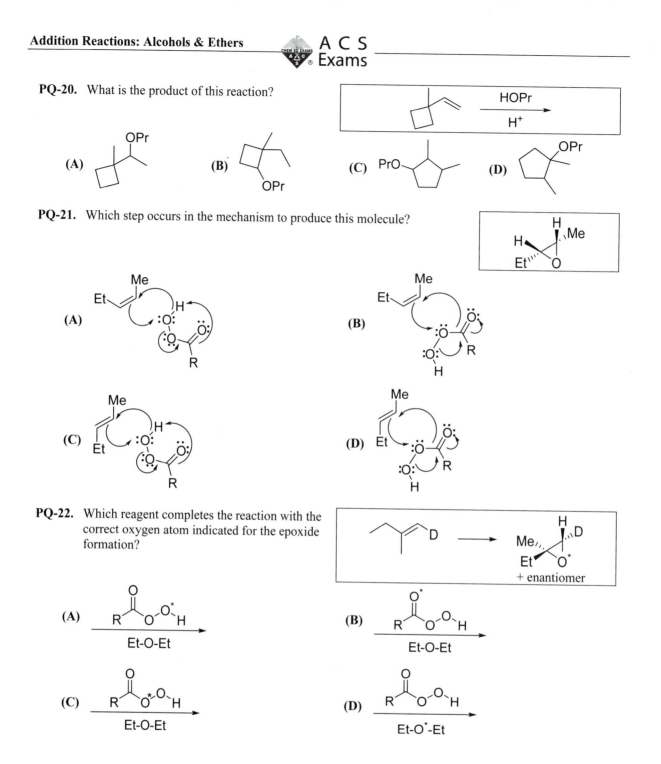

(A)

(B)

(C) PrO

(D)

PQ-21. Which step occurs in the mechanism to produce this molecule?

(A)

(B)

(C)

(D)

PQ-22. Which reagent completes the reaction with the correct oxygen atom indicated for the epoxide formation?

(A) Et-O-Et

(B) Et-O-Et

(C) Et-O-Et

(D) Et-O*-Et

PQ-23. Which reagents yield this product?

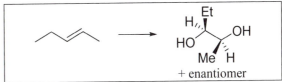

(A) Hg(OAc)₂, H₂O followed by NaBH₄, NaOH

(B) O₃ followed by (CH₃)₂S

(C) 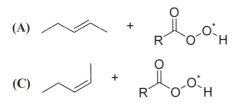, followed by NaOH/H₂O

(D) OsO₄/NMO

PQ-24. How is this reaction characterized?

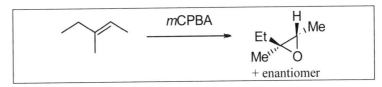

(A) only regioselective

(B) only stereospecific

(C) both regioselective and stereospecific

(D) neither regioselective nor stereospecific

PQ-25. Which reagents would yield this product?

(A)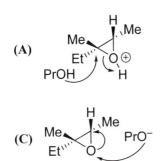

(B)

(C)

(D)

PQ-26. What is a step in the mechanism for this reaction?

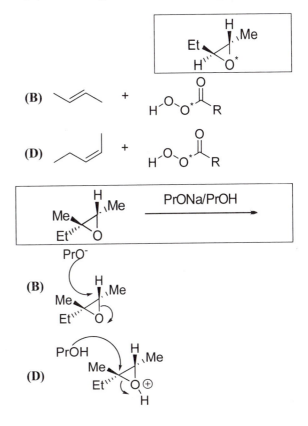

(A)

(B)

(C)

(D)

PQ-27. What is the first step of this mechanism?

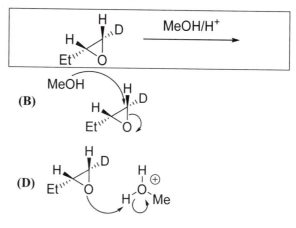

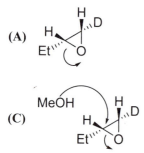

(A)

(B)

(C)

(D)

PQ-28. How would you characterize this reaction?

(A) only regioselective

(B) only stereospecific

(C) both regioselective and stereospecific

(D) neither regioselective nor stereospecific

PQ-29. What are the products of this reaction?

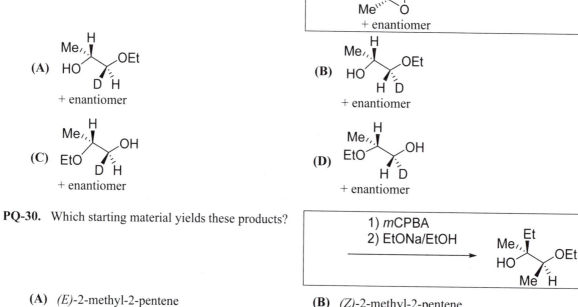

(A) + enantiomer

(B) + enantiomer

(C) + enantiomer

(D) + enantiomer

PQ-30. Which starting material yields these products?

1) *m*CPBA
2) EtONa/EtOH

(A) *(E)*-2-methyl-2-pentene

(B) *(Z)*-2-methyl-2-pentene

(C) *(E)*-3-methyl-2-pentene

(D) *(Z)*-3-methyl-2-pentene

Answers to Study Questions

SQ-1.	C	SQ-5.	C	SQ-9.	D
SQ-2.	C	SQ-6.	B	SQ-10.	B
SQ-3.	A	SQ-7.	B		
SQ-4.	A	SQ-8.	C		

Answers to Practice Questions

PQ-1.	C	PQ-11.	C	PQ-21.	A
PQ-2.	D	PQ-12.	D	PQ-22.	A
PQ-3.	C	PQ-13.	C	PQ-23.	D
PQ-4.	B	PQ-14.	B	PQ-24.	B
PQ-5.	C	PQ-15.	A	PQ-25.	A
PQ-6.	D	PQ-16.	B	PQ-26.	B
PQ-7.	C	PQ-17.	C	PQ-27.	D
PQ-8.	C	PQ-18.	D	PQ-28.	C
PQ-9.	D	PQ-19.	A	PQ-29.	D
PQ-10.	C	PQ-20.	D	PQ-30.	D

Chapter 9 –Spectroscopy

Chapter Summary:

This chapter will focus on how to interpret instrumental data for the determination of organic structure, including mass spectrometry (MS), ^1H and ^{13}C nuclear magnetic resonance spectroscopy (NMR), and infrared spectrophotometry (IR). Each method can be used independently, often allowing the determination of the structure of simple compounds but can also be used together to determine the structure of complicated unknowns. Also included in this chapter are questions related to the type of data supplied by these modern instrumental methods, especially with regard to molecular constitution.

Specific topics covered in this chapter are:
- Mass spectrometry (MS)
- ^1H nuclear magnetic resonance spectroscopy (^1H NMR)
- ^{13}C nuclear magnetic resonance spectroscopy (^{13}C NMR)
- Infrared spectrophotometry (IR)
- Solving spectroscopic problems with combinations of the methods listed above

Previous material that is relevant to your understanding of questions in this chapter includes:
- Structure: Molecular Orbital, Hybridization, Valence Bond Theory, Resonance (***Chapter 1***)
- Structure: Nomenclature and Functional Groups (***Chapter 2***)
- Structure: Isomers (stereochemical, conformational, constitutional) of Alkanes, Cycloalkanes, Alkenes (***Chapter 3***)

Where you might see this material in upcoming Study Guide chapters:
- Spectral Problems in Application of Organic Chemistry (***Chapter 16***)

Where to find this in your textbook:

The material in this chapter typically aligns to "Mass Spectrometry (MS)," "^1H and ^{13}C Nuclear Magnetic Resonance (NMR)," and "Infrared Spectrophotometry (IR)" in your textbook. The name of your chapter may vary.

Practice exam:

There may be practice exam questions aligned to the material in this chapter. Because there are a limited number of questions on the practice exam, a review of the breadth of the material in this chapter is advised in preparation for your exam.

How this fits to the big picture:

The material in this chapter aligns to the Big Ideas of Structure and Function (III), Experiments, Measurement, and Data (IX), and Visualization (X) as listed on page 13 of this study guide.

Study Questions (SQ)

SQ-1. Which structure would give a molecular ion (M^+) at 114 *m/z* and a major fragment at *m/z* at 71 in mass spectrometry?

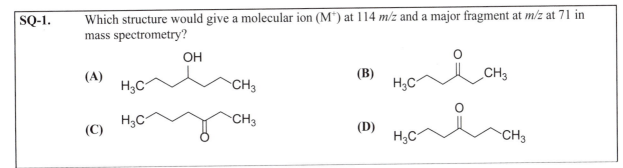

Knowledge Required: (1) Theory of mass spectrometry and molecular ions. (2) Fragmentation patterns in mass spectrometry.

Thinking it Through: You know that the molar mass of a structure in g/mol corresponds directly to the mass of the molecular ion (M^+) in mass spectrometry measured in *m/z* units. You also know that fragmentation reactions take place in mass spectrometry according to known carbocation and radical stability principles.

You recall that for both carbocations and radicals, stability decreases as the number of –R groups attached to the reactive carbon decreases. You know that 3° (carbocations/radicals) are more stable than 2°, which are more stable than 1°. You recall that generally, an allylic (or benzylic) radical is more stable than a 3° radical, while an allylic (or benzylic) carbocation is slightly less stable than a 3° carbocation. You note that in this prompt, the high stability of acyl cations (positive carbon of a carbonyl) will be important in fragmentation.

Choice **(D)** is correct. The molar mass that corresponds to $C_7H_{14}O$ is 114 g/mol and the acyl cation generated by fragmentation of this structure (carbonyl with propyl group) has a mass of 71 g/mol.

Choices **(A)** and **(B)** are not correct. Their molar masses are either more or less than the supplied molecular ion of 114 *m/z*. Choice **(C)** is not correct. Although its molar mass is 114 g/mol, its two acyl carbocation fragments do not have masses of 71 g/mol.

Practice Problems: PQ-1 and **PQ-2**

SQ-2. Each molecular formula corresponds to molecular ion (M^+) of 158 *m/z* EXCEPT one. What is the EXCEPTION?

(A) $C_{10}H_{10}N_2$ **(B)** $C_{12}H_{14}$ **(C)** $C_{11}H_{13}N$ **(D)** $C_8H_5F_3$

Knowledge Required: (1) Theory of mass spectrometry and molecular ions. (2) Use of the nitrogen rule in MS.

Thinking it Through: You know that the molar mass of a structure in g/mol corresponds directly to the mass of the molecular ion (M^+) in mass spectrometry measured in *m/z* units. You also know that because nitrogen has an odd-numbered valence in its neutral state, the molecular ions of structures with odd numbers of nitrogen atoms are always odd-numbered. You recall that in cases with zero nitrogen atoms M^+ is an even number.

Choice **(C)** is correct. It is the only choice with an odd number of nitrogen atoms that could not correspond to an even-numbered molecular ion in *m/z*. The molecular weight of this molecule is 159 g/mol.

Choices **(A)**, **(B)**, and **(D)** are not correct. They all involve zero or even numbers of nitrogen atoms, which would give rise to an even-numbered molecular ion value in *m/z*.

Practice Problems: PQ-3

SQ-3. How many unique signals would be observed in the ^1H NMR spectrum for the structure?

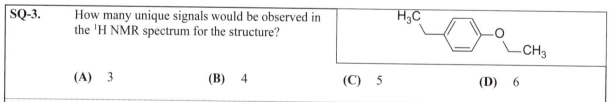

(A) 3   **(B)** 4   **(C)** 5   **(D)** 6

Knowledge Required: (1) Theory of ^1H NMR with regard to molecular symmetry.

Thinking it Through: You know that ^1H NMR spectroscopy gives data related to symmetrically unique proton or hydrogen sets in a structure. You recall that symmetrically unique hydrogens and carbons are magnetically or chemically nonequivalent, and therefore, give rise to unique NMR signals. You also know that three-dimensional mirror planes which bisect organic structures are one way to track whether the ^1H NMR experiment will present a symmetrically unique set of protons.

The presence of the oxygen atom alters the symmetry of the given structure, making protons closer and further from it magnetically/chemically nonequivalent. There is one plane of symmetry in this molecule that goes through both alkyl chains and the benzene ring. This means there are only four unique carbon atoms in the benzene ring and only two pairs of equivalent proton environments in the ring.

Choice **(D)** is correct. The answer accounts for the six different sets of protons in the structure: two different methyl (CH₃) groups, two different methylene (CH₂) groups, and two different sets of CH groups in the aromatic ring.

Choice **(A)** is not correct. This would be the answer if there were two ethyl substituents *para* to each other on the aromatic ring. The oxygen disrupts the symmetry and thus the two ethyl groups are not equivalent, nor are all the protons on the aromatic ring.

Choices **(B)**, and **(C)** are not correct. They do not take into account all the symmetrically unique proton sets in the given structure.

***Practice Problems:* PQ-4, PQ-5**, and **PQ-6**

SQ-4. Which structure could have given rise to this ¹H NMR spectrum?

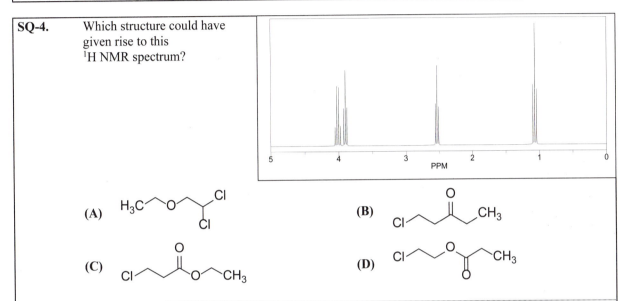

(A) H₃C—O—CHCl₂ (with Cl shown)

(B) Cl—CH₂CH₂—C(=O)—CH₂—CH₃

(C) Cl—CH₂CH₂—C(=O)—O—CH₂CH₃

(D) Cl—CH₂CH₂—O—C(=O)—CH₂CH₃

Knowledge Required: (1) Chemical shift of functional groups in ¹H NMR. (2) Signal splitting (neighbor rule) in ¹H NMR.

Thinking it Through: You recognize the following splitting patterns in the spectrum presented in order, from highest to lowest ppm (δ, chemical shift): quartet, two equal/smaller triplets, one larger triplet. You know that each of these split signals corresponds to one set of protons/hydrogen atoms in an organic structure, and that the splitting signals correspond to how many proton neighbors a proton set has plus one. Thus, you are looking for four unique proton environments with 3, 2, 2 and 2 equivalent protons per environment. You realize this eliminates choice **(A)**.

You also know a signal's relative placement on the chemical shift scale corresponds to the proton's electronic environment. You know that proton sets closer to electronegative atoms or multiple bonds tend to have higher relative chemical shifts for their split signals:

H bonded to	δ (ppm)
sp³ C atom	1
C atom bonded to π system	2
C atom bonded to O atom	3-4
sp² C atom	5-6
aromatic C atom	7-8
aldehyde C atom	10
carboxylic acid O atom	11-12

Choice **(C)** is correct. It is the only structure which would give rise to a quartet signal higher than 4 ppm which would correspond to a methylene (–CH₂–) group bonded to one oxygen atom and one methyl (–CH₃) group and has the correct other splitting patterns.

Choice **(A)** is not correct. One of its methylene (–CH_2–) groups would give a doublet signal (one proton neighbor). Choice **(B)** is not correct. Although this structure would give the number and type of signals presented, the methylene (–CH_2–) group bonded to the ketone carbonyl and one methyl (–CH_3) group would display a quartet closer to 2-3 ppm. Choice **(D)** is not correct. Although this structure would give the number and type of signals presented, the highest ppm signal (most deshielded) would be a triplet and correspond to the methylene (–CH_2–) group bonded to the oxygen atom and one other methylene group.

Practice Problems: **PQ-7**, **PQ-8**, and **PQ-9**

SQ-5.   Which structure could have
given rise to this ^{1}H NMR
spectrum?

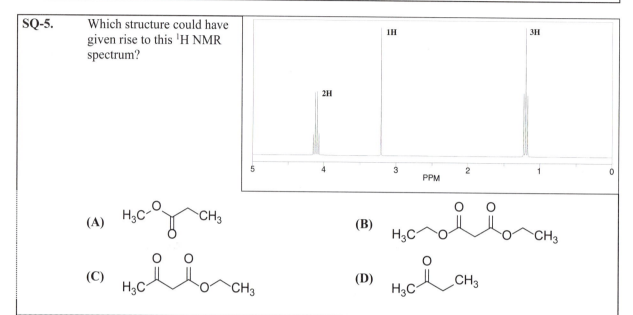

(A)   **(B)**

(C)   **(D)**

Knowledge Required: (1) Chemical shift of functional groups in ^{1}H NMR. (2) Signal splitting (neighbor rule) in ^{1}H NMR. (3) Peak height or integral in ^{1}H NMR.

Thinking it Through: You know that the spectrum presents signals in this order, from highest to lowest ppm (δ, chemical shift): quartet, singlet, triplet. You know that each of these split signals corresponds to one set of protons/hydrogen atoms in an organic structure, and that the splitting signals correspond to how many proton neighbors a proton set has plus one (thus 3, 0 and 2 neighbors respectively).

You also know a signal's relative placement on the chemical shift scale corresponds to the proton's electronic environment. You know that proton sets closer to electronegative atoms or multiple bonds tend to have higher relative chemical shifts for their split signals.

You also know that integrations in ^{1}H NMR relates to the total number of individual hydrogen atoms represented in that signal. If you consider the answer options, you note that there are no single hydrogen peaks; therefore, the integrations must be at least a multiple of 2 (i.e., 4H for the quartet, 2H for the singlet, and 6H for the triplet.

Choice **(B)** is correct. The order of signals based on splitting and chemical shift matches the given ^{1}H NMR spectrum. The peak group at 1.2 ppm corresponds to the methyl (–CH_3) group and the two other signals are of relatively the same height, corresponding to the two methylene (–CH_2–) groups.

Choice **(A)** is not correct. The methyl (–CH_3) group bonded to the oxygen atom would be at the highest ppm value as a singlet. Choice **(C)** is not correct. Its structure gives rise to four unique ^{1}H NMR signals. This structure would have two higher integrating signals signifying the two methyl (–CH_3) groups. Choice **(D)** is not correct. While the number and type of the signals matches the data, the quartet and singlet signals would appear at different chemical shifts than the given data: closer to 2 ppm in both cases, and the integrations would be different.

Practice Problems: **PQ-10**, **PQ-11**, and **PQ-12**

SQ-6. How many signals would be expected in the proton-decoupled ^{13}C NMR spectrum for this structure?

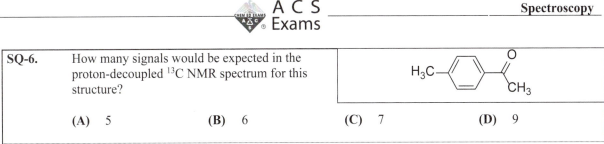

(A) 5   (B) 6   (C) 7   (D) 9

Knowledge Required: (1) Theory of ^{13}C NMR with regard to molecular symmetry.

Thinking it Through: You know that the ^{13}C NMR spectrum of a compound displays a resonance for each symmetrically unique carbon atom in its structure. Symmetrically unique carbons are magnetically or chemically nonequivalent, and therefore, give rise to unique NMR signals. You also know that three-dimensional mirror planes which bisect organic structures are one way to track whether the ^{13}C NMR experiment will present a symmetrically unique carbon atom. You note that this structure has one mirror plane that cuts through the methyl group, cuts the aromatic ring in two and proceeds through the R group *para* to the methyl. You recall that proton-decoupled refers to standard ^{13}C NMR spectra where the peaks are not split by neighboring hydrogen atoms. In some questions "proton decoupled" may be omitted.

Choice (C) is correct. It accounts for the seven different sets of carbons in the structure: two different methyl ($-CH_3$) groups, two different sets of "CH" groups in the aromatic ring, and three carbons lacking hydrogen atoms (one carbonyl and two aromatic).

Choices (A), (B), and (D) are not correct. They do not take into account all of the symmetrically-unique carbons in the given structure.

Practice Problems: **PQ-13, PQ-14, PQ-15,** and **PQ-16**

SQ-7. Which structure is consistent with this ^{13}C NMR spectrum?

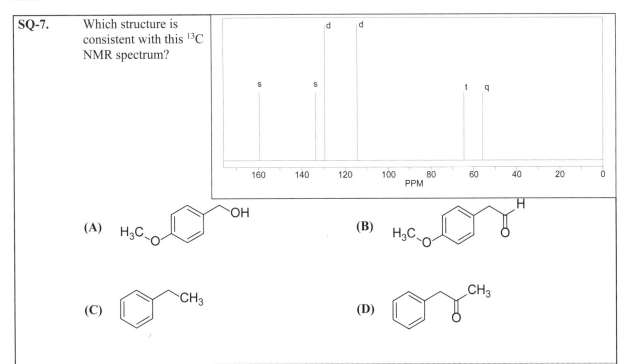

Knowledge Required: (1) Chemical shift of functional groups in ^{13}C NMR. (2) Proton-coupled or DEPT ^{13}C NMR data.

Thinking it Through: You know that the spectrum presents six total signals. You know that each of these signals corresponds to one set of carbon atoms in an organic structure, and that the proton-coupled symbols at the top of each signal correspond to the number of hydrogen atoms bonded to the symmetrically-unique carbon: s = 0 H, or C_q; d = 1 H, or CH; t = 2 H, or CH_2; q = 3 H, or CH_3. You also know the signals' relative placement on the chemical shift scale corresponds to a carbon atom's electronic environment. You know that carbon atoms closer to electronegative atoms or multiple bonds tend to have higher relative chemical shifts for their signals:

C environment	δ (ppm)
sp³ alkyl C atom	10-30
sp³ alkyl C atom bonded to O/N/X	50-70
sp alkynyl C atom	75-90
sp² alkenyl C atom	100-160
ester, amide, carboxyl C=O	160-180
aldehyde or ketone C=O	190-200

Choice **(A)** is correct. The structure has two different C signals without hydrogen atoms attached, two different aromatic CH signals, and one each of CH_2 and CH_3.

Choice **(C)** is not correct. While the structure has one each of CH_2 and CH_3, it only has one C signal without an H atom attached and three different aromatic CH signals. Choices **(B)** and **(D)** are not correct. Both structures have seven symmetrically unique carbons. In addition, these two choices have C signals without Hs attached that are carbonyls, not present in the supplied spectrum.

Practice Problems: **PQ-17, PQ-18, PQ-19**, and **PQ-20**

SQ-8. What effect does the conjugation of a carbonyl group with a carbon-carbon double bond (alkenyl functional group) have on the IR absorption due to the C=O stretch?

(A) It shifts to a lower frequency (longer wavelength).

(B) It shifts to a higher frequency (shorter wavelength).

(C) It has no effect.

(D) The absorption due to C=O disappears.

Knowledge Required: (1) Theory of IR spectrophotometry based on relationships between frequency/wavelength and energy of electromagnetic radiation. (2) Effect of resonance on the nature of double bonds.

Thinking it Through: You know that there is a resonance interaction between the C=C and C=O when they are conjugated:

You also know less energy is required to stretch a carbon-oxygen single bond than a carbonyl. You recall that less energy is associated with lower frequencies. Because in the resonance hybrid of this structure the C–O bond would be more than a single bond, but less than a double bond, you realize that it would take less energy to stretch this C=O.

Choice **(A)** is correct. The reduced double bond character of the conjugated carbonyl will result in a lower stretching frequency.

Choices **(B)**, **(C)**, and **(D)** are not correct. They do not follow the logic of increased single-bond character leading to lower frequency bond stretching.

Practice Problems: **PQ-21, PQ-22**, and **PQ-23**

SQ-9. Which structure is consistent with this IR spectrum?

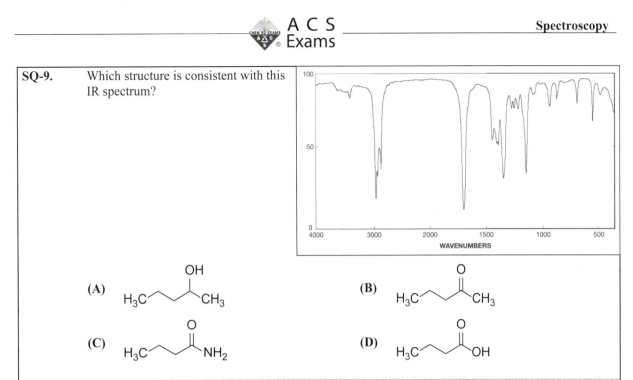

Knowledge Required: (1) Approximate IR absorption frequencies for O–H, N–H, and C=O bonds.
(2) Recognition of the absence of characteristic IR absorption bands for various bonds allows structure containing those bonds to be ruled out.

Thinking it Through: You know that the given IR spectrum shows a strong absorption band at approximately 1720 cm^{-1}. You know that certain bonds stretch, bend, and vibrate according to the differences in atomic size and electronegativity and generate a list of IR-active bonds important in organic chemistry:

Bond Type	Frequency (cm^{-1})
O–H and N–H	3400
sp C–H	3300
sp^2 C–H	3100-3000
sp^3 C–H	3000-2850
C≡C and C≡N	2100
C=O	1700
C=C, aromatic C–C	1600
aromatic C–C	1500

Choice **(B)** is correct. It contains a C=O bond, but not an O–H or N–H bond.
Choice **(A)** is not correct. It contains an O–H bond, but not a C=O bond. Choices **(C)** and **(D)** are not correct. They contain bonds not represented in the IR spectrum, N–H and O–H, respectively.

Practice Problems: PQ-24, PQ-25, PQ-26, and **PQ-27**

A C S
Exams

SQ-10. Which structure is in agreement with both of these ^1H and ^{13}C NMR spectra?

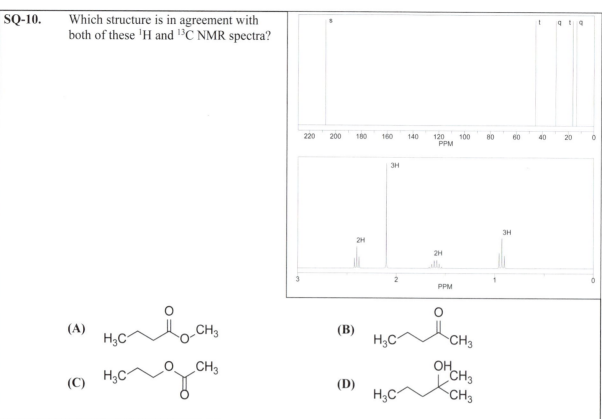

(A) H₃C——————O——CH₃ with O double bond

(B) H₃C——————CH₃ with O double bond

(C) H₃C——————O——CH₃ with O double bond below

(D) H₃C——————CH₃ with OH and CH₃

Knowledge Required: (1) Integration of spectral data from multiple sources.

Thinking it Through: You know that when examining data from multiple spectroscopic sources, the correct structure must match all the given data. You also know that process of elimination works best in this case, and structural choices missing key pieces of spectral data can be eliminated.

You recognize that key data in this case would include information from both the ^{13}C NMR (top image) and the ^1H NMR (bottom image). In the ^{13}C NMR you notice five unique carbon environments, specifically a C that is a C=O above 200 ppm, 2 –CH₃ groups and 2 –CH₂– groups. From the ^1H NMR you notice four unique proton environments and most notably, nothing above 2.5 ppm. Thus, a CH attached to an electronegative oxygen can be ruled out.

Choice **(B)** is correct. It has five total ^{13}C NMR signals (one is a C=O) and four total ^1H NMR signals with the correct splitting pattern (one is a –CH₃ singlet), and no ether or ester link.

Choice **(A)** is not correct. Although it has the correct number and type of signals, its –CH₃ group bonded to the oxygen atom would deshield the corresponding ^{13}C (q at 30 ppm) and ^1H (singlet at 2.1 ppm) NMR signals to larger (60 and 4 ppm, respectively) values. Choice **(C)** is not correct. For similar reasons as above, however the functional group affected most by the oxygen atom would be a methylene (–CH₂–). Choice **(D)** is not correct. It does not contain the carbonyl (C=O) C indicated in the ^{13}C NMR data. There is also no evidence of a proton bonded to an oxygen (hydroxyl functional group) in the ^1H NMR spectrum.

Practice Problems: PQ-28, PQ-29, and PQ-30

Practice Questions (PQ)

PQ-1. Which structure would show major fragment ions at 59 and 73 *m/z* in its mass spectrum?

(A) H₃C ⌁ OH ⌁ CH₃

(B) H₃C ⌁ CH₃ / OH

(C) H₃C ⌁ OH ⌁ CH₃ / CH₃

(D) H₃C ⌁ OH ⌁ CH₃ / CH₃

PQ-2. Which structure would show major fragments in its mass spectrum at 57 and 85 *m/z*?

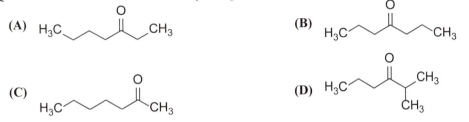

(A) H₃C ⌁ O ⌁ CH₃

(B) H₃C ⌁ O ⌁ CH₃

(C) H₃C ⌁ O ⌁ CH₃

(D) H₃C ⌁ O ⌁ CH₃ / CH₃

PQ-3. Which molecular formula corresponds to a compound with a molecular ion (M+) of 117 *m/z* in its mass spectrum?

(A) C_8H_7N (B) $C_7H_5N_2$ (C) $C_7H_{14}F$ (D) $C_6H_{13}O_2$

PQ-4. Which structure is consistent with this ¹H NMR spectrum?

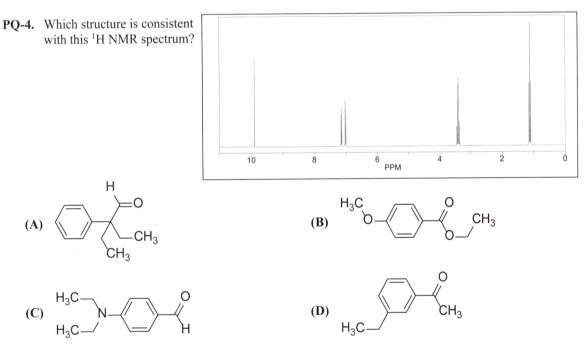

(A) phenyl group with C(CH₂CH₃)(CH₃) and CHO

(B) H₃C—O—C₆H₄—C(=O)—O—CH₂CH₃

(C) H₃C—CH₂—N(—CH₂—CH₃)—C₆H₄—CHO

(D) H₃C—C₆H₄—C(=O)—CH₃

PQ-5. Signals from how many sets of protons should be observed in the ^{1}H NMR spectrum for this structure?

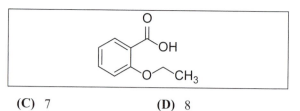

(A) 5   (B) 6   (C) 7   (D) 8

PQ-6. How many ^{1}H NMR signals should appear in the spectrum of this structure?

(A) 2   (B) 3   (C) 4   (D) 5

PQ-7. What is the correct order (from lowest to highest ppm) for the chemical shifts of labeled sets of protons in the ^{1}H NMR spectrum of this structure?

(A) **I < II < III**   (B) **III < I < II**   (C) **III < II < I**   (D) **I < III < II**

PQ-8. Which structure(s) would give two triplets in their ^{1}H NMR spectra (other signals with different multiplicities allowed)?

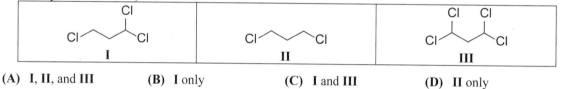

(A) **I, II, and III**   (B) **I** only   (C) **I and III**   (D) **II** only

PQ-9. What is the first-order splitting pattern for the indicated hydrogen?

(A) singlet   (B) doublet   (C) triplet   (D) quartet

PQ-10. Which structure is consistent with this ^{1}H NMR spectrum?

(A)

(B)

(C)

(D)

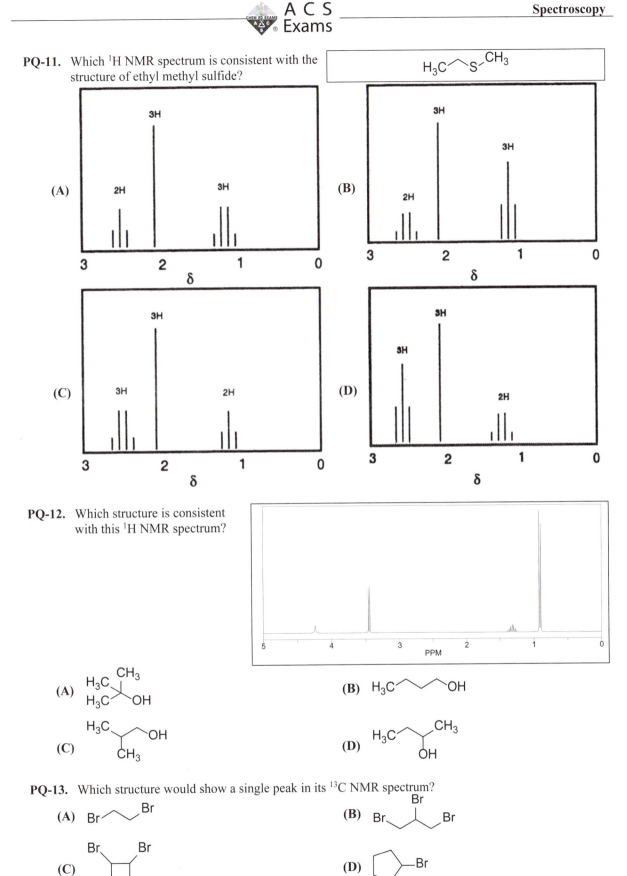

PQ-11. Which ^{1}H NMR spectrum is consistent with the structure of ethyl methyl sulfide?

PQ-12. Which structure is consistent with this ^{1}H NMR spectrum?

(A)

(B) H₃C ⌢⌣ OH

(C)

(D)

PQ-13. Which structure would show a single peak in its ^{13}C NMR spectrum?

(A) Br ⌢⌣ Br

(B) Br ⌢ Br

(C)

(D)

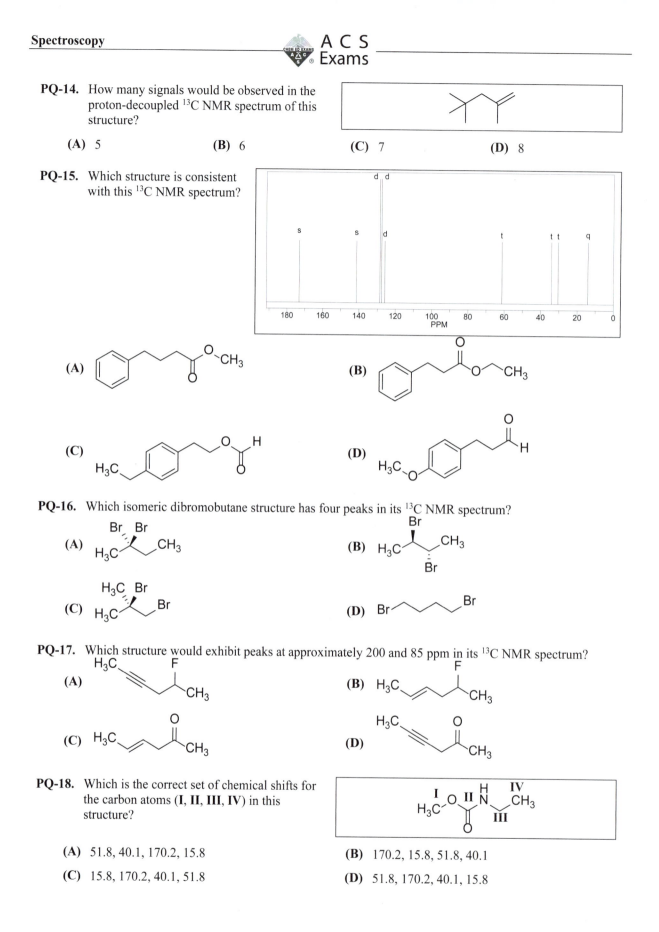

PQ-14. How many signals would be observed in the proton-decoupled ^{13}C NMR spectrum of this structure?

(A) 5   (B) 6   (C) 7   (D) 8

PQ-15. Which structure is consistent with this ^{13}C NMR spectrum?

(A)

(B)

(C)

(D)

PQ-16. Which isomeric dibromobutane structure has four peaks in its ^{13}C NMR spectrum?

(A)

(B)

(C)

(D)

PQ-17. Which structure would exhibit peaks at approximately 200 and 85 ppm in its ^{13}C NMR spectrum?

(A)

(B)

(C)

(D)

PQ-18. Which is the correct set of chemical shifts for the carbon atoms (**I, II, III, IV**) in this structure?

(A) 51.8, 40.1, 170.2, 15.8

(B) 170.2, 15.8, 51.8, 40.1

(C) 15.8, 170.2, 40.1, 51.8

(D) 51.8, 170.2, 40.1, 15.8

PQ-19. Which structure is consistent with this ^{13}C NMR spectrum?

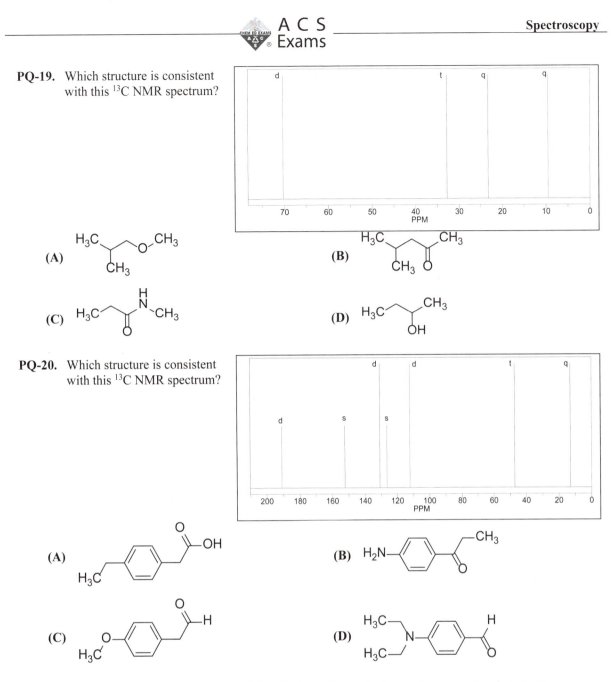

(A) H₃C—CH(CH₃)—CH₂—O—CH₃

(B) H₃C—CH(CH₃)—C(=O)—CH₃

(C) H₃C—CH₂—C(=O)—NH—CH₃

(D) H₃C—CH(OH)—CH₂—CH₃ [with CH₃]

PQ-20. Which structure is consistent with this ^{13}C NMR spectrum?

(A) H₃C— substituted benzene ring —CH₂—C(=O)—OH

(B) H₂N— benzene ring —C(=O)—CH₂—CH₃

(C) H₃C—O— benzene ring —CH₂—C(=O)—H

(D) (H₃C—CH₂)₂N— benzene ring —C(=O)—H

PQ-21. Which ketone will show a carbonyl (C=O) absorption at the lowest frequency (cm^{-1}) in its IR spectrum?

(A) cyclohexyl—C(=O)—CH₃

(B) cyclohexenyl (1-ene)—C(=O)—CH₃

(C) cyclohexenyl (2-ene)—C(=O)—CH₃

(D) cyclohexyl—C(=O)—CH₂—CH₃

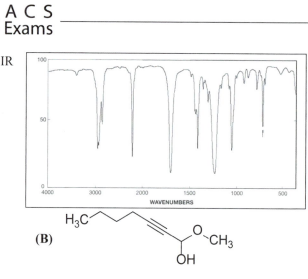

PQ-22. Which structure is most consistent with this IR spectrum?

(A)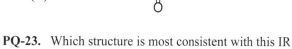

(B)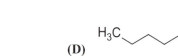

(C)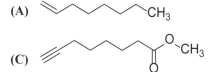

(D)

PQ-23. Which structure is most consistent with this IR spectrum?

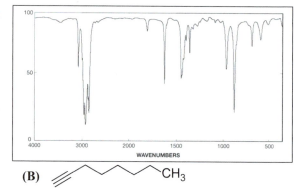

(A)

(B)

(C)

(D) H₃C

PQ-24. Which structure is most consistent with this IR spectrum?

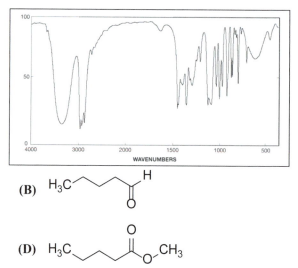

(A)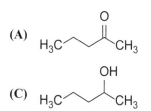

(B) H₃C

(C) H₃C

(D) H₃C

PQ-25. Which structure is most consistent with this IR spectrum?

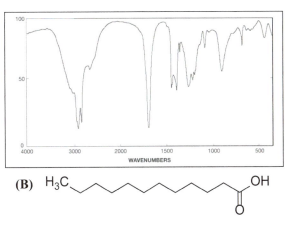

(A) 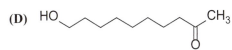 H₃C ～～～～～～O CH₃

(B) H₃C ～～～～～～～OH

(C) H₃C ～～～～～～H

(D) HO ～～～～～～CH₃

PQ-26. Which structure is most consistent with this IR spectrum?

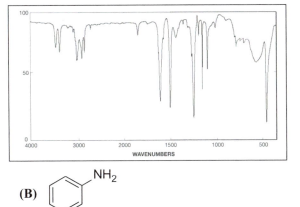

(A)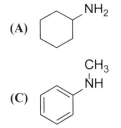

(B)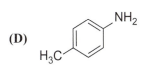

(C)

(D)

PQ-27. Which structure is most consistent with this IR spectrum?

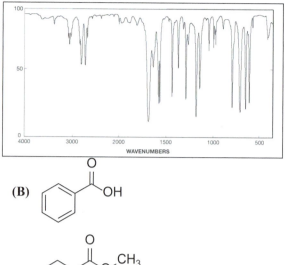

(A)

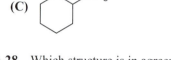

(B)

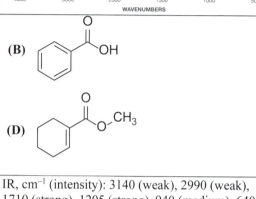

(C)

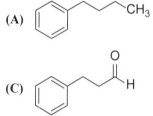

(D)

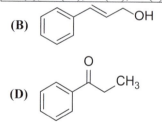

PQ-28. Which structure is in agreement with both of these MS and IR data?

IR, cm^{-1} (intensity): 3140 (weak), 2990 (weak), 1710 (strong), 1205 (strong), 940 (medium), 640 (medium)

MS, m/z (intensity): 134 (16), 106 (8), 105 (100), 78 (6), 77 (59), 51 (22), 50 (9)

(A)

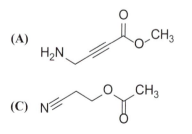

(B)

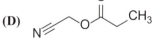

(C)

(D)

PQ-29. Which structure is in agreement with both of these IR and ^{1}H NMR data?

IR, cm^{-1} (intensity): 3000 (medium), 2270 (weak), 1745 (strong)

^{1}H NMR, δ (splitting, #H): 5.2 (singlet, 2H); 2.3 (quartet, 2H); 1.1 (triplet, 3H)

(A)

(B)

(C)

(D)

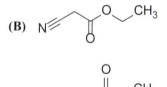

PQ-30. An unknown compound was found to be unreactive towards chromic acid (Jones' reagent = CrO₃, aqueous H₂SO₄, acetone) and gave this IR spectrum. What is the structure of the compound?

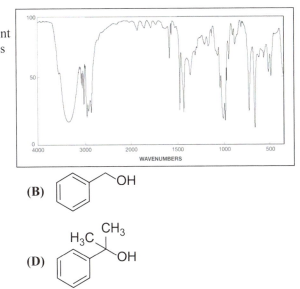

(A)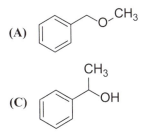

(B)

(C)

(D)

Answers to Study Questions

SQ-1.	D	SQ-5.	B	SQ-9.	B
SQ-2.	C	SQ-6.	C	SQ-10.	B
SQ-3.	D	SQ-7.	A		
SQ-4.	C	SQ-8.	A		

Answers to Practice Questions

PQ-1.	D	PQ-11.	B	PQ-21.	B
PQ-2.	A	PQ-12.	C	PQ-22.	A
PQ-3.	A	PQ-13.	A	PQ-23.	A
PQ-4.	C	PQ-14.	B	PQ-24.	C
PQ-5.	C	PQ-15.	B	PQ-25.	B
PQ-6.	B	PQ-16.	A	PQ-26.	D
PQ-7.	C	PQ-17.	D	PQ-27.	A
PQ-8.	C	PQ-18.	D	PQ-28.	D
PQ-9.	C	PQ-19.	D	PQ-29.	D
PQ-10.	A	PQ-20.	D	PQ-30.	D

Chapter 10 – Radical Reactions

Chapter Summary:
This chapter will focus on reactions involving radicals.

Specific topics covered in this chapter are:
- Radical reaction mechanisms
- Functionalization of alkanes
- Formation of polymers

Previous material that is relevant to your understanding of questions in this chapter include:
- Bond-line structures (*Chapter 1*)
- Structure: Isomers (*Chapter 3*)

Where to find this in your textbook:
The material in this chapter typically aligns to "Radical Reactions" in your textbook. The name of your chapter may vary.

Practice exam:
There may be practice exam questions aligned to the material in this chapter. Because there are a limited number of questions on the practice exam, a review of the breadth of the material in this chapter is advised in preparation for your exam.

How this fits to the big picture:
The material in this chapter aligns to the Big Idea of "Chemical Reactions" (V) as listed on page 13 of this study guide.

Study Questions (SQ)

SQ-1. Which represents a termination step of a radical reaction?

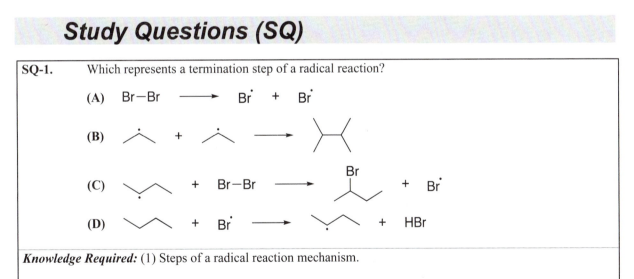

Knowledge Required: (1) Steps of a radical reaction mechanism.

Thinking it Through: You are asked to evaluate four reaction steps to determine which step is a termination step. You recall that an initiation step is when radicals are formed from starting materials that do not contain radicals. A propagation step is when one or more starting materials has a radical and one or more products has a radical. Finally, a termination step is when two radicals combine to form a product that does not include a radical.

Choice **(B)** is correct because it fits the definition of a termination step where two radicals combine to form a neutral species.

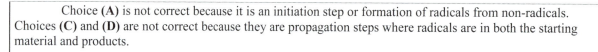
Choice **(A)** is not correct because it is an initiation step or formation of radicals from non-radicals. Choices **(C)** and **(D)** are not correct because they are propagation steps where radicals are in both the starting material and products.

Practice Problems: **PQ-1, PQ-2, PQ-3, PQ-4,** and **PQ-5**

SQ-2.   What is the major product of this reaction?

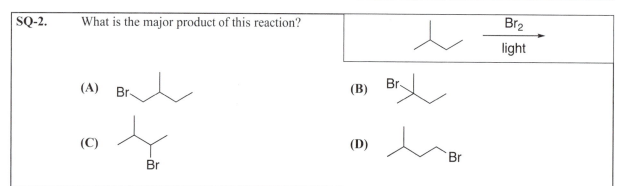

(A)   (B)

(C)   (D)

Knowledge Required: (1) Functionalization of alkanes through free-radical halogenation. (2) Stability trend of radical intermediates.

Thinking it Through: You are asked to determine which product is formed from the free-radical bromination of 2-methylbutane. You recall that the initiation step of this reaction is the homolytic cleavage of bromine (Br_2) to form two bromine radicals. The first propagation step is the abstraction of a proton from 2-methylbutane. There are four possible abstraction sites leading to four unique radical intermediates:

Each of these radical intermediates can lead to a different monobrominated alkane upon reaction with a bromine (Br_2):

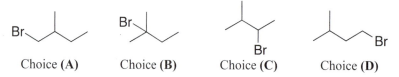

Choice **(A)**   Choice **(B)**   Choice **(C)**   Choice **(D)**

You recall that free-radical bromination proceeds through the most stable free-radical intermediate. Choices **(A)** and **(D)** are formed from primary radicals. Choice **(C)** is formed from a secondary radical. Choice **(B)** is formed from a tertiary radical. Of primary, secondary, and tertiary radicals, you recall that radicals follow the same stability trend as carbocations (resonance stabilized > 3° > 2° > 1° > methyl).
Choice **(B)** is correct because it is formed from the most stable, or tertiary radical intermediate.
Choices **(A), (C),** and **(D)** are not correct because they are formed from less stable radical intermediates.

Practice Problems: **PQ-6, PQ-7, PQ-8, PQ-9,** and **PQ-10**

SQ-3.   What two monomers are used to form the polymer via a free-radical reaction?

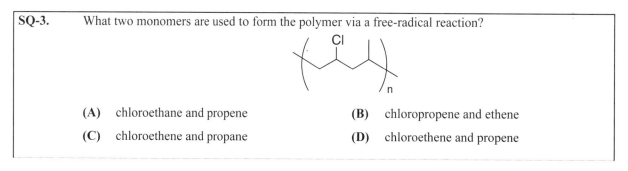

(A)   chloroethane and propene   (B)   chloropropene and ethene

(C)   chloroethene and propane   (D)   chloroethene and propene

Knowledge Required: (1) Formation of polymers via a free radical mechanism.

Thinking it Through: You are asked to consider which two monomers are used to form a given polymer. You note that there are four carbons in the backbone of the polymer unit provided, and thus assume that the polymer is formed from two monomers that include an ethenyl, or alkene, moiety (–CHCH–). You draw a dotted line through the central carbon-carbon bond to determine the two monomers:

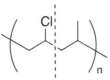

You conclude that chloroethene (CH_2CHCl) is the monomer on the left side of the dotted line. You conclude that propene (CH_2CHCH_3) is the monomer on the right side of the dotted line.

Choice **(D)** is correct because the two monomers both contain alkenes and the chlorine group is on the correct monomer.

Choice **(A)** is not correct because the two monomers do not both contain an alkene. Choice **(B)** is not correct because the chlorine group is on the wrong monomer. Choice **(C)** is not correct because the two monomers do not both contain an alkene.

Practice Problems: PQ-11, PQ-12, PQ-13, PQ-14, and PQ-15

Practice Questions (PQ)

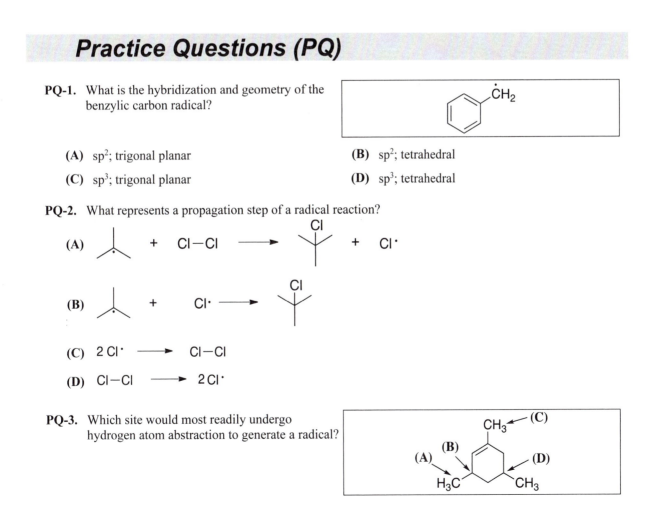

PQ-1. What is the hybridization and geometry of the benzylic carbon radical?

(A) sp^2; trigonal planar

(B) sp^2; tetrahedral

(C) sp^3; trigonal planar

(D) sp^3; tetrahedral

PQ-2. What represents a propagation step of a radical reaction?

(A)

(B)

(C) $2\,Cl\cdot \longrightarrow Cl-Cl$

(D) $Cl-Cl \longrightarrow 2\,Cl\cdot$

PQ-3. Which site would most readily undergo hydrogen atom abstraction to generate a radical?

PQ-4. What is the expected stereochemistry of the organic product from this reaction?

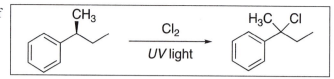

(A) (*S*)-isomer only

(B) (*R*)-isomer only

(C) equal amounts of (*R*)-isomer and (*S*)-isomer

(D) unequal amounts of (*R*)-isomer and (*S*)-isomer

PQ-5. How is the regioselectivity and stereospecificity in the hydrobromination of an alkene with catalytic peroxide best described?

(A) Markovnikov orientation with both *syn* and *anti* products

(B) Anti-Markovnikov orientation with both *syn* and *anti* products

(C) Markovnikov orientation with only *syn* product(s)

(D) Anti-Markovnikov orientation with only *anti* product(s)

PQ-6. What is the major product obtained from radical monobromination of this molecule?

(A) 1-bromo-2-methylbutane

(B) 2-bromo-2-methylbutane

(C) 2-bromo-3-methylbutane

(D) 1-bromo-3-methylbutane

PQ-7. How many products, including stereoisomers, result from this monochlorination?

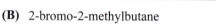

(A) 3

(B) 4

(C) 5

(D) 6

PQ-8. What is the major monochlorination product of this reaction?

(A)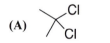

(B)

(C)

(D)

PQ-9. What is the major product of this reaction?

(A)

(B)

(C)

(D)

PQ-10. Which reagents would be used to carry out this transformation?

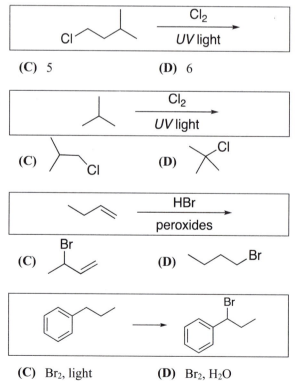

(A) Br$_2$, FeBr$_3$

(B) HBr, HOOH

(C) Br$_2$, light

(D) Br$_2$, H$_2$O

PQ-11. Free-radical polymerization of 2-chloro-1,3-butadiene would produce which polymer?

(A)   (B)

(C)   (D)

PQ-12. The copolymerization of vinyl chloride and vinylidene chloride by free radical catalysis produces a polymer used in food wrap. Which structural unit could appear in this polymer?

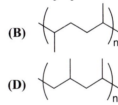

vinyl chloride   **vinylidene chloride**

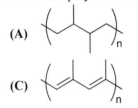

(A)   (B)

(C)   (D)

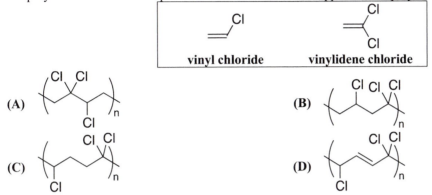

PQ-13. Which polymer is formed by free-radical polymerization of propene?

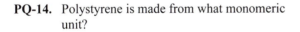

(A)   (B)

(C)   (D)

PQ-14. Polystyrene is made from what monomeric unit?

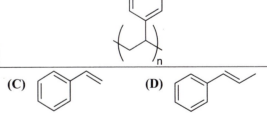

(A)   (B)   (C)   (D)

PQ-15. Polyvinyl chloride is made from what monomeric unit?

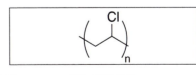

(A) CH_2CHCl (B) CH_3CH_2Cl (C) $CHClCHCl$ (D) $HCCCl$

Answers to Study Questions

SQ-1.	B	SQ-2.	B	SQ-3.	D

Answers to Practice Questions

PQ-1.	A	PQ-6.	B	PQ-11.	D
PQ-2.	A	PQ-7.	C	PQ-12.	B
PQ-3.	B	PQ-8.	C	PQ-13.	D
PQ-4.	C	PQ-9.	D	PQ-14.	C
PQ-5.	B	PQ-10.	C	PQ-15.	A

Additional material for full-year exam begins here

Additional material for full-year exam begins here

Chapter 11 – Conjugated Systems & Aromaticity

Chapter Summary:

This chapter will focus on the conjugated and aromatic properties of molecules. This chapter will also include questions related to the reactivity of conjugated systems.

Specific topics covered in this chapter are:
- Definition of conjugation and resonance stabilization of conjugated systems
- Definitions of aromatic, antiaromatic, and nonaromatic molecules
- Conjugate addition: 1,2- vs 1,4- and kinetic vs thermodynamic control
- Diels-Alder Reaction
- UV-Vis spectroscopy
- Molecular Orbital Theory as it applies to conjugated and aromatic molecules
- Benzylic and allylic cations in substitution and elimination reactions
- Acid-base properties of molecules related to aromaticity or conjugation
- Electron-donating and electron-withdrawing substituent effects

Previous material that is relevant to your understanding of questions in this chapter include:
- Resonance **(Chapter 1)**
- Acid and base strength **(Chapter 4)**
- Nucleophilic substitution reactions **(Chapter 5)**
- Elimination reactions **(Chapter 6)**
- Addition reactions **(Chapter 7)**

Where you might see this material in upcoming Study Guide chapters:
- Aromatic reactions **(Chapter 12)**

Where to find this in your textbook:

The material in this chapter typically aligns to "Conjugated Unsaturated Systems" and "Aromatic Compounds" in your textbook. The name of your chapter may vary.

Practice exam:

There may be practice exam questions aligned to the material in this chapter. Because there are a limited number of questions on the practice exam, a review of the breadth of the material in this chapter is advised in preparation for your exam.

How this fits to the big picture:

The material in this chapter aligns to the Big Idea of Structure and Function (III), Chemical Reactions (V), Energy and Thermodynamics (VI), and Kinetics (VII) as listed on page 13 of this study guide.

Study Questions (SQ)

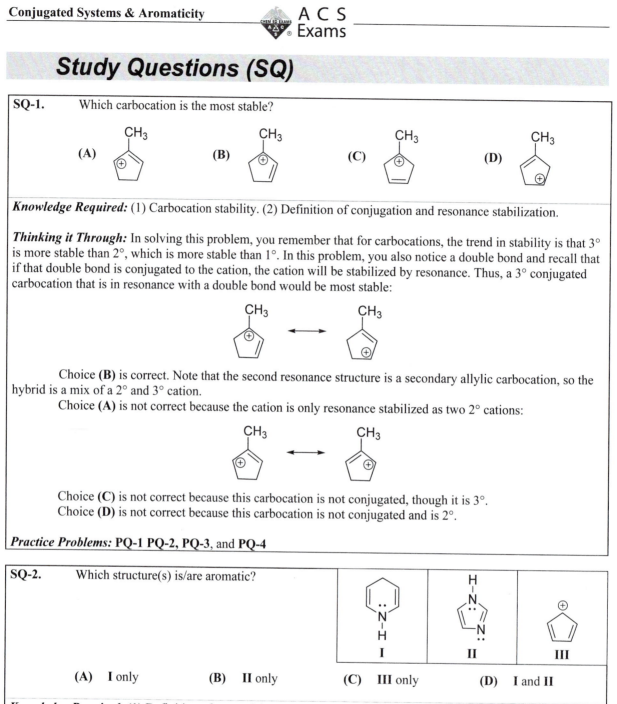

SQ-1. Which carbocation is the most stable?

(A)   (B)   (C)   (D)

Knowledge Required: (1) Carbocation stability. (2) Definition of conjugation and resonance stabilization.

Thinking it Through: In solving this problem, you remember that for carbocations, the trend in stability is that 3° is more stable than 2°, which is more stable than 1°. In this problem, you also notice a double bond and recall that if that double bond is conjugated to the cation, the cation will be stabilized by resonance. Thus, a 3° conjugated carbocation that is in resonance with a double bond would be most stable:

Choice **(B)** is correct. Note that the second resonance structure is a secondary allylic carbocation, so the hybrid is a mix of a 2° and 3° cation.
Choice **(A)** is not correct because the cation is only resonance stabilized as two 2° cations:

Choice **(C)** is not correct because this carbocation is not conjugated, though it is 3°.
Choice **(D)** is not correct because this carbocation is not conjugated and is 2°.

Practice Problems: **PQ-1** PQ-2, **PQ-3**, and **PQ-4**

SQ-2. Which structure(s) is/are aromatic?

I   II   III

(A) I only   (B) II only   (C) III only   (D) I and II

Knowledge Required: (1) Definition of aromaticity.

Thinking it Through: You are asked in this problem to evaluate three structures and determine which are aromatic. You recall that for a molecule to be aromatic it must contain ring, and every atom in that ring must contain a p orbital that can overlap to form an extended π-system. You also recall Hückel's rule which states that a system will be aromatic if the overall energy of the system is stabilized by the delocalization of the electrons, which occurs if there are $4n+2$ π electrons in the delocalized π-system.
For **I**, the carbon-atom at the top of the structure is sp^3-hybridized and thus cannot contribute a p orbital to the system. Therefore, this molecule is nonaromatic because it lacks a ring of p orbitals.
You recognize that in **II**, the nitrogen that does not contain a double bond has a lone pair of electrons that can be placed into a p orbital and delocalized in the π-system. These two electrons plus the four electrons in the π bonds total six, following the $4n+2$ rule and making the molecule aromatic. Note that a lone pair of electrons on the other nitrogen atom are in an sp^2 hybridized orbital, because only one p orbital can be part of the π system for each atom in the ring. Therefore, **II** is aromatic.

For **III**, the carbocation is an empty p orbital and contributes zero electrons to the extended π-system. Thus, the molecule has four π electrons from the π bonds. This molecule fits the 4n rule making **III** antiaromatic, assuming planarity.

Choice (**B**) is correct because compound **II** is the only molecule that is aromatic.

Choices (**A**) and (**D**) are not correct because **I** is nonaromatic. Choice (**C**) is not correct because **III** is antiaromatic

Practice Problems: **PQ-5, PQ-6, PQ-7,** and **PQ-8**

SQ-3.   What is the major product of this reaction?

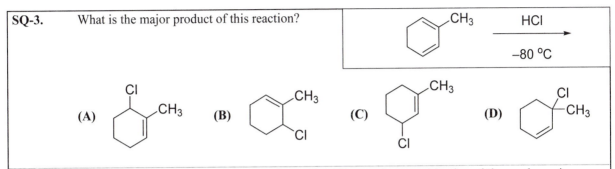

(A)   (B)   (C)   (D)

Knowledge Required: (1) Conjugate addition reactions. (2) Difference between kinetic and thermodynamic products.

Thinking it Through: You are asked to predict which of four products is formed. Looking at the reaction, you notice that HX is added to a π bond. You recall that this happens via a Markovnikov addition, and furthermore with conjugated systems, the cation should be conjugated to the remaining π bond. This resonance-stabilized allylic cation is the most energetically favorable of the possible carbocation intermediates:

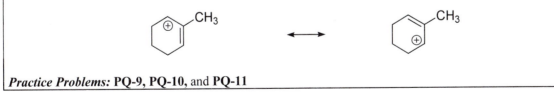

You realize that carbocation resonance structure **I** is the greatest contributor and thus the 3° carbon has the most partial positive charge. You recall this results in the transition state from the attack at this position being the lowest energy, thus leading to the kinetic product. You note that the reaction takes place at –80 °C. You remember that performing reactions in the absence of heat favors the kinetic product.

Choice (**D**) is the correct answer.

Choices (**A**), (**B**), and (**C**) are not correct because they are formed from less energetically stable carbocation intermediates. Choice (**C**) would be formed from the carbocation **II**. Choices (**A**) and (**B**) would be formed from a less stable carbocation intermediate:

Practice Problems: **PQ-9, PQ-10,** and **PQ-11**

SQ-4. Rank the compounds from slowest to fastest rate of S$_N$1 substitution.

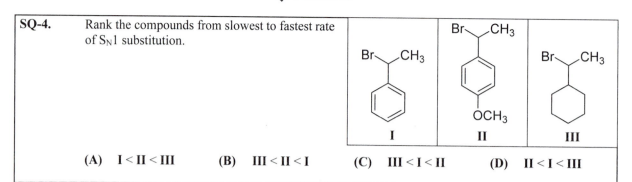

I   II   III

(A) I < II < III   (B) III < II < I   (C) III < I < II   (D) II < I < III

Knowledge Required: (1) Rate-Determining Step in an S$_N$1 is formation of the carbocation. (2) Carbocation stability, including benzylic carbocations. (3) Electron-donating effects on carbocation stability.

Thinking it Through: You are asked in the prompt to evaluate three compounds and determine their relative rate in an S$_N$1 reaction. Given that you are considering an S$_N$1 reaction, you know that the stability of the carbocation intermediate, formed in the rate-limiting step, will determine the overall rate of the reaction. You recognize that these carbocations are formed when the bromide leaving group leaves:

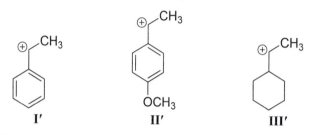

I′   II′   III′

The carbocations formed from **I** and **II** are benzylic, meaning the cation is conjugated to the benzene ring and can be delocalized, and thus stabilized. The carbocation formed from compound **III** is not resonance-stabilized and thus it is the least reactive in an S$_N$1 reaction.

The carbocation formed from the removal of the bromine from **II** is further stabilized by the electron-donating methoxy (–OCH$_3$) group attached at the *para*-position:

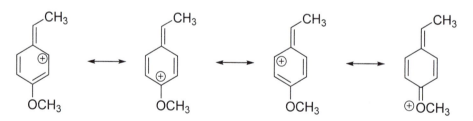

Note that similar resonance-stabilized cations can be drawn for the cation formed from **I**; however, there is no substituent to further stabilize the carbocation as was the case for **II**.

Choice **(C)** is correct. The methoxy substituent will stabilize the carbocation intermediate.

Choice **(A)** is not correct because **I** is not the slowest. Choice **(B)** is not correct because **I** is not the fastest. Choice **(D)** is not correct because it is the reverse order of reactivity.

Practice Problems: **PQ-12** and **PQ-13**

SQ-5.	Rank the compounds from least to most basic.	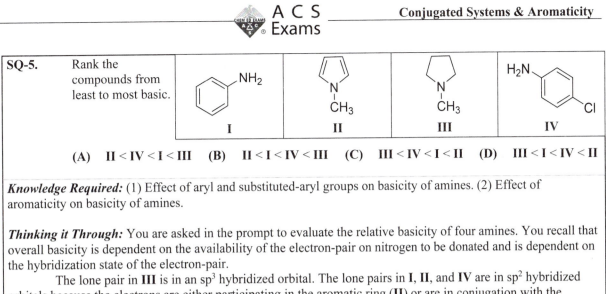

(A) II < IV < I < III   **(B)** II < I < IV < III   **(C)** III < IV < I < II   **(D)** III < I < IV < II

Knowledge Required: (1) Effect of aryl and substituted-aryl groups on basicity of amines. (2) Effect of aromaticity on basicity of amines.

Thinking it Through: You are asked in the prompt to evaluate the relative basicity of four amines. You recall that overall basicity is dependent on the availability of the electron-pair on nitrogen to be donated and is dependent on the hybridization state of the electron-pair.

The lone pair in **III** is in an sp^3 hybridized orbital. The lone pairs in **I**, **II**, and **IV** are in sp^2 hybridized orbitals because the electrons are either participating in the aromatic ring (**II**) or are in conjugation with the aromatic ring (**I** and **IV**). Given these observations, you conclude that **III** is the most "available" lone pair and thus **III** is the most basic compound. Additionally, you conclude that **II** is the least "available" lone pair because of its involvement in the aromatic ring and thus **II** is the least basic compound.

While the lone pairs of **I** and **IV** are in conjugation with the ring, the electrons are somewhat "available". You consider the structures of both molecules to make a determination of relative basicity. You note that halide substituents are electron-withdrawing groups and thus the chlorine in **IV** would pull electron density out of the ring and allow for the nitrogen lone pair to be further donated into the ring. Compound **I** does not have substituents on the aryl ring. You conclude that the nitrogen lone pair in **IV** is less "available" than **I**.

Choice **(A)** is correct.

Choice **(B)** is not correct because the two amines with aryl substituents are in reverse order. Choices **(C)** and **(D)** are not correct because **II** is the least basic of the amines.

Practice Problems: PQ-14 and **PQ-15**

SQ-6.	What is the major product of this reaction?	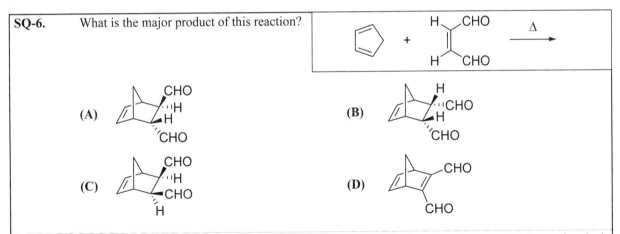

Knowledge Required: (1) The Diels-Alder Reaction. (2) *Endo-Exo* positions on bicyclic rings. (3) Stereochemical outcomes of a Diels-Alder Reaction.

Thinking it Through: You are asked in the question to determine which of four compounds is formed in the given reaction. You note that the reaction is between a diene and a dienophile at high temperature and thus are clued that this is a Diels-Alder reaction, (i.e. a [4+ 2] cycloaddition). You recall that this means that all six π electrons move in one concerted mechanism. The movement of these π electrons will result in the formation of two new σ bonds and one new π bond, as well as a new ring. Because the diene starting material is a ring, you realize that your product will be a bicyclic molecule. You also note that the diene in a ring has the s-*cis* conformation, which is required in order for the reaction to proceed. It is also important that the substituents be matched, and you note the diene is electron-rich with an electron-donating alkyl group (–CH₂–), while the dienophile has two electron-withdrawing aldehyde groups (–CHO).

Other details you recall about Diels-Alder reaction is that stereochemistry of the dienophile must be retained when the ring is formed. Because you note that the dienophile is *cis* or a (*Z*)-alkene, the –COH substituents must remain on the same side of the newly formed ring. Also, because you are forming a bicyclic ring, you determine that the substituents will be in the *endo* position, meaning pointing towards the forming π bond in the product.

Choice (**B**) is correct. The bicyclic ring contains one π bond. The substituents are *cis* and *endo*.

Choice (**A**) is not correct because the substituents are *trans*. Choice (**C**) is not correct because the substituents are *exo*. Choice (**D**) is not correct because there is an extra π-bond in the ring. This would be the product if the dienophile contained and alkyne instead of an alkene.

Practice Problems: **PQ-16, PQ-17, PQ-18, PQ-19, PQ-20,** and **PQ-21**

SQ-7. Which molecule absorbs light at the longest wavelength?

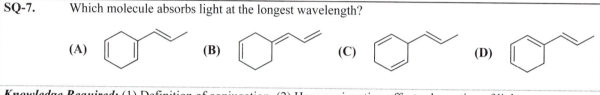

(A)   **(B)**   **(C)**   **(D)**

Knowledge Required: (1) Definition of conjugation. (2) How conjugation effects absorption of light.

Thinking it Through: To solve this problem, you recall that the wavelength of light a molecule absorbs is related to the degree of conjugation found within the molecule. You remember that the more conjugated a molecule is, the lower the energy gap between the HOMO and LUMO of the molecule. The smaller energy required to absorb a photon of light means the longer the wavelength of that absorbed light, because $E = hc / \lambda$.

Choice (**D**) is correct because it has three conjugated π bonds.

Choices (**A**) and (**B**) are not correct because they only have two conjugated π bonds. Choice (**C**) is not correct because it lacks conjugated π bonds.

Practice Problems: **PQ-22** and **PQ-23**

SQ-8. How many electrons are in bonding π-molecular orbitals (π-MOs) for the molecule in the ground state?

(A) 2   **(B)** 4   **(C)** 6   **(D)** 10

Knowledge Required: (1) Conjugated system MO diagrams. (2) Labeling π-MOs as bonding, antibonding, and non-bonding. (3) Counting electrons in π-system and properly populating a MO diagram.

Thinking it Through: You notice that the system in question is conjugated, with five atoms contributing to the delocalized π-system. You recall that this means there will be five π-molecular orbitals (MOs). You also determine that there are six electrons in the delocalized π-system. You recall, however, that in an MO diagram, half the molecular orbitals are bonding MOs and half are antibonding MOs. If there is an odd number of MOs, the middle MO is non-bonding. You note that the question asked how many electrons are in bonding π-MOs. There are two bonding π-MOs for this molecule.

Choice (**B**) is correct because the two bonding MOs are filled with two electrons each.

Choice (**A**) is not correct because it is the number of bonding MOs and not the number of electrons in the bonding MOs. Choice (**C**) is not correct because it is the total number of electrons in the π-system, and the HOMO is a non-bonding orbital. Choice (**D**) is not correct because it is the maximum number of electrons that could be in the π-system if all bonding, non-bonding, and antibonding MOs were filled.

Practice Problems: **PQ-24, PQ-25, PQ-26,** and **PQ-27**

SQ-9. Which is the correct π-system molecular orbital diagram for this molecule?

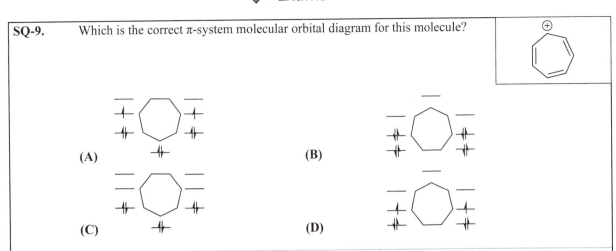

(A) (B) (C) (D)

Knowledge Required: (1) MO diagrams of aromatic rings: Frost circles (i.e., inscribed polygon method). (2) Counting number of π electrons and populating the MO diagram correctly.

Thinking it Through: In this problem, you recognize that you need to draw the MO levels of a ring, decide how many electrons are in the delocalized π-system, and populate the MO levels appropriately. You recall that in the Frost circle approach (also called the inscribed polygon method), you need to place the molecular shape so that a vertex is pointed downward. This is important because the π_1-MO, which will be drawn at the bottom vertex, is never degenerate. You draw MOs at the other vertices. To solve this problem, you note that the system contains six π electrons: two from each of the double bonds and the carbocation denotes the absence of, or zero, electrons.

Choice **(C)** is correct because the inscribed heptagon is pointed downward and there are 6 π electrons.

Choice **(A)** is not correct because there are too many π electrons. Choices **(B)** and **(D)** are not correct because the inscribed heptagon is not pointed downward.

Practice Problems: **PQ-28**, **PQ-29**, and **PQ-30**

Practice Questions (PQ)

PQ-1. Which carbon atom(s) share(s) the positive charge in the carbocation formed by protonation of 1,3-butadiene?

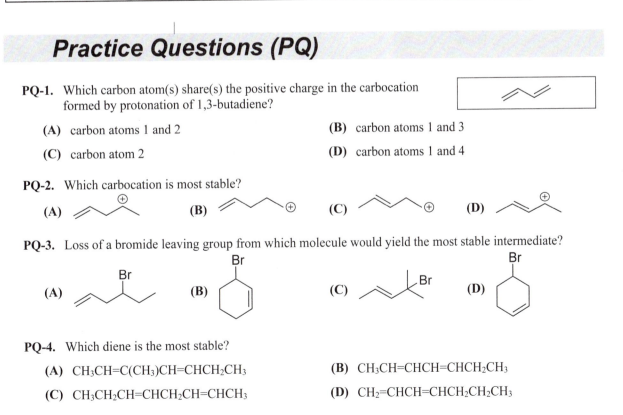

(A) carbon atoms 1 and 2   (B) carbon atoms 1 and 3

(C) carbon atom 2   (D) carbon atoms 1 and 4

PQ-2. Which carbocation is most stable?

(A)   (B)   (C)   (D)

PQ-3. Loss of a bromide leaving group from which molecule would yield the most stable intermediate?

(A)   (B)   (C)   (D)

PQ-4. Which diene is the most stable?

(A) $CH_3CH=C(CH_3)CH=CHCH_2CH_3$ (B) $CH_3CH=CHCH=CHCH_2CH_3$

(C) $CH_3CH_2CH=CHCH_2CH=CHCH_3$ (D) $CH_2=CHCH=CHCH_2CH_2CH_3$

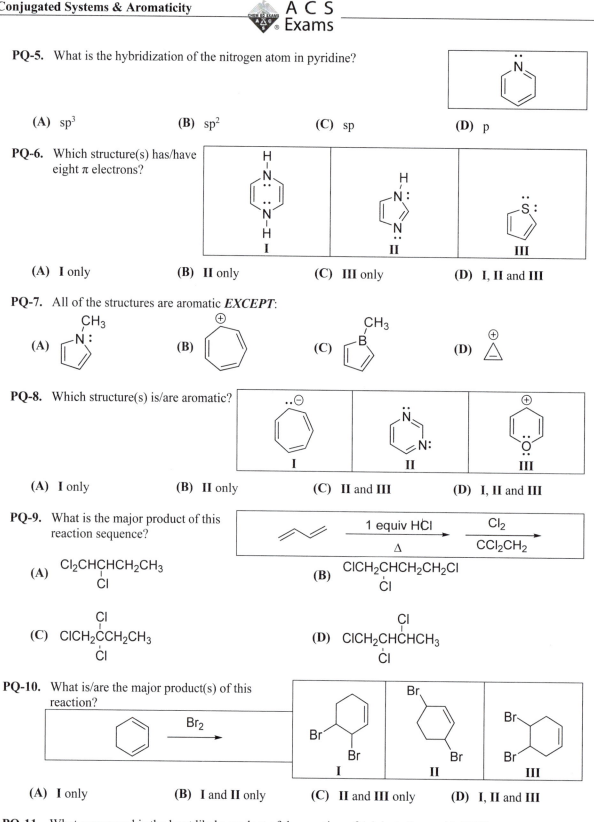

PQ-5. What is the hybridization of the nitrogen atom in pyridine?

(A) sp^3 (B) sp^2 (C) sp (D) p

PQ-6. Which structure(s) has/have eight π electrons?

I   II   III

(A) **I** only   (B) **II** only   (C) **III** only   (D) **I, II and III**

PQ-7. All of the structures are aromatic *EXCEPT*:

(A)   (B)   (C)   (D)

PQ-8. Which structure(s) is/are aromatic?

I   II   III

(A) **I** only   (B) **II** only   (C) **II and III**   (D) **I, II and III**

PQ-9. What is the major product of this reaction sequence?

$$\xrightarrow[\Delta]{1\ equiv\ HCl} \xrightarrow[CCl_2CH_2]{Cl_2}$$

(A) $Cl_2CHCHCH_2CH_3$ with Cl

(B) $ClCH_2CHCH_2CH_2Cl$ with Cl

(C) $ClCH_2CCH_2CH_3$ with Cl and Cl

(D) $ClCH_2CHCHCH_3$ with Cl and Cl

PQ-10. What is/are the major product(s) of this reaction?

$$\xrightarrow{Br_2}$$

I   II   III

(A) **I** only   (B) **I and II** only   (C) **II and III** only   (D) **I, II and III**

PQ-11. What compound is the least likely product of the reaction of 1,3-butadiene with HCl?

(A) (*S*)-3-chloro-1-butene   (B) (*R*)-3-chloro-1-butene

(C) (*E*)-1-chloro-2-butene   (D) (*Z*)-2-chloro-2-butene

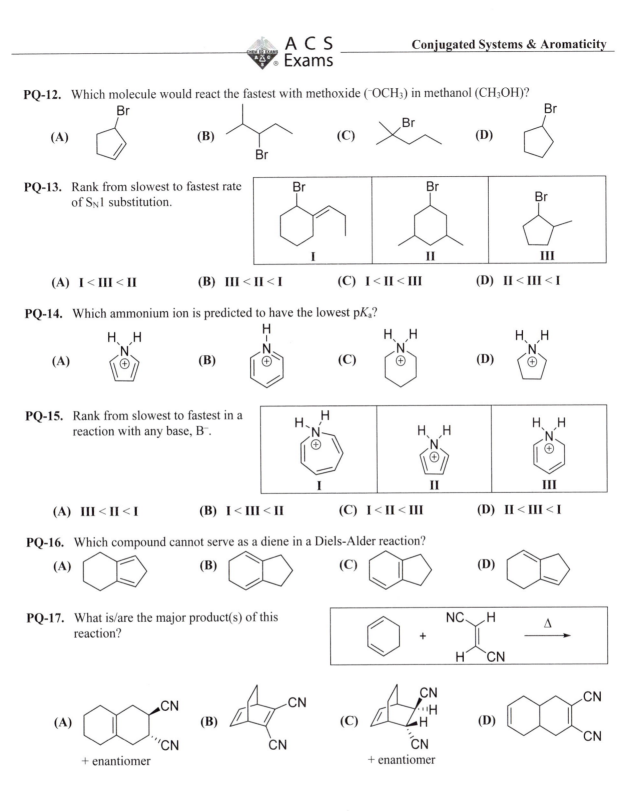

PQ-12. Which molecule would react the fastest with methoxide ($^-OCH_3$) in methanol (CH_3OH)?

(A)

(B)

(C)

(D)

PQ-13. Rank from slowest to fastest rate of S_N1 substitution.

I   II   III

(A) I < III < II   (B) III < II < I   (C) I < II < III   (D) II < III < I

PQ-14. Which ammonium ion is predicted to have the lowest pK_a?

(A)

(B)

(C)

(D)

PQ-15. Rank from slowest to fastest in a reaction with any base, B^-.

I   II   III

(A) III < II < I   (B) I < III < II   (C) I < II < III   (D) II < III < I

PQ-16. Which compound cannot serve as a diene in a Diels-Alder reaction?

(A)

(B)

(C)

(D)

PQ-17. What is/are the major product(s) of this reaction?

(A) + enantiomer

(B)

(C) + enantiomer

(D)

PQ-18. Which reagents would yield this product when reacted with heat?

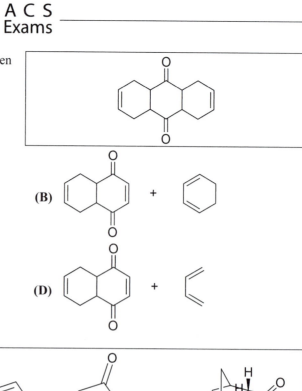

(A)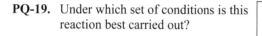

(B)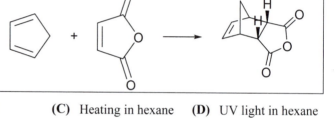

(C)

(D)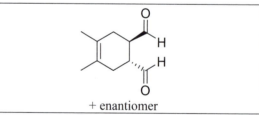

PQ-19. Under which set of conditions is this reaction best carried out?

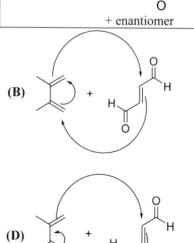

(A) 6 M H₂SO₄   **(B)** 6 M NaOH   **(C)** Heating in hexane   **(D)** UV light in hexane

PQ-20. Which mechanism produces this product?

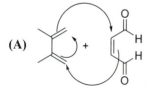

+ enantiomer

(A)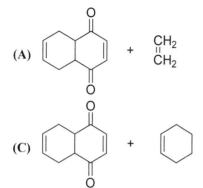

(B)

(C)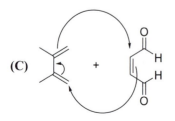

(D)

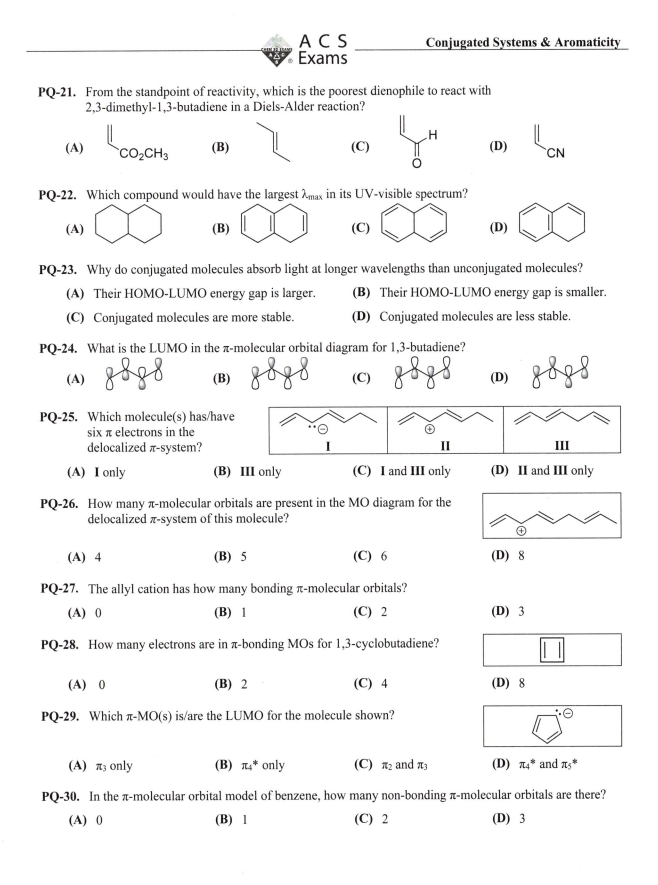

PQ-21. From the standpoint of reactivity, which is the poorest dienophile to react with 2,3-dimethyl-1,3-butadiene in a Diels-Alder reaction?

(A) CO_2CH_3 (B)   (C) H, O   (D) CN

PQ-22. Which compound would have the largest λ_{max} in its UV-visible spectrum?

(A)   (B)   (C)   (D)

PQ-23. Why do conjugated molecules absorb light at longer wavelengths than unconjugated molecules?

(A) Their HOMO-LUMO energy gap is larger.   (B) Their HOMO-LUMO energy gap is smaller.

(C) Conjugated molecules are more stable.   (D) Conjugated molecules are less stable.

PQ-24. What is the LUMO in the π-molecular orbital diagram for 1,3-butadiene?

(A)   (B)   (C)   (D)

PQ-25. Which molecule(s) has/have six π electrons in the delocalized π-system?

I   II   III

(A) **I** only   (B) **III** only   (C) **I** and **III** only   (D) **II** and **III** only

PQ-26. How many π-molecular orbitals are present in the MO diagram for the delocalized π-system of this molecule?

(A) 4   (B) 5   (C) 6   (D) 8

PQ-27. The allyl cation has how many bonding π-molecular orbitals?

(A) 0   (B) 1   (C) 2   (D) 3

PQ-28. How many electrons are in π-bonding MOs for 1,3-cyclobutadiene?

(A) 0   (B) 2   (C) 4   (D) 8

PQ-29. Which π-MO(s) is/are the LUMO for the molecule shown?

(A) π_3 only   (B) π_4^* only   (C) π_2 and π_3 (D) π_4^* and π_5^*

PQ-30. In the π-molecular orbital model of benzene, how many non-bonding π-molecular orbitals are there?

(A) 0   (B) 1   (C) 2   (D) 3

Answers to Study Questions

SQ-1.	B	SQ-4.	C	SQ-7.	D
SQ-2.	B	SQ-5.	A	SQ-8.	B
SQ-3.	D	SQ-6.	B	SQ-9.	C

Answers to Practice Questions

PQ-1.	B	PQ-11.	D	PQ-21.	B
PQ-2.	D	PQ-12.	A	PQ-22.	D
PQ-3.	C	PQ-13.	D	PQ-23.	B
PQ-4.	A	PQ-14.	A	PQ-24.	A
PQ-5.	B	PQ-15.	B	PQ-25.	A
PQ-6.	A	PQ-16.	D	PQ-26.	B
PQ-7.	C	PQ-17.	C	PQ-27.	B
PQ-8.	C	PQ-18.	D	PQ-28.	B
PQ-9.	D	PQ-19.	C	PQ-29.	D
PQ-10.	B	PQ-20.	D	PQ-30.	A

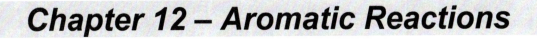
Chapter 12 – Aromatic Reactions

Chapter Summary:
    This chapter will focus on reactions that involve aromatic rings including benzene, benzene derivatives, and heterocycles.

    Specific topics covered in this chapter are:
- Electrophilic aromatic substitution
- Nucleophilic aromatic substitution
- Directing groups and activation/deactivation
- Order of substituent addition
- Benzyne intermediates
- Diazonium salts

    Previous material that is relevant to your understanding of questions in this chapter include:
- Elimination (E) Reactions (**Chapter 6**)
- Addition Reactions: Alkenes and Alkynes (**Chapter 7**)
- Conjugated Systems and Aromaticity (***Chapter 11***)

Where to find this in your textbook:
    The material in this chapter typically aligns to "Aromatic Substitution Reactions" in your textbook. The name of your chapter may vary.

Practice exam:
    There may be practice exam questions aligned to the material in this chapter. Because there are a limited number of questions on the practice exam, a review of the breadth of the material in this chapter is advised in preparation for your exam.

How this fits to the big picture:
    The material in this chapter aligns to the Big Idea of "Chemical Reactions" (V) as listed on page 13 of this study guide.

Study Questions (SQ)

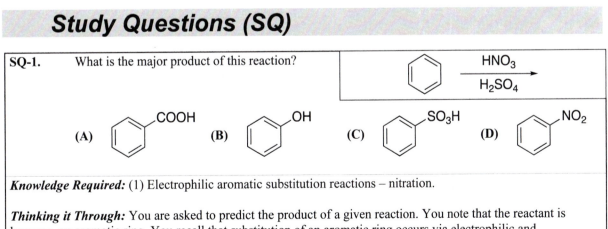

SQ-1. What is the major product of this reaction?

Knowledge Required: (1) Electrophilic aromatic substitution reactions – nitration.

Thinking it Through: You are asked to predict the product of a given reaction. You note that the reactant is benzene, an aromatic ring. You recall that substitution of an aromatic ring occurs via electrophilic and nucleophilic mechanisms. You recall that HNO_3 and H_2SO_4 are reagents that lead to the nitration of aromatic rings (i.e., substitution of $-NO_2$ for an $-H$).
    Choice **(D)** is correct, nitrobenzene.

Choice **(A)** is not correct because different reagents are necessary to produce benzoic acid. Choice **(B)** is not correct because different reagents are necessary to produce phenol. Choice **(C)** is not correct because different reagents are necessary to product benzenesulfonic acid.

Practice Problems: **PQ-1, PQ-2, PQ-3, PQ-4, PQ-5, PQ-6** and **PQ-7**

SQ-2.   What is the major product?

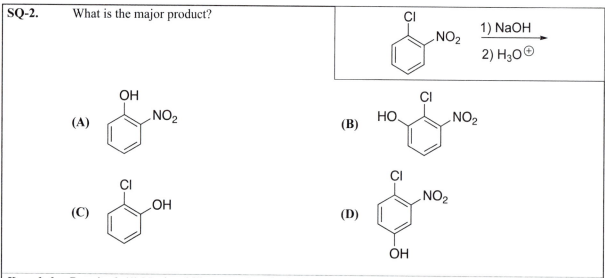

Knowledge Required: (1) Nucleophilic aromatic substitution reactions.

Thinking it Through: You are asked to predict the product of a given reaction. You note that the reactant contains an aromatic ring. You recall that substitution of an aromatic ring can occur via electrophilic and/or nucleophilic mechanisms. You recall that NaOH is a reagent that can lead to the nucleophilic aromatic substitution of a leaving group such as –Cl with an –OH group when an electron-withdrawing group is *ortho* or *para* to the leaving group.
    Choice **(A)** is correct, 2-nitrophenol.
    Choice **(B)** is not correct because hydride ion is not a good leaving group. Choice **(C)** is not correct because the nitro group is not a good leaving group. Choice **(D)** is not correct because hydride ion is not a good leaving group.

Practice Problems: **PQ-8, PQ-9,** and **PQ-10**

SQ-3.   Which substituent would be classified as a deactivating, *meta*- director in an electrophilic aromatic substitution reaction?

   (A)   –COOH   **(B)**   –OCH₃   **(C)**   –Cl   **(D)**   –NH₂

Knowledge Required: (1) Structure-function relationship between substituents and activation/deactivation of electrophilic aromatic substitution reactions. (2) Structure-function relationship between substituents and *ortho/meta/para* direction of electrophilic aromatic substitution reactions.

Thinking it Through: You are asked to determine which of a series of substituents is a deactivator and *meta*-director. You choose to evaluate each characteristic separately.
    You recall that substituents that activate the aromatic ring in electrophilic aromatic substitution reactions donate electron density to the ring either through resonance or induction. Example activators are –OH or –CH₃ which donate electron density via resonance with the oxygen lone pair or induction, respectively. You recall that substituents that deactivate the aromatic ring in electrophilic aromatic substation reactions withdraw electron density from the ring either through resonance or induction. Example deactivators are –NO₂ or –NH₃⁺ which withdraw electron density via resonance with the cationic nitrogen atom of the nitro group or induction from the positively charged substituent, respectively. You evaluate the answer options and determine that choices **(A)** and **(C)** are deactivators; choices **(B)** and **(D)** are activators.

Next, you recall that with the exception of halide substituents, electron-donating substituents are *ortho/para* directors and electron withdrawing substituents are *meta* directors. Halogens are electron-withdrawing substituents but *ortho/para* directors. You evaluate the answer options and determinate that choice (**A**) is a *meta* director, and choices (**B**), (**C**), and (**D**) are *ortho/para* directors.

Therefore, choice (**A**) is correct.

Choices (**B**) and (**D**) are not correct because they are activating, *ortho/para* directors. Choice (**C**) is not correct because it is an *ortho/para* director.

Practice Problems: **PQ-11, PQ-12, PQ-13, PQ-14, PQ-15, PQ-16** and **PQ-17**

SQ-4.	Which reagents best lead to this transformation?	

(**A**)	1. SO₃, H₂SO₄ 2. CH₃CH₂Cl, AlCl₃	(**B**)	1. CH₃CH₂Cl, AlCl₃ 2. SO₃, H₂SO₄

(**A**) 1. SO$_3$, H$_2$SO$_4$
        2. CH$_3$CH$_2$Cl, AlCl$_3$

(**B**) 1. CH$_3$CH$_2$Cl, AlCl$_3$
        2. SO$_3$, H$_2$SO$_4$

(**C**) 1. CH$_3$COCl, AlCl$_3$
        2. Zn(Hg), conc. HCl
        3. SO$_3$, H$_2$SO$_4$

(**D**) 1. CH$_3$COCl, AlCl$_3$
        2. SO$_3$, H$_2$SO$_4$
        3. Zn(Hg), conc. HCl

Knowledge Required: (1) Friedel-Crafts alkylation reactions. (2) Friedel-Crafts acylation reactions. (3) Sulfonation reactions. (4) Structure-function relationship between substituents and activation/deactivation of electrophilic aromatic substitution reactions. (5) Structure-function relationship between substituents and *ortho/meta/para* direction of electrophilic aromatic substitution reactions.

Thinking it Through: You are asked to evaluate a series of reaction conditions to determine which leads to the desired product. You note that the reagents in all the answer options include sulfonation of an aromatic ring, Friedel-Crafts alkylation or acylation, and reduction of a ketone to an alkane. You note that the substituents in the desired product have a *meta* relationship and, thus, you note that the addition order of the two substituents will be important.

Choice (**A**): The first set of reagents results in sulfonated benzene. The second set of reagents typically leads to an alkylation of the aromatic ring; however, you recall that Friedel-Crafts alkylation does not readily occur on strongly deactivated aromatic rings such as the sulfonated benzene produced from the first reaction. Therefore, the alkyl group will not add in the second step to a significant degree.

Choice (**B**): The first set of reagents lead to alkylation and produce ethylbenzene. The second set of reagents sulfonates the aromatic ring; you note that an alkyl group is an *ortho/para* director and thus conclude that the resulting product would be *para*-substituted.

Choice (**C**): The first set of reagents lead to acylation and produces acetophenone. The second set of reagents reduces the ketone and produces ethyl benzene. The third set of reagents sulfonates the aromatic ring; you note that an alkyl group is an *ortho/para* director and thus conclude that the resulting product would be *para*-substituted.

Choice (**D**): The first set of reagents lead to acylation and produces acetophenone. The second set of reagents sulfonates the aromatic ring; you note that an acyl group is a *meta* director and thus conclude that the resulting product is *meta*-substituted. The third set of reagents reduces the ketone and produces the desired product.

Therefore, choice (**D**) is correct.

Choice (**A**) is not correct because it will not undergo a Friedel-Crafts reaction. Choice (**B**) and (**C**) are not correct because they will produce *para*-substituted products.

Practice Problems: **PQ-18, PQ-19, PQ-20, PQ-21, PQ-22, PQ-23** and **PQ-24**

SQ-5. Which intermediate is formed in the mechanism of this reaction?

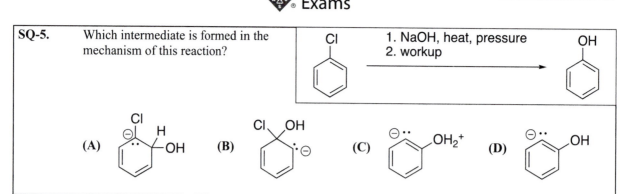

(A) 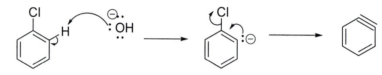 (B) (C) (D)

Knowledge Required: (1) Nucleophilic aromatic substitution – benzyne intermediates.

Thinking it Through: You are asked to determine which of a series of intermediates is formed in the mechanism for this reaction. You note from the starting material and product that this is a substitution reaction; you further note from the reaction conditions that this is a nucleophilic aromatic substitution reaction that proceeds through a benzyne intermediate.

You decide to sketch each of the mechanistic steps before selecting your answer. The first step of a nucleophilic aromatic substitution reaction that proceeds through a benzyne intermediate is the formation of the benzyne intermediate from an elimination:

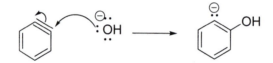

Next, the nucleophile attaches to the ring creating a carbanion intermediate:

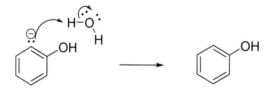

Next, the carbanion and a proton from a water molecule created from the elimination in the first step lead to the formation of the desired product:

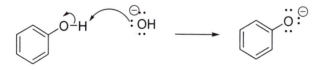

However, you note that the reaction conditions are basic and the resulting phenol has an acidic proton. Therefore, you conclude phenoxide is an additional intermediate for the reaction conditions.

Finally, the "workup" step adds the proton back on to form the desired product, (i.e. phenol).

Based on this evaluation, there are several intermediates formed in this reaction from which to evaluate the given answer options.

Choices **(A)** and **(B)** are not correct because hydroxide does not add to the aromatic ring until chloride is eliminated.

Choice **(C)** is not correct because the reaction conditions are basic and thus the phenol group will not be protonated in the presence of sodium hydroxide. It also does not make sense that the adjacent carbon atom would be deprotonated (making it anionic) while the oxygen is protonated (making it cationic).

Choice **(D)** is correct because a carbanion is formed after the hydroxide anion (i.e., the nucleophile) adds to the benzyne intermediate.

Practice Problems: **PQ-25, PQ-26,** and **PQ-27**

SQ-6. Which set of reagents lead to the formation of *o*-xylene ($CH_3C_6H_4CH_3$) in the highest yield from aniline ($NH_2C_6H_5$)?

(A) 1. CH_3Cl, $AlCl_3$
2. HONO, 3 °C
3. CuBr
4. Mg
5. CH_3Br

(B) 1. HONO, 3 °C
2. CuBr
3. CH_3Cl, $AlCl_3$
4. Mg
5. CH_3Br

(C) 1. HONO, 3 °C
2. CH_3Cl, $AlCl_3$
3. CuBr
4. Mg
5. CH_3Br

(D) 1. HONO, 3 °C
2. CuBr
3. Mg
4. CH_3Br
5. CH_3Cl, $AlCl_3$

Knowledge Required: (1) Formation and use of diazonium salts. (2) Friedel-Crafts alkylation. (3) Grignard reactions. (4) Amines as nucleophiles in substitution reactions.

Thinking it Through: You are asked to evaluate a series of reaction conditions to determine which lead to the formation of aniline from *o*-xylene ($CH_3C_6H_4CH_3$). You consider each answer option:

Choice **(A)**: You note that the first step is a Friedel-Crafts alkylation reaction and that the amine group of aniline is an *ortho/para* director and activator. However, you also note that the amine functional group interacts with the reaction conditions to methylate the amine in competition with alkylation of the ring. Thus, you conclude that the first reagents of choice **(A)** will lead to a mixture of products and thus not the desired product in the highest yield as requested.

Choice **(B)**: You note that the first set of reaction conditions is the formation of a diazonium salt from aniline. This is followed by copper(I) bromide leading to the formation of bromobenzene. The next set of reaction conditions is the alkylation of bromobenzene. You note that bromine is an *ortho/para* director; however, it is also a deactivator and thus may not produce the highest yield. You continue to predict the products of the next two steps but note the deficiency in this answer option. The resulting 4-bromo-toluene is converted to a Grignard reagent with the addition of magnesium. Finally, the Grignard reagent is used as a nucleophile in an S_N2 reaction to form the desired *o*-xylene product.

Choice **(C)**: You note that the first set of reaction conditions is the formation of a diazonium salt from aniline. The next set of reaction conditions is intended to alkylate the aromatic ring; however, the diazonium salt interacts with the alkylation reagents in competition with the alkylation and thus leads to a mixture of products. Thus, you conclude that the second reagents of choice **(C)** will not lead to the desired product in the highest yield, as requested.

Choice **(D)**: You note that the first set of reaction conditions is the formation of a diazonium salt from aniline. This is followed by copper(I)bromide leading to the formation of bromobenzene. The resulting bromobenzene is converted to a Grignard reagent with the addition of magnesium; the Grignard reagent is used as a nucleophile in an S_N2 reaction to form toluene. The final set of reaction conditions is an alkylation; you note that the methyl substituent is an *ortho/para* director and activator. You conclude that this answer option leads to the formation of the desired product, (i.e. *o*-xylene).

Therefore, choice **(D)** is correct.

Choices **(A)** and **(C)** are not correct because they involve a reaction step that forms a mixture of products. Choice **(B)** is not correct because it involves the alkylation of a weakly deactivated ring.

Practice Problems: **PQ-28, PQ-29,** and **PQ-30**

Practice Questions (PQ)

PQ-1. What type of reaction is this?

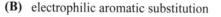

(A) nucleophilic aromatic substitution

(B) electrophilic aromatic substitution

(C) nucleophilic aromatic addition

(D) electrophilic aromatic addition

PQ-2. What is the major product?

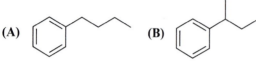

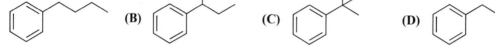

(A)   **(B)**   **(C)**   **(D)**

PQ-3. Which sequence of reagents would produce *n*-propylbenzene as the major product from benzene?

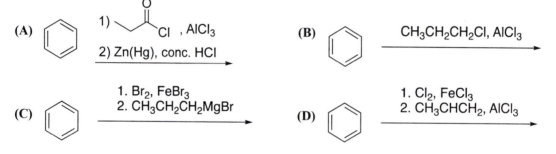

(A) 1) (image), AlCl$_3$ 2) Zn(Hg), conc. HCl

(B) CH$_3$CH$_2$CH$_2$Cl, AlCl$_3$

(C) 1. Br$_2$, FeBr$_3$ 2. CH$_3$CH$_2$CH$_2$MgBr

(D) 1. Cl$_2$, FeCl$_3$ 2. CH$_3$CHCH$_2$, AlCl$_3$

PQ-4. Which reaction will NOT produce *tert*-butylbenzene in high yield?

(A) (CH$_3$)$_3$CCl, AlCl$_3$

(B) CH$_3$CH$_2$CH(Cl)CH$_3$, AlCl$_3$

(C) (CH$_3$)$_2$CHCH$_2$OH, H$_2$SO$_4$

(D) (CH$_3$)$_2$CCH$_2$, H$_3$PO$_4$

PQ-5. What is the electrophile that adds to the benzene ring during sulfonation in electrophilic aromatic substitution?

(A) SO$_3$H$^+$ **(B)** SH$_2$ **(C)** SO$_3$ **(D)** $^+$SH$_2$

PQ-6. What causes this product to form as the major organic product rather than butylbenzene in this reaction?

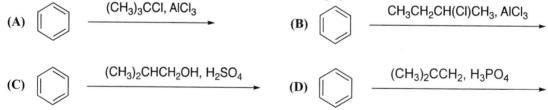

1) CH$_3$CH$_2$CH$_2$CH$_2$Cl/AlCl$_3$

2) H$_2$O

(A) 1,2-methyl shift produces a more stable electrophile

(B) 1,2-hydride shift produces a more stable electrophile

(C) 1,2-methyl shift produces a more stable nucleophile

(D) 1,2 hydride shift produces a more stable nucleophile

PQ-7. What is a mechanistic step for this reaction?

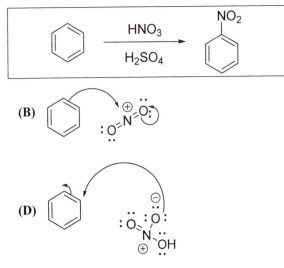

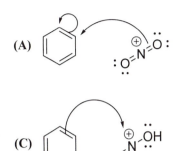

(A)

(B)

(C)

(D)

PQ-8. Which description is most applicable to the mechanism of this reaction?

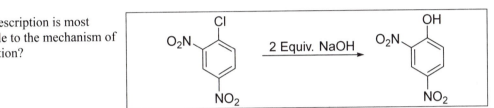

(A) It takes place in one step with no ionic intermediates.

(B) It takes place in two steps: elimination then addition.

(C) It takes place in two steps: addition then elimination.

(D) It takes place in three steps and involves a carbocation intermediate.

PQ-9. Which aryl chloride reacts the fastest with NaOH?

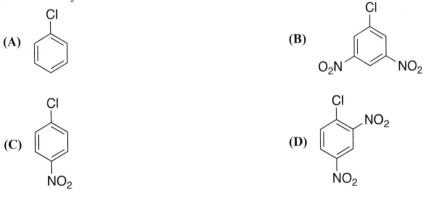

(A)

(B)

(C)

(D)

PQ-10. What is the major product?

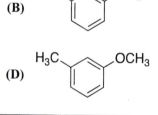

CH₃ONa (1 eq.)

(A)

(B)

(C)

(D)

PQ-11. Which benzene derivative would be the most reactive in an electrophilic aromatic substitution reaction?

(A)

(B)

(C)

(D)

PQ-12. Which substrate is the most reactive with respect to nitration by electrophilic aromatic substitution?

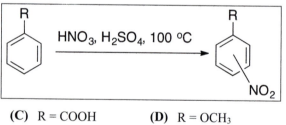

HNO₃, H₂SO₄, 100 °C

(A) R = NO₂   (B) R = Cl   (C) R = COOH   (D) R = OCH₃

PQ-13. Which substituent would be classified as an activating *ortho/para* director in an electrophilic aromatic substitution reaction?

(A) –COOH   (B) –OCOCH₃   (C) –Cl   (D) –NH₃⁺

PQ-14. Rank the compounds from slowest to fastest reactivity towards electrophilic aromatic substitution.

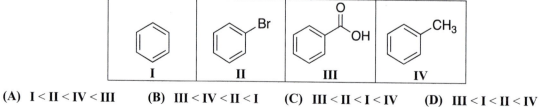

I   **II**   **III**   **IV**

(A) I < II < IV < III   (B) III < IV < II < I   (C) III < II < I < IV   (D) III < I < II < IV

PQ-15. What is a major product of this reaction?

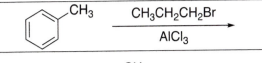

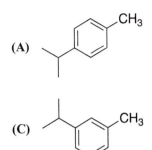

(A)

(B)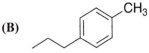

(C)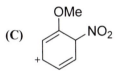

(D)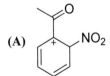

PQ-16. What is the most stable resonance contributor for the arenium ion in this reaction?

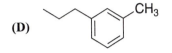

(A)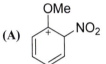

(B)

(C)

(D)

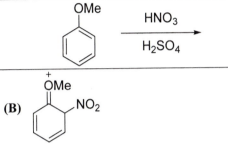

PQ-17. What is the most stable resonance contributor for the arenium ion that leads to the major product in this reaction?

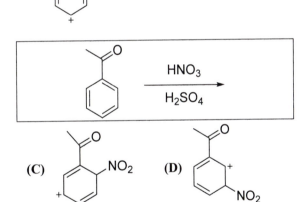

(A)

(B)

(C)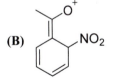

(D)

PQ-18. What is a major product of this reaction?

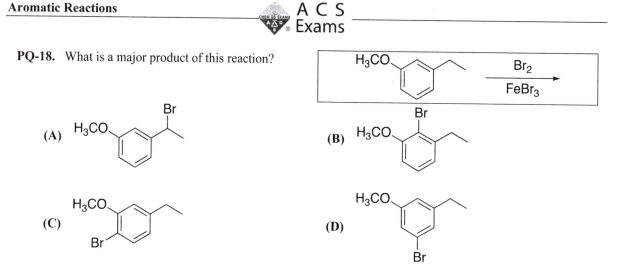

(A)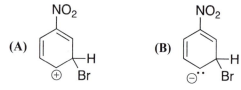

(B) H₃CO structure with Br and ethyl

(C) H₃CO structure with Br

(D) H₃CO structure with ethyl and Br

PQ-19. Which structure represents a major intermediate in the bromination of nitrobenzene?

(A) (B) (C) (D)

PQ-20. What is the major product of this reaction?

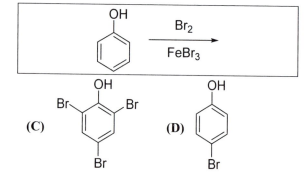

(A) (B) (C) (D)

PQ-21. Which reagents lead to this transformation?

(A) 1. Br₂, FeBr₃
2. Mg
3. CH₃CHO
3. HNO₃, H₂SO₄

(B) 1. CH₃Cl, AlCl₃
2. HNO₃, H₂SO₄
3. KMnO₄, H₂O, heat

(C) 1. HNO₃, H₂SO₄
2. Br₂, FeBr₃
3. Mg
4. CO₂
5. H⁺

(D) 1. KMnO₄, H₂O, heat
2. HNO₃, H₂SO₄

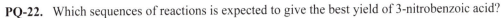

PQ-22. Which sequences of reactions is expected to give the best yield of 3-nitrobenzoic acid?

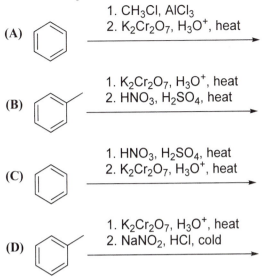

(A)
1. CH_3Cl, $AlCl_3$
2. $K_2Cr_2O_7$, H_3O^+, heat

(B)
1. $K_2Cr_2O_7$, H_3O^+, heat
2. HNO_3, H_2SO_4, heat

(C)
1. HNO_3, H_2SO_4, heat
2. $K_2Cr_2O_7$, H_3O^+, heat

(D)
1. $K_2Cr_2O_7$, H_3O^+, heat
2. $NaNO_2$, HCl, cold

PQ-23. What is the purpose of the first step in this synthesis?

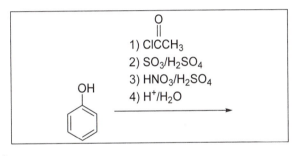

1) $ClCCH_3$
2) SO_3/H_2SO_4
3) HNO_3/H_2SO_4
4) H^+/H_2O

(A) transforming the phenol into a stronger activating group

(B) transforming the phenol into a weaker activating group

(C) transforming the phenol into a *meta* directing group

(D) transforming the phenol into benzoic acid

PQ-24. What is the product of this synthesis?

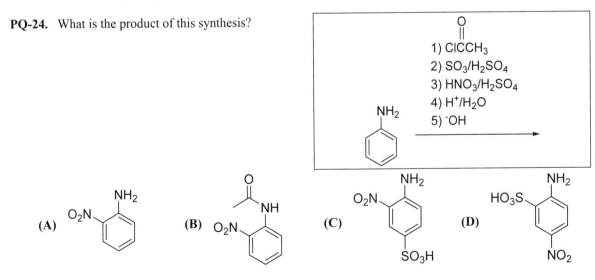

1) $ClCCH_3$
2) SO_3/H_2SO_4
3) HNO_3/H_2SO_4
4) H^+/H_2O
5) ^-OH

(A)

(B)

(C)

(D)

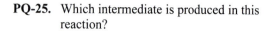

PQ-25. Which intermediate is produced in this reaction?

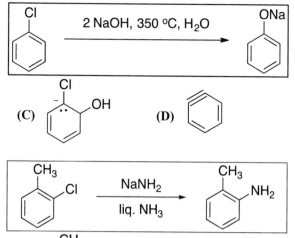

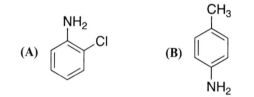

(A)   (B)   (C)   (D)

PQ-26. In addition to the product shown, what other compound is expected to be formed in this reaction?

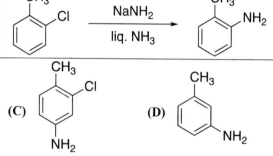

(A)   (B)   (C)   (D)

PQ-27. Which description is most applicable to the mechanism of the reaction between chlorobenzene and sodium amide to produce aniline?

(A) It takes place in one step with no ionic intermediates.

(B) It takes place in two steps: elimination then addition.

(C) It takes place in two steps: addition then elimination.

(D) It takes place in three steps and involves an anionic intermediate.

PQ-28. Which reagents will yield this diazonium salt from aniline?

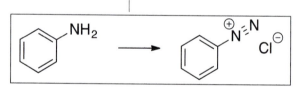

(A) $HClO_2$, N_2 (B) $HClO_2$, N_2H_4 (C) $NaCl$, N_2 (D) $NaNO_2$, HCl

PQ-29. What is the product of this reaction?

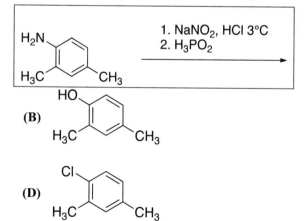

(A) 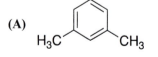   (B)

(C) 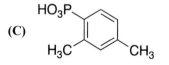   (D)

PQ-30. Which set of reagents synthesizes phenol from benzene?

(A) 1) HONO 3°C 2) CuCl 3) NaOH

(B) 1) HONO 3°C 2) CuCl 3) Cu^{+2}, Cu_2OH H_2O

(C) 1) HNO_3/H_2SO_4 2) HONO 3° C 3) Fe/HCl 4) NaOH 5) H_2O

(D) 1) HNO_3/H_2SO_4 2) Fe/HCl 3) NaOH 4) HONO 3° C 5) H_2O

Answers to Study Questions

SQ-1.	D	SQ-3.	A	SQ-5.	D
SQ-2.	A	SQ-4.	D	SQ-6.	D

Answers to Practice Questions

PQ-1.	B	PQ-11.	D	PQ-21.	C
PQ-2.	B	PQ-12.	D	PQ-22.	B
PQ-3.	A	PQ-13.	B	PQ-23.	B
PQ-4.	B	PQ-14.	C	PQ-24.	A
PQ-5.	C	PQ-15.	A	PQ-25.	D
PQ-6.	B	PQ-16.	B	PQ-26.	D
PQ-7.	B	PQ-17.	D	PQ-27.	D
PQ-8.	C	PQ-18.	C	PQ-28.	D
PQ-9.	D	PQ-19.	A	PQ-29	A
PQ-10.	C	PQ-20.	C	PQ-30	D

Chapter 13 – Carbonyl Chemistry: Aldehydes, Ketones, Carboxylic Acids and Derivatives

Chapter Summary:

This chapter will focus on how the carbonyl carbon is electrophilic and reacts with different functional groups. Specifically, this chapter will look at the nucleophilic addition reactions with ketones and aldehydes, as well as nucleophilic acyl substitution reactions for carboxylic acids and their derivatives.

Specific topics covered in this chapter are:
- Reactivity of aldehydes and ketones
- Nucleophilic addition to the carbonyl carbon
- Hemiacetal and acetal reactions
- Imine, enamine, oxime, hydrazine and semi-carbazone reactions
- Reductions of all carbonyl compounds
- Wittig reaction
- Organometallic reagents: Grignard, organolithium and organocuprate (Gilman reagents)
- Reactivity trends of the carboxylic acid derivatives
- Nucleophilic acyl substitution reactions of carboxylic acid and its derivatives

Previous material that is relevant to your understanding of questions in this chapter include:
- Structures of molecules (*Chapter 1*)
- Functional groups (*Chapter 2*)
- Addition reactions of alcohols and ethers (*Chapter 8*)

Where to find this in your textbook:

The material in this chapter typically aligns to "Carbonyl Chemistry", "Aldehydes and Ketones", "Nucleophilic Addition to the Carbonyl", "Carboxylic Acids and their Derivatives", or "Nucleophilic Acyl Substitution" in your textbook. The name of your chapter may vary.

Practice exam:

There may be practice exam questions aligned to the material in this chapter. Because there are a limited number of questions on the practice exam, a review of the breadth of the material in this chapter is advised in preparation for your exam.

How this fits to the big picture:

The material in this chapter aligns to the Big Idea of Structure and Function (III) and Chemical Reactions (V) as listed on page 13 of this study guide.

Study Questions (SQ)

SQ-1.	Arrange these molecules from slowest to fastest substrate in a nucleophilic addition reaction.	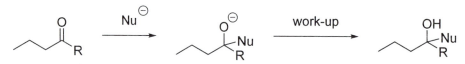

(A) I < III < II < IV   **(B)** I < III < IV < II   **(C)** II < IV < III < I   **(D)** IV < II < I < III

Knowledge Required: (1) Reactivity of aldehydes and ketones. (2) Reaction mechanism for nucleophilic addition to a carbonyl group. (3) Electron-donating and electron-withdrawing substituent effects. (4) Steric factors.

Thinking it Through: You note that the problem asks you to evaluate several compounds and determine the relative rate at which these molecules are susceptible to nucleophilic addition. To solve this problem, you must consider numerous factors that affect how a carbonyl reacts in a nucleophilic addition reaction. First, you recall the general reaction mechanism for an aldehyde or ketone with a nucleophile (Nu):

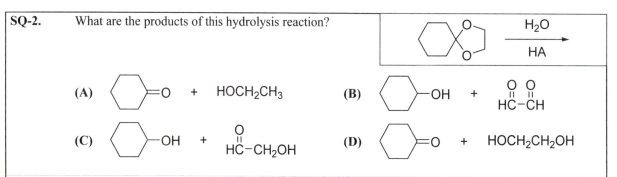

      Reactivity of the carbonyl, you remember, will be affected by both electronic and steric factors. Aldehydes are more reactive than ketones because the alkyl groups of the ketones donate electron density towards the carbon center making them less electropositive; the more δ^+ on the carbon the faster the reaction. Also, you remember that steric hindrance is important; and thus, the small size of the aldehyde hydrogen allows for the nucleophile to approach and attack the carbonyl of an aldehyde easier than a ketone.

      You also note that when comparing two ketones, steric hindrance can have a further effect, in that less hindered ketones like **III** will be more reactive than the hindered ketone **I**.

      Finally, you recall that electron-withdrawing groups increase the $\delta+$ of the carbonyl carbon by induction; thus, an aldehyde like **II** would be more reactive than **IV**.

      Choice **(B)** is correct because all the steric and electronic factors are considered.

      Choice **(A)** is not correct because the order of aldehyde reactivity is reversed. Choice **(C)** is not correct because it is the reverse order. Choice **(D)** is not correct because aldehydes are more reactive than ketones.

Practice Problems: **PQ-1, PQ-2**, and **PQ-3**

SQ-2.	What are the products of this hydrolysis reaction?	

(A) ⬡=O + HOCH$_2$CH$_3$

(B) ⬡–OH + $\underset{HC-CH}{\overset{O\ \ O}{}}$

(C) ⬡–OH + $\underset{HC-CH_2OH}{\overset{O}{}}$

(D) ⬡=O + HOCH$_2$CH$_2$OH

Knowledge Required: (1) Mechanism of nucleophilic addition to a carbonyl group. (2) Mechanism of acid-catalyzed hydrolysis of acetals.

Thinking it Through: You are asked to determine the products of the given reaction in this problem. You note that the reactant is an acetal, and that the reagents hydrolyze that acetal. One approach to solving this problem is to determine what the starting materials would be for an acetal reaction; you know that acetals start with an aldehyde (or ketone) and add an alcohol molecule twice, thus you need one carbonyl and either two alcohol functional groups in one molecule or two alcohols. You also note from the problem that the acetal is cyclic and thus must form from a diol. This particular acetal is familiar, as it is used to protect aldehydes and ketones, by forming the acetal with ethylene glycol:

Thus, the necessary ketone is cyclohexanone.

To confirm your answer, you consider the mechanism in the forward direction, using your presumed starting materials. This reaction is taking place in acidic conditions. You first protonate the carbonyl, the nucleophile then attacks, two proton transfers occur to form a good leaving group (i.e., water), water will leave, forming an electropositive oxygen on the carbonyl, the second alcohol attacks, and the molecule is deprotonated:

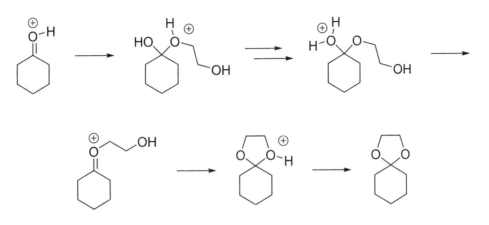

Choice **(D)** is correct because it includes ethylene glycol and cyclohexanone.

Choice **(A)** is not correct because the necessary alcohol is ethylene glycol. Choice **(B)** is not correct because there are too many carbonyls. Choice **(C)** is not correct because it would lead to the formation of a mixture of incorrect products.

Practice Problems: **PQ-4**, **PQ-5**, **PQ-6**, and **PQ-7**

SQ-3. What is the major product of this reaction?

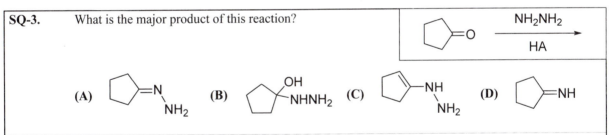

Knowledge Required: (1) Mechanism of imine (enanmine and other derivatives) formation.

Thinking it Through: You are asked to predict the product of a given reaction. You recognize from the starting material and reagents that this is the reaction of a nitrogen-based nucleophile with a ketone. Thus, this reaction follows either an imine-like mechanism or an enamine-like mechanism. You recall that if the nucleophilic nitrogen is primary you will form an imine-like product:

If the nucleophilic nitrogen is secondary you will form an enamine-like product:

Choice (**A**) is correct because the nucleophilic nitrogen is primary and thus the imine product is formed. Choice (**B**) is incorrect because it is an intermediate in the imine formation mechanism. Choice (**C**) is incorrect because it is the enamine-like product, which does not form with a primary nucleophilic nitrogen. Choice (**D**) is incorrect because the N-N bond is not broken in this mechanism.

Practice Problems: **PQ-8** and **PQ-9**

SQ-4. What is the major product of this reaction?

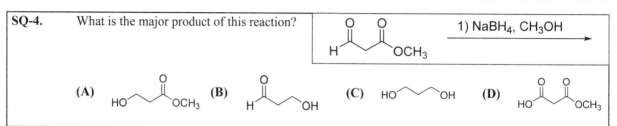

Knowledge Required: (1) Reduction of aldehydes and ketones. (2) Reduction of carboxylic acids and their derivatives. (3) Strength of reducing agents.

  Thinking it Through: You are asked in the problem to consider which of four possible products are formed by the given reaction conditions. You note that the main reagent is NaBH$_4$, a reducing agent. Sodium borohydride will reduce an aldehyde or a ketone to an alcohol via nucleophilic addition to the carbonyl, where hydride (H$^-$) is the effective nucleophile. You further recall that NaBH$_4$ is not strong enough to reduce carboxylic acids or carboxylic acid derivatives. If LiAlH$_4$ had been used as the reducing agent, aldehydes, ketones and all carboxylic acids and derivatives would be transformed into alcohols.
  Choice (**A**) is correct because the aldehyde is reduced, but not the ester.
  Choice (**B**) is not correct because the aldehyde is not reduced and the ester is reduced. Choice (**C**) is not correct because both the aldehyde and the ester are reduced. Choice (**D**) is not correct because the product shown would result from an oxidation.

Practice Problems: **PQ-10**, **PQ-11**, **PQ-12**, **PQ-13**, and **PQ-14**

SQ-5. What alkyl halide would be the starting reactant for this reaction?

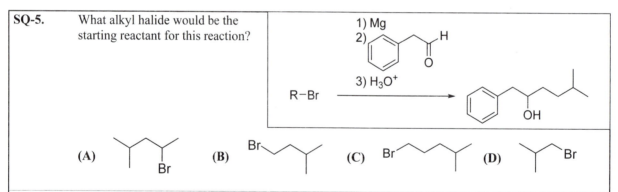

Knowledge Required: (1) Formation of Grignard reagents. (2) Reaction of organometallic reagents with aldehydes and ketones.

Thinking it Through: You are asked to determine which of four alkyl halides would produce the desired product with the given reagents. You note this is an organometallic reaction. You recall that the Grignard reagent will add the nucleophilic carbon to a carbonyl and transform the carbonyl into an alcohol. Using retrosynthetic analysis, you identify the portion of the molecule that comes from the aldehyde and the portion that must come from the Grignard reagent:

From the aldehyde:

From the Grignard:

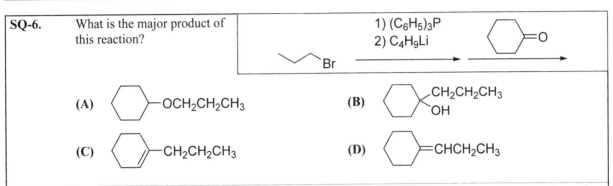

Choice (**B**) is correct because the alkyl halide contains the necessary 3′-methylbutyl R-group.

Choice (**A**) is not correct because the alkyl R-group would contain an extra –CH₃ group. Choice (**C**) is not correct because the alkyl R-group would contain an extra –CH₂– group. Choice (**D**) is not correct because the alkyl R-group is missing a –CH₂– group.

Practice Problems: **PQ-15**, **PQ-16**, **PQ-17**, and **PQ-18**

SQ-6. What is the major product of this reaction?

$$\text{1) } (C_6H_5)_3P$$
$$\text{2) } C_4H_9Li$$

(A) ⬡–OCH₂CH₂CH₃

(B) ⬡ with CH₂CH₂CH₃ and OH

(C) ⬡=CH₂CH₂CH₃

(D) ⬡=CHCH₂CH₃

Knowledge Required: (1) The formation of Wittig reagents. (2) Reaction of Wittig reagents with aldehydes and ketones.

Thinking it Through: You are asked to predict the product for a given starting material and two sets of reagents. You recognize that the reaction step with triphenyl phosphine is the start of a Wittig reaction. You recall that in a Wittig reaction, you react a phosphonium ylide with an aldehyde or ketone to make an alkene. You recall that an ylide is a species that has a positive and negative charge on adjacent atoms. The product after the first two steps forms:

The ylide is a nucleophile that attacks the carbonyl carbon of the ketone. A new carbon-carbon bond is formed in the attack. The intermediate forms a carbon-carbon double bond with the elimination of triphenyl phosphine oxide. Formally, one carbon of the alkene came from the carbon of the initial carbonyl, while the other carbon came from the alkyl halide to which the halogen was originally attached.

Choice (**D**) is correct because it includes an alkene between the two reacting carbon atoms.

Choice (**A**) is not correct because the carbonyl oxygen is not the nucleophile in this reaction. Choice (**B**) is not correct because it is the product one would expect from an organometallic reaction. Choice (**C**) is not correct because the π bond is in the wrong position.

Practice Problem: **PQ-19**

SQ-7. Rank the molecules from least to most reactive with aqueous ammonia.

I	II	III

(A) I < II < III   (B) II < I < III   (C) III < I < II   (D) II < III < I

Knowledge Required: (1) Relative reactivity of carboxylic acid derivatives to nucleophilic acyl substitution (i.e., nucleophilic acyl addition/elimination reactions).

Thinking it Through: You are asked to evaluate the given structures and determine the relative order of reactivity to ammonia (NH_3). You note that all three molecules are carboxylic acid derivatives. You recall that the reactivity of carboxylic acid derivatives depends on the leaving group, with a halide being the best leaving group (thus acid chlorides being the most reactive) and an amine being the worst leaving group (thus amides are the least reactive).

Choice **(B)** is correct because ethoxide is the worst leaving group, followed by carboxylate and then chloride (best leaving group).

Choice **(A)** is not correct because the anhydride is more reactive than the ester. Choice **(C)** is not correct because the order is reversed. Choice **(D)** is not correct because the acid chloride is more reactive than the anhydride.

Practice Problems: **PQ-20** and **PQ-21**

SQ-8.   What is the major product of this reaction?

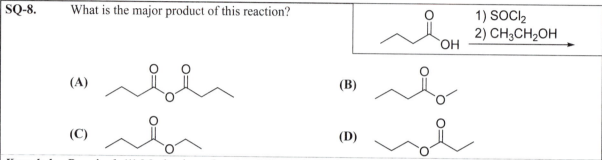

Knowledge Required: (1) Mechanism of nucleophilic acyl substitution. (2) Forming an acid chloride from carboxylic acid using thionyl chloride.

Thinking it Through: You are asked to determine which of four possible products are formed from the starting materials and two sets of reagents. You recognize that the first step of this reaction is the conversion of an –OH group to an –Cl group; for the given starting material, this is a transformation from a carboxylic acid to an acid chloride. The second step of the sequence is the formation of an ester from the acid chloride formed in the first step and the alcohol in the second step through nucleophilic acyl substitution.

Choice **(C)** is correct because it is the resulting ester from when butanoic acid is reacted with sulfonyl chloride followed by ethanol.

Choice **(A)** is not correct because it is the product for when a carboxylic acid or carboxylate anion is reacted with an acid chloride, for example. Choices **(B)** and **(D)** are not correct because the alkyl groups have an incorrect number of carbon atoms.

Practice Problems: **PQ-22, PQ-23, PQ-24, PQ-25, PQ-26,** and **PQ-27**

SQ-9.   What is the major product of this reaction?

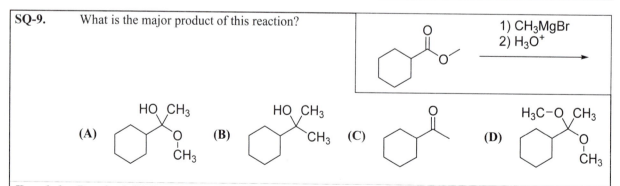

Knowledge Required: (1) Reaction products formed when a carboxylic acid derivative reacts with an organometallic reagent. (2) Mechanism for organometallic reactions with carboxylic acid derivatives.

Thinking it Through: You are asked to predict the product from the given starting material and two sets of reagents. You recognize the first step as an organometallic reaction of an ester with a Grignard reagent. You recall that Grignard reagents have a nucleophilic carbon that attacks the carbon of the carbonyl group. In this case,

because the carbonyl is an ester, you know that a nucleophilic substitution will occur via nucleophilic addition, followed by elimination of ⁻OCH₃ as a leaving group. This will form a ketone.

You recall, also, that when a ketone is formed in the presence of the Grignard reagent, a second equivalent of Grignard reagent will add via nucleophilic addition to the ketone, thus forming a tertiary alcohol, with two R groups from the organometallic reagent (in this case, two methyl groups).

Choice (**B**) is correct because it is a tertiary alcohol with two methyl groups originating from the Grignard reagent in step one.

Choice (**A**) is not correct because it is a protonated form of the anionic intermediate that is short-lived in the mechanism. Choice (**C**) is not correct because it is the ketone intermediate in the reaction. Choice (**D**) is not correct because it is formed from reagents not available in the reaction.

Practice Problems:* PQ-28** and **PQ-29

*You recall that this is different from when a carboxylic acid reacts with a Grignard. The acid has an acidic hydrogen on the acid group which is deprotonated by the Grignard. Next, you know one equivalent of the Grignard will add and a dianion will form. That is the end of step 1 when you begin with a carboxylic acid. You recall the acidic workup (step 2) then forms a diol which dehydrates to a ketone as a final product.

SQ-10. What reagent is best suited for this transformation?

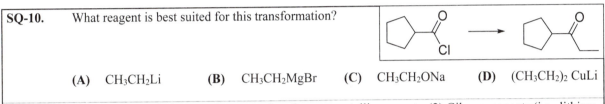

(A) CH₃CH₂Li (B) CH₃CH₂MgBr (C) CH₃CH₂ONa (D) (CH₃CH₂)₂ CuLi

Knowledge Required: (1) Relative reactive strengths of organometallic reagents. (2) Gilman reagents (i.e., lithium dialkylcuprates) as organometallic reagents.

Thinking it Through: You are asked to identify which reagents lead to the given transformation. You note that this reaction forms a new carbon-carbon bond and is thus likely an organometallic reaction. You recognize that the starting material is an acid chloride and thus if you used a strong organometallic reagent you would end with a tertiary alcohol. Thus, you recall that you must use a milder organometallic reagent that works with acid chlorides.

Choice (**D**) is correct. Gillman reagents (i.e., lithium dialkylcuprate) will only add once to the acid chloride via an addition-elimination mechanism.

Choice (**A**) and (**B**) are not correct because both reagents will add twice, first to the acid chloride and second to the resultant elimination product. Choice (**C**) is not correct because it will lead to the formation of an ester.

***Practice Problem:* PQ-30**

Practice Questions (PQ)

PQ-1. Arrange the ketones in order of increasing reactivity toward cyanohydrin formation with HCN/KCN.

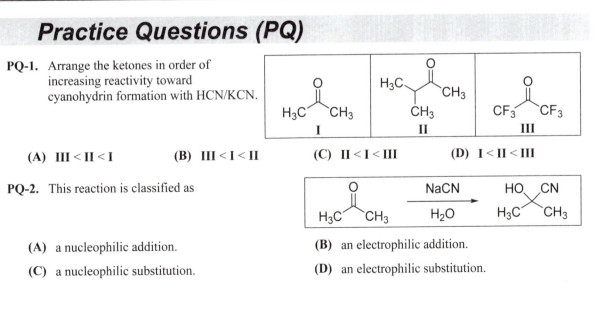

(A) III < II < I (B) III < I < II (C) II < I < III (D) I < II < III

PQ-2. This reaction is classified as

(A) a nucleophilic addition. (B) an electrophilic addition.
(C) a nucleophilic substitution. (D) an electrophilic substitution.

PQ-3. What is the major product of this reaction?

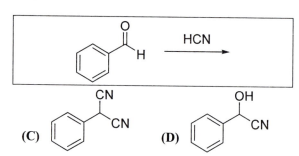

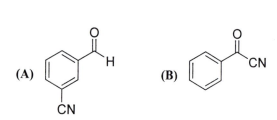

(A)   (B)   (C)   (D)

PQ-4. What is the principal product of the acid-catalyzed reaction of cyclopentanone with ethylene glycol (HOCH₂CH₂OH)?

(A) 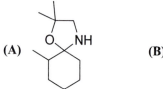 OCH₂CH₂OH / OCH₂CH₂OH

(B)

(C)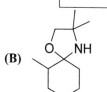

(D) —OCH₂CH₂OH

PQ-5. What is the major product of this reaction?

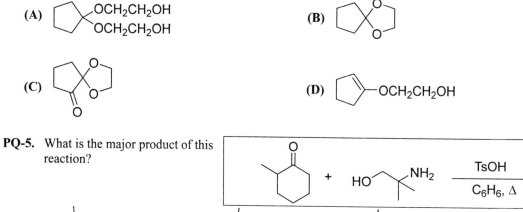

(A)   (B)   (C)   (D)

PQ-6. What is the major product of this reaction?

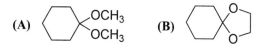

NaOCH₃
CH₃OH

(A) OCH₃ / OCH₃   (B)   (C) OCH₃ / OH   (D) OH / OH

PQ-7. What is the starting material of this reaction?

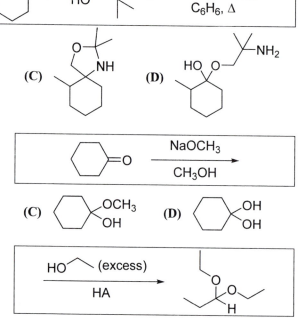

HO⌒ (excess)
HA

(A)   (B)   (C) ⌒OH   (D)

PQ-8. What is the major product of this reaction?

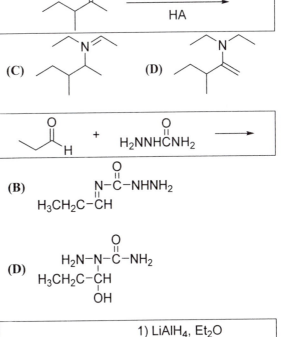

(A) 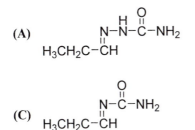 **(B)** 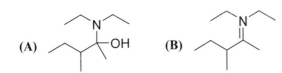 **(C)** **(D)**

PQ-9. What is the major product of this reaction?

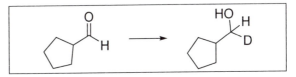

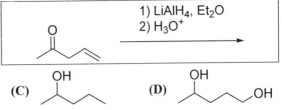

(A)
H
N–N–C–NH₂
‖   ‖
     O
H₃CH₂C–CH
        ‖

(B)
N–C–NHNH₂
‖   ‖
     O
H₃CH₂C–CH
        ‖

(C)
N–C–NH₂
‖   ‖
     O
H₃CH₂C–CH
        ‖

(D)
H₂N–N–C–NH₂
      | ‖
          O
H₃CH₂C–CH
        |
        OH

PQ-10. What is the major product of this reaction?

1) LiAlH₄, Et₂O
2) H₃O⁺

(A) **(B)** OH **(C)** OH **(D)** OH ... OH

PQ-11. What is the best reagent for this conversion?

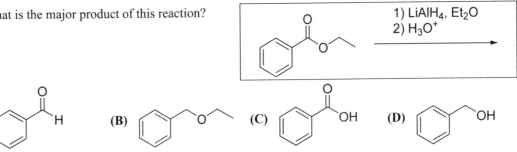

(A) D₂O, catalytic HCl

(B) NaBD₄, ethanol (and aqueous workup)

(C) NaOD, ethanol (and aqueous workup)

(D) D₂O₂, CH₃CO₂H

PQ-12. What is the major product of this reaction?

1) LiAlH₄, Et₂O
2) H₃O⁺

(A) **(B)** **(C)** OH **(D)** OH

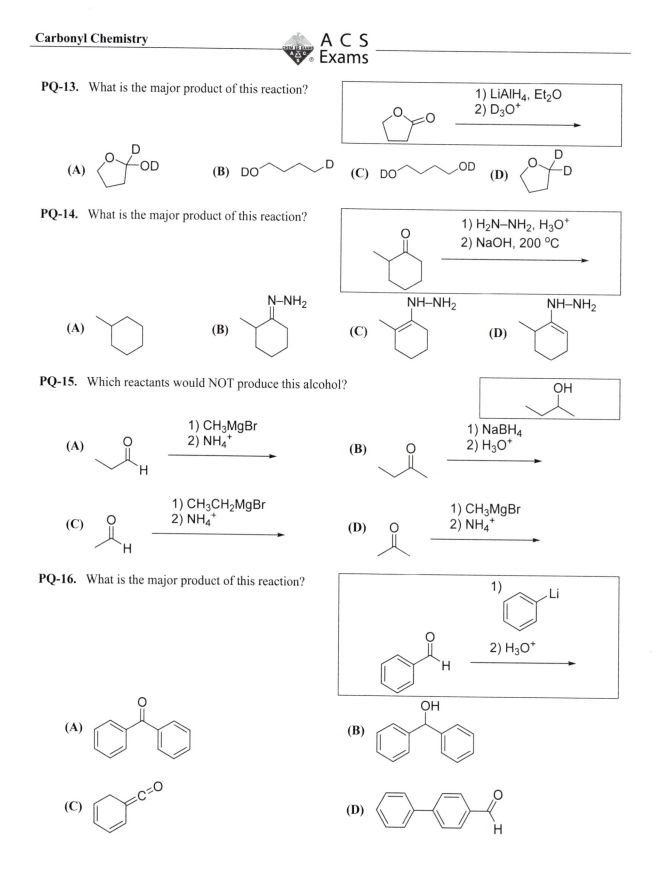

PQ-13. What is the major product of this reaction?

1) LiAlH$_4$, Et$_2$O
2) D$_3$O$^+$

(A)

(B) DO

(C) DO OD

(D)

PQ-14. What is the major product of this reaction?

1) H$_2$N–NH$_2$, H$_3$O$^+$
2) NaOH, 200 °C

(A)

(B) N–NH$_2$

(C) NH–NH$_2$

(D) NH–NH$_2$

PQ-15. Which reactants would NOT produce this alcohol?

OH

(A) 1) CH$_3$MgBr
    2) NH$_4$$^+$

(B) 1) NaBH$_4$
    2) H$_3$O$^+$

(C) 1) CH$_3$CH$_2$MgBr
    2) NH$_4$$^+$

(D) 1) CH$_3$MgBr
    2) NH$_4$$^+$

PQ-16. What is the major product of this reaction?

1) Li

2) H$_3$O$^+$

(A)

(B) OH

(C) C=O

(D) H

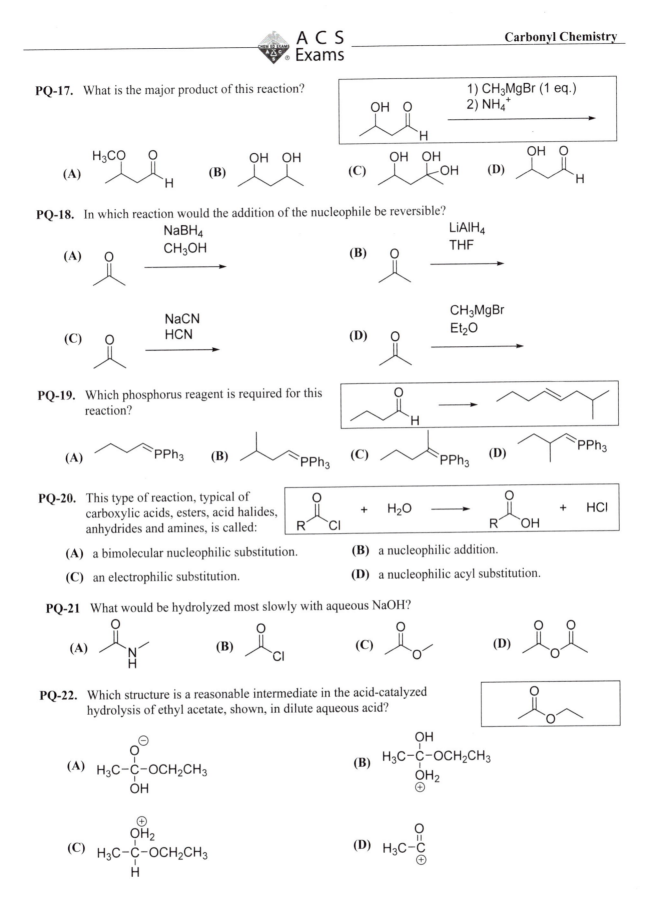

PQ-17. What is the major product of this reaction?

1) CH₃MgBr (1 eq.)
2) NH₄⁺

(A)

(B)

(C)

(D)

PQ-18. In which reaction would the addition of the nucleophile be reversible?

(A) NaBH₄ / CH₃OH

(B) LiAlH₄ / THF

(C) NaCN / HCN

(D) CH₃MgBr / Et₂O

PQ-19. Which phosphorus reagent is required for this reaction?

(A) ⁼PPh₃

(B) ⁼PPh₃

(C) ⁼PPh₃

(D) ⁼PPh₃

PQ-20. This type of reaction, typical of carboxylic acids, esters, acid halides, anhydrides and amines, is called:

$$R-COCl + H_2O \longrightarrow R-COOH + HCl$$

(A) a bimolecular nucleophilic substitution.

(B) a nucleophilic addition.

(C) an electrophilic substitution.

(D) a nucleophilic acyl substitution.

PQ-21 What would be hydrolyzed most slowly with aqueous NaOH?

(A)

(B)

(C)

(D)

PQ-22. Which structure is a reasonable intermediate in the acid-catalyzed hydrolysis of ethyl acetate, shown, in dilute aqueous acid?

(A) $H_3C-\overset{\underset{|}{O^-}}{\underset{|}{C}}-OCH_2CH_3$, OH below

(B) $H_3C-\overset{\underset{|}{OH}}{\underset{|}{C}}-OCH_2CH_3$, $\overset{+}{O}H_2$ below

(C) $H_3C-\overset{\underset{|}{\overset{+}{O}H_2}}{\underset{|}{C}}-OCH_2CH_3$, H below

(D) $H_3C-\overset{+}{C}=O$

PQ-23. What are the major products of this reaction?

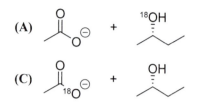

(A) 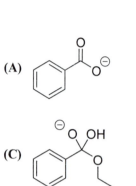 + (structure with ^{18}OH)

(B) (structure) + ^{18}OH (structure)

(C) (structure with ^{18}O) + OH (structure)

(D) (structure with ^{18}O) + OH (structure)

PQ-24. Which intermediate is involved in the mechanism of this base-promoted hydrolysis?

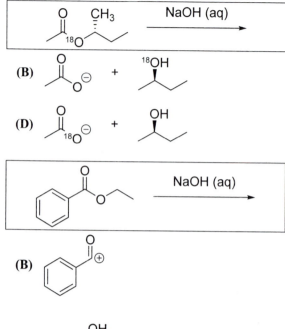

(A) (structure)

(B) (structure)

(C) 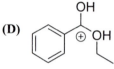 (structure)

(D) (structure)

PQ-25. What are the major products of this reaction?

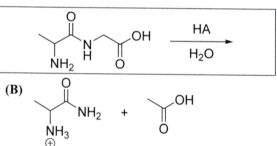

(A) 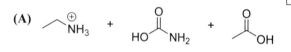 (structures)

(B) (structures)

(C) 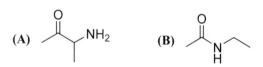 (structures) + NH_4^+

(D) (structures)

PQ-26. What is the major product of this reaction?

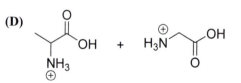

(A) (structure) NH_2

(B) (structure)

(C) (structure)

(D) (structure)

PQ-27. What is the major product of this reaction?

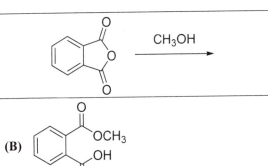

(A)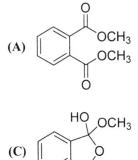

(B)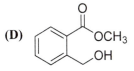

(C)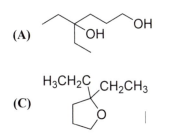

(D)

PQ-28. What is the major product of this reaction?

1) CH₃CH₂MgBr
2) NH₄⁺

(A)

(B)

(C) H₃CH₂C CH₂CH₃

(D) HO CH₂CH₃

PQ-29. What is the major product of this reaction?

1) excess CH₃Li
2) H₃O⁺

(A)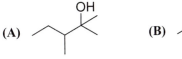

(B)

(C)

(D)

PQ-30. Which reaction sequence is preferred for this conversion?

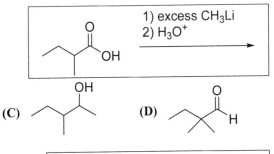

(A)
1) CH₃MgBr
2) H₃O⁺

(B)
1) SOCl₂
2) CH₃Li
3) H₃O⁺

(C)
1) SOCl₂
2) (CH₃)₂CuLi

(D)
1) SOCl₂
2) CH₃MgBr
3) H₃O⁺

ACS
Exams

Answers to Study Questions

SQ-1.	B	SQ-5.	B	SQ-9.	B
SQ-2.	D	SQ-6.	D	SQ-10.	D
SQ-3.	A	SQ-7.	B		
SQ-4.	A	SQ-8.	C		

Answers to Practice Questions

PQ-1.	C	PQ-11.	B	PQ-21.	A
PQ-2.	A	PQ-12.	D	PQ-22.	B
PQ-3.	D	PQ-13.	C	PQ-23.	B
PQ-4.	B	PQ-14.	A	PQ-24.	C
PQ-5.	B	PQ-15.	D	PQ-25.	D
PQ-6.	C	PQ-16.	B	PQ-26.	B
PQ-7.	B	PQ-17.	D	PQ-27.	B
PQ-8.	D	PQ-18.	C	PQ-28.	A
PQ-9.	A	PQ-19.	B	PQ-29.	B
PQ-10.	B	PQ-20.	D	PQ-30.	C

Chapter 14 – Enol and Enolate Chemistry and Conjugate Additions

Chapter Summary:

This chapter will focus on how the alpha-carbon to the carbonyl carbon reacts in different functional groups. Also included in this chapter are many famous reactions of the alpha-carbon to a carbonyl. Additionally, the conjugate additions to α,β-unsaturated carbonyls are covered here.

Specific topics covered in this chapter are:
- Enols and enolates as intermediates
- Keto-enol tautomerization
- Racemization of the α-carbon
- Halogenation and haloform reactions
- Alkylations at the α-carbon
- Aldol reactions
- Claisen and Dieckmann condensations
- β-dicarbonyl reactions and decarboxylation
- Michael addition and Robinson annulation
- Conjugate additions

Previous material that is relevant to your understanding of questions in this chapter include:
- Structures of molecules (**Chapter 1**)
- Carbonyl chemistry (**Chapter 13**)

Where to find this in your textbook:

The material in this chapter typically aligns to "Reactions at the α-carbon of a carbonyl" and "carbonyl condensation and conjugate addition reactions of carbonyls" in your textbook. The name of your chapter may vary.

Practice exam:

There may be practice exam questions aligned to the material in this chapter. Because there are a limited number of questions on the practice exam, a review of the breadth of the material in this chapter is advised in preparation for your exam.

How this fits to the big picture:

The material in this chapter aligns to the Big Idea of Structure and Function (III) and Chemical Reactions (V) as listed on page 13 of this study guide.

Study Questions (SQ)

SQ-1. What represents keto-enol tautomerization?

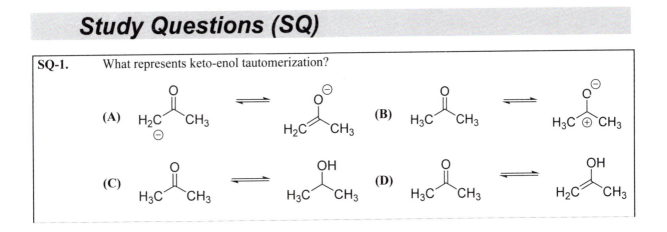

Knowledge Required: (1) Definition of enol/enolate. (2) Resonance stability of the enol tautomer with a ketone.

Thinking it Through: You realize that to answer this question you are looking for a compound that has had a hydrogen abstracted from an α–carbon to the carbonyl. The α-carbon atom forms a double bond with the carbon of the carbonyl and the oxygen of the carbonyl becomes a hydroxyl group, this is an enol.

You recall that an equilibrium exists between this enol and the ketone made by formally moving the hydrogen of the –OH group to the α-carbon and re-forming the carbonyl. The ketone is favored in the equilibrium, unless the enol is formed between 2 carbonyls (a β-dicarbonyl compound). Enols are formed in acidic solutions.

You also recall that similar chemistry occurs in basic conditions, only the enolate ion is formed. The enolate ion of acetone is given here for reference:

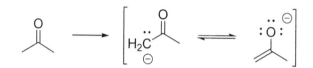

Choice **(D)** is correct. You recognize the ketone of acetone and its corresponding enol.

Choice **(A)** is not correct. These are the two resonance stabilized forms of the enolate anion. Choice **(B)** is not correct. This shows the ketone and its resonance structure showing a δ^+ carbon-atom and a δ^- oxygen-atom. Choice **(C)** is not correct. Though acetone is the correct ketone, the second structure is isopropanol, which is the product of the reduction of acetone.

Practice Problems: PQ-1, PQ-2, and PQ-3

SQ-2.   What is the major product of this reaction?

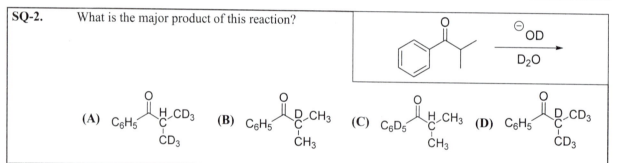

Knowledge Required: (1) The identity and acidity of hydrogen atoms α to a carbonyl group. (2) The ability of α-hydrogens to undergo racemization (deuterium exchange).

Thinking it Through: You recognize that to start this problem you need to form an enolate from the given ketone. There is only one α–hydrogen on this molecule and drawing the intermediate you get:

Next, you realize that in D_2O, DO^-, you are being asked to simply show racemization of the α–carbon (despite not being a stereocenter). Therefore, you put a deuterium (–D) in the place of the abstracted proton (–H).

Choice **(B)** is correct. This shows one proton exchanged for a deuterium at the α–carbon.

Choices **(A)**, **(C)**, and **(D)** are not correct because the compounds have deuterium atoms on carbons other than the α–carbon being exchanged for deuterium. There is no mechanism for these exchanges in D_2O, DO^-.

Practice Problems: PQ-4

SQ-3. What is the major product of this reaction?

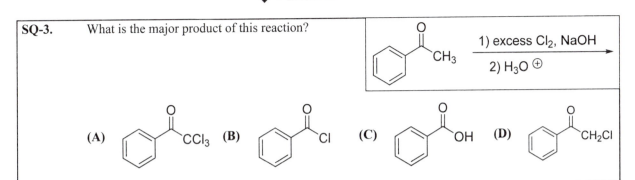

Knowledge Required: (1) Halogenation of the α-carbon. (2) Products of halogenation in the presence of base (including the haloform reaction) and acid.

Thinking it Through: You recognize that this question is asking about halogenation at the α-carbon. You recall that the number of halogens that add to the α-carbon is dependent on whether you are in acidic or basic solution. In acidic media (if step 1 of the reaction included acid) you recall that only one chlorine atom would add to the α–carbon. Because this reaction takes place in base, you recall that you will substitute all of the hydrogens on the α–carbon and get to:

Because this is a methylketone, you remember that you will now do a nucleophilic acyl substitution reaction where hydroxide is the nucleophile and ⁻CCl₃ is the leaving group. You recall that this is termed the haloform reaction, and that the acid in the second step is to work up the reaction and protonate the carboxylate anion to form carboxylic acid.

Choice (C) is correct. A methyl ketone halogenated in base ends as a carboxylic acid.

Choice (A) is not correct. Substitution of all three hydrogens on the α–carbon in base is correct, but this reaction should have gone further. Choice (B) is not correct. The methyl group does not get substituted for a chlorine. Choice (D) is not correct. This is the product of an acid-promoted halogenation.

Practice Problems: **PQ-5** and **PQ-6**

SQ-4. What is the major product of this reaction?

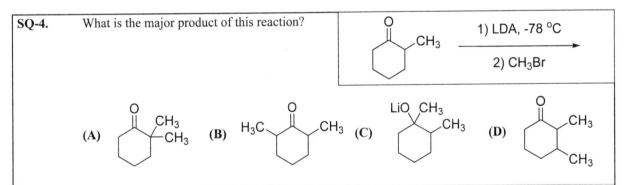

Knowledge Required: (1) Formation of the kinetic and thermodynamic enolate. (2) Reaction and mechanism of the enolate with a ketone or aldehyde in an alkylation reaction.

Thinking it Through: You recognize this two-step reaction as the alkylation of a ketone (or aldehyde), and thus you must first identify the enolate formed by the base in step one, and then the alkylation product formed in step two.

You recall that there are two possible enolates that will form in the first step, the thermodynamic enolate (more stable enolate) formed when an alkoxide base is used, or the kinetic enolate (the enolate that forms faster) formed when LDA is used:

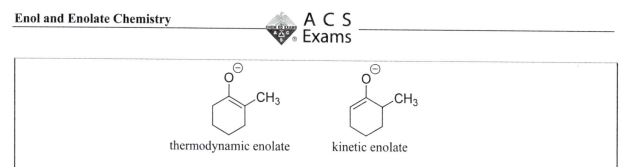

thermodynamic enolate   kinetic enolate

Because this reaction takes place with LDA, the kinetic enolate will form. You also recall that unlike thermodynamic enolates, LDA converts the ketone completely (close to 100 % yield) to the kinetic enolate.
In the second step the α-carbon where the enolate formed is alkylated via an S_N2 reaction.
Choice (**B**) is correct because alkylation occurred at the kinetic enolate α-carbon atom.
Choice (**A**) is not correct. This is the product of a thermodynamic enolate. Choice (**C**) is not correct. The CH_3 does not add to the carbonyl. Choice (**D**) is not correct. This appears to come from a conjugate addition, but there is not a π-bond between the α and β-carbon atoms.

Practice Problems: **PQ-7**, **PQ-8**, **PQ-9**, and **PQ-10**

SQ-5.   What is the major product of this reaction?

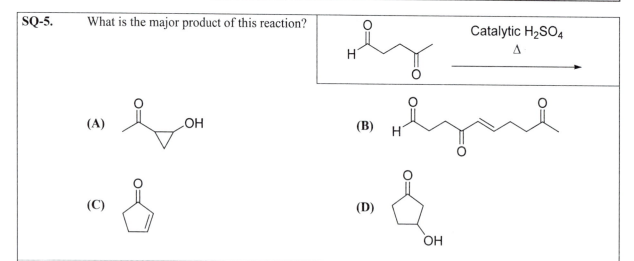

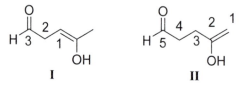

Knowledge Required: (1) Reaction and mechanism of the enol with a ketone or aldehyde in an aldol reaction. (2) Understanding of reactivity of an aldehyde versus ketone. (3) Stability of products when rings form.

Thinking it Through: You recognize that the starting material in the reaction has both an aldehyde and a ketone functional group. Because both of these functional groups react similarly, you realize you can identify the reaction based on the reagents. In this case with catalytic acid and heat, the molecule will undergo an intramolecular aldol reaction.
You realize you need to identify where the enol will form, and which carbonyl will be the site for the nucleophilic (enol) attack. You recall that aldehydes are more reactive than ketones and are therefore more likely to be the site for nucleophilic attack.
This means the enol will form on the carbonyl of the ketone. There are two different α-carbon atoms, and so there are two different enols that can form:

Finally, you decide that after drawing the two possible enols, intermediate **II** is more likely to react via an aldol mechanism as it will form a more stable five-membered ring instead of the three-membered ring that would form from intermediate **I**.

The final step in the reaction mechanism when acid is present is that the alcohol formed in the aldol once the enol attacks (shown below) will dehydrate.

Choice **(C)** is correct because it shows the correct aldol condensation product.
Choice **(A)** is not correct. It is the beta-hydroxyketone that would form from intermediate **I**. Choice **(B)** is not correct. This is the aldol condensation product that would form from two of the starting materials reacting instead of an intramolecular attack. This is not thermodynamically favored. Choice **(D)** is not correct. It is an intermediate in the reaction which will dehydrate in the presence of acid.

Practice Problems: **PQ-11, PQ-12, PQ-13, PQ-14, PQ-15, PQ-16, PQ-17**, and **PQ-18**

SQ-6.	What is the major product of this reaction?	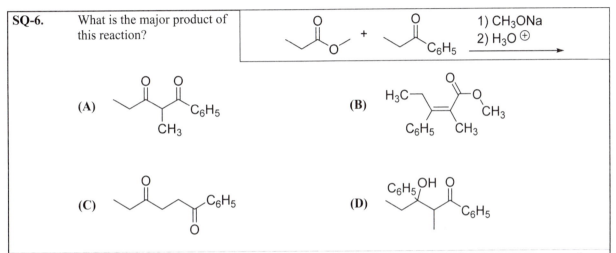

Knowledge Required: (1) Formation of the enolate ions in solutions that contain α–hydrogen atoms on more than one compound. (2) Reaction product and mechanism of a Claisen condensation reaction.

Thinking it Through: You evaluate the starting materials and the reagent for step one to decide which type of reaction will take place. An ester is reacting with a ketone in the presence of a strong unhindered base. You decide that the first step of the reaction will be to form an enolate, and you note that both the ketone and the ester have α-hydrogens available.

To figure out the major product you recall that you need to think about which functional group will form more product upon nucleophilic (enolate) attack. Neither the ketone nor the ester initially prefers to undergo nucleophilic attack, but you remember that when an enolate attacks an ester, a subsequent step is the formation of an enolate between two carbonyls such as:

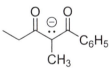

The formation of this enolate drives the reaction forward and you know, therefore, that the enolate will form at the ketone and nucleophilic attack will happen at the ester (a Claisen condensation). An acidic workup is then needed as a final step to isolate the organic product.

Choice **(A)** is correct. This is the product resulting from forming an enolate at the ketone and attacking the ester.

Choice **(B)** is not correct. This is the product of an aldol condensation that would occur if the enolate formed on the ester and attacked the ketone. There is no energetic driving force for this reaction. Choice **(C)** is not correct. This assumes you deprotonate the β-hydrogen instead of the α-hydrogen. Choice **(D)** is not correct. This is the aldol addition reaction of the ketone reacting with itself. This reaction is not favored energetically.

Practice Problems: **PQ-19, PQ-20, PQ-21, PQ-22**, and **PQ-23**

SQ-7.   What is the major product of this reaction sequence?

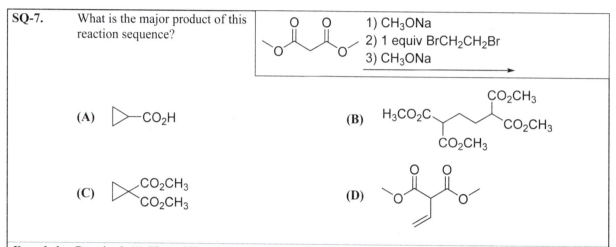

1) CH₃ONa
2) 1 equiv BrCH₂CH₂Br
3) CH₃ONa

(A) ▷—CO₂H

(B) H₃CO₂C ⟍⟍⟍ CO₂CH₃ / CO₂CH₃ / CO₂CH₃

(C) ▷⟨CO₂CH₃ / CO₂CH₃

(D)

Knowledge Required: (1) The acidity of the α-hydrogen between two carbonyls in a β-dicarbonyl. (2) Alkylation of the α-carbon in a β-dicarbonyl. (3) Assessing for decarboxylation in a β-dicarbonyl.

Thinking it Through: You realize that this problem combines knowledge from previous questions in this chapter. You first identify the α-carbon atom from which a hydrogen atom will be abstracted to form the enolate ion. In this case you note that there is a β-dicarbonyl, and thus a hydrogen on the carbon between the two carbonyls is a million times more acidic than a normal α-hydrogen. This is where the enolate forms, and it forms completely.

In step 2, you notice that you are doing an S_N2 displacement and, thus, alkylating the enolate. In the third, step another molecule of base is introduced, and, thus, you realize a second enolate will form, in the same location. Finally, that enolate will do an intramolecular attack on the chain to form the three-membered ring:

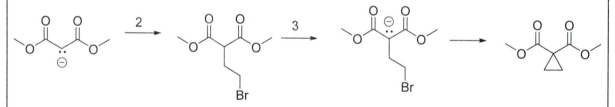

You also notice that in this case once the final alkylation (the closing of the ring) occurs there is no further workup. If an acidic work-up with heat was present, you would turn both of the esters into carboxylic acids and one of the acids would be lost to decarboxylation.

Choice **(C)** is correct because it shows the correct final product.

Choice **(A)** is not correct. This is the product you would get if you had acid and heat as a final step to cause decarboxylation. Choice **(B)** is not correct. This would be the product if a second equivalent of the β-dicarbonyl nucleophile displaced the second Br. Choice **(D)** is not correct. This implies that after the initial alkylation the second reaction of base eliminates the remaining bromine in an E2 pathway, whereas the formation of the second enolate is favored.

Practice Problems: **PQ-24**, and **PQ-25**

SQ-8. What is the major product of this reaction?

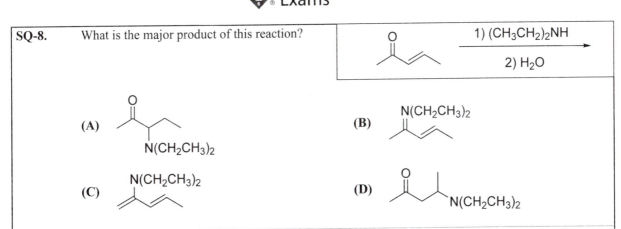

(A)

(B)

(C)

(D)

Knowledge Required: (1) Factors that control whether 1,2-addition or 1,4-addition is the major product of nucleophilic addition to α,β-unsaturated carbonyl compounds. (2) Products of a 1,4-addition to an α,β-unsaturated carbonyl compound.

Thinking it Through: You recognize that the starting material is an α,β-unsaturated carbonyl, and you are adding a nitrogen-based nucleophile, an amine, to it. You recall that you need to decide whether the nucleophile will add to the carbonyl (a 1,2-addition) or whether a conjugate addition (1,4-addition) will occur. 1,2-Additions are kinetic products favored by strongly basic nucleophiles (because the addition is not reversible). 1,4-Additions are thermodynamic products and, when the initial 1,2-addition is reversible (with less basic nucleophiles), the 1,4-product is preferred.

Strongly basic nucleophiles are usually negatively charged species and strong bases like hydride, Grignards/organolithiums and Wittig reagents. Less basic nucleophiles include anionic species that are weaker bases (hydroxide, alkoxide, enolates, organocuprates and cyanide) and neutral species (amines and enamines).

Because this is a less basic nucleophile, a conjugate addition (or 1,4-addition) will occur.

Choice **(D)** is correct because it depicts the product of a 1,4-conjugate addition.

Choice **(A)** is not correct. This would be a 1,3-addition product that would result from the nucleophile adding to the wrong side of the carbon-carbon double bond. Choice **(B)** is not correct. This is an attempt at the kinetic 1,2-product, meant to look like an imine, but the nitrogen would have a positive charge. This product doesn't form. Choice **(C)** is not correct. This is the kinetic 1,2-product, the result of nucleophilic addition to a ketone (the enamine).

Practice Problems: **PQ-26, PQ-27,** and **PQ-28**

SQ-9. What is the major product of this reaction?

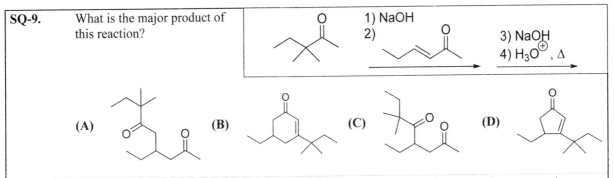

(A) **(B)** **(C)** **(D)**

Knowledge Required: (1) Michael addition reaction (conjugate addition of an enolate to a α,β-unsaturated carbonyl compound). (2) Robinson annulation (a Michael addition followed by an aldol condensation).

Thinking it Through: You recognize this as a multi-step reaction that starts with the formation of an enolate (and there is only one source of α-hydrogens). The enolate reacts with an α,β-unsaturated carbonyl. You recognize this as a conjugate 1,4-addition, named the Michael addition. The product at the end of the Michael addition is:

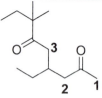

In the third step of the reaction, base is added to form a second enolate. There are three potential sites from which to take an α-hydrogen, as numbered above.

If the enolate formed at either position **2** or **3**, then you realize a three-membered ring would form; this is not favorable. However, the reaction of the enolate at position **1** with the other ketone forms a six-membered ring, which is favorable. The acid in the final step dehydrates the alcohol of the aldol. You recall that this reaction: a Michael addition followed by an aldol condensation is sometimes referred to as a Robinson annulation.

Choice **(B)** is correct because this is the product of the aldol condensation when an enolate forms at carbon-1 and attacks the other ketone.

Choice **(A)** is not correct. This is the Michael addition product at the end of steps 1 and 2. Choice **(C)** is not correct. This is close to the Michael addition product but is missing a carbon atom. Choice **(D)** is not correct. It is not possible to form a five-membered ring.

Practice Problems: **PQ-29**, and **PQ-30**

Practice Questions (PQ)

PQ-1. Rank the indicated hydrogen atoms from least to most acidic.

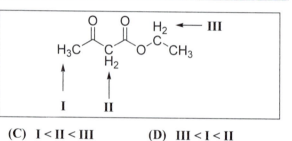

(A) III < II < I   (B) I < III < II   (C) I < II < III   (D) III < I < II

PQ-2. What is the enol intermediate formed in this reaction?

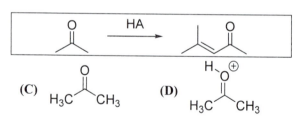

PQ-3 Which compound forms the greatest equilibrium concentration of the enol tautomer?

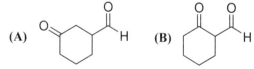

PQ-4. Which sets of hydrogen atoms can undergo deuterium exchange with CH₃ONa in CH₃OD?

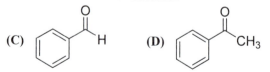

(A) II and III   (B) I, II and III   (C) II, III and IV   (D) I and IV

PQ-5. What is the major product of this reaction?

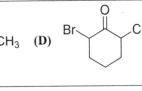

(A)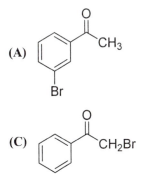

(B) + CHBr₃

(C)

(D)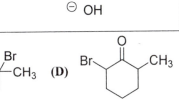

PQ-6. What is the major product of this reaction?

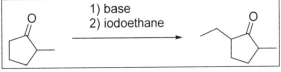

(A) 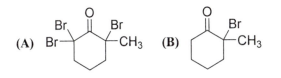 (B) (C) (D)

PQ-7. Which base would be the best for completing this α-substitution?

(A) sodium amide

(B) lithium diisopropyl amide

(C) lithium amide

(D) sodium ethoxide

PQ-8. What is the major product of this reaction?

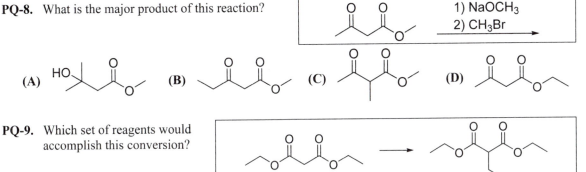

PQ-9. Which set of reagents would accomplish this conversion?

(A) NaH followed by CH₃CH₂OH

(B) CH₃CH₂ONa followed by CH₃CH₂Br

(C) NaH followed by CH₂=CH₂

(D) CH₃CH₂OH with H⁺ as a catalyst

PQ-10. Which base should be used to quantitatively convert the given molecule to its enolate form?

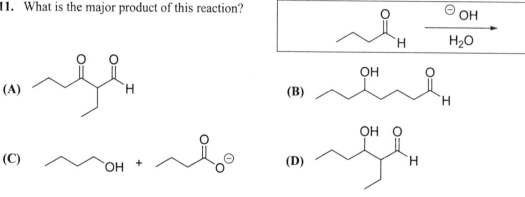

(A) LiO—C(=O)—CH₃

(B) LiO—CH₃

(C) LiN[CH(CH₃)₂]₂

(D) LiOH

PQ-11. What is the major product of this reaction?

(A) (structure)

(B) (structure)

(C) (structure) + (structure)

(D) (structure)

PQ-12. Which statement is NOT true of an aldol reaction between two simple aldehydes?

(A) It accomplishes the formation of a new carbon-carbon bond.

(B) The key step in the mechanism is the attack of the α-carbon atom of an enolate ion on the carbon atom of a carbonyl carbon atom.

(C) Dehydration of the aldol product is often observed (an aldol condensation).

(D) The enolate is favored over the ketone at equilibrium.

PQ-13. What is the major product of this reaction when propanal is added slowly to the reaction mixture?

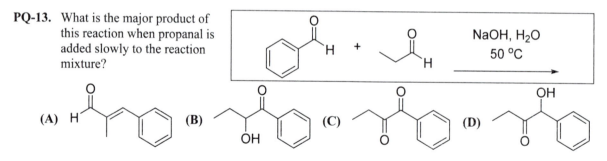

(A) (structure)

(B) (structure)

(C) (structure)

(D) (structure)

PQ-14. Which compound is the product of an aldol condensation?

(A) (structure)

(B) (structure)

(C) (structure)

(D) (structure)

PQ-15. What is the major product of this reaction?

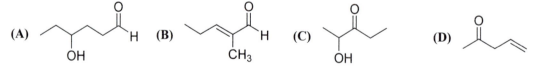

(A) (structure)

(B) (structure)

(C) (structure)

(D) (structure)

PQ-16. Which compound CANNOT undergo an aldol reaction in the presence of dilute base?

(A) C₆H₅CH₂CH (with O double bond) (B) (CH₃)₃CCH (with O double bond) (C) (CH₃)₂CHCH (with O double bond) (D) CH₃CH₂CH (with O double bond)

PQ-17. Which reactant can be used to make this compound by an intramolecular aldol reaction?

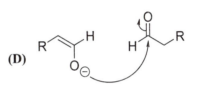

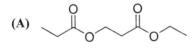

(A) 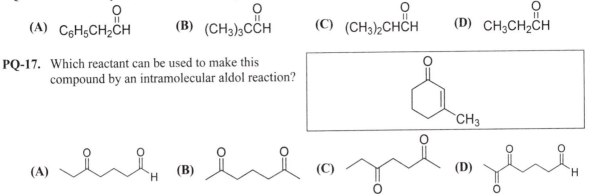 (B) (C) (D)

PQ-18. What is NOT a step in the mechanism of the aldol reaction?

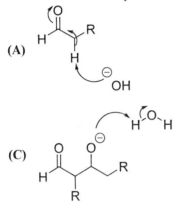

(A) (B)

(C) (D)

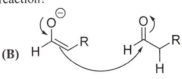

PQ-19. What is the major product of this reaction?

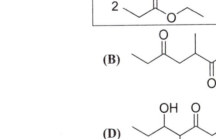

1) NaOCH₂CH₃
2) H₃O⁺

(A) (B)

(C) (D)

PQ-20. What starting material will yield this compound when treated with CH₃CH₂ONa in CH₃CH₂OH?

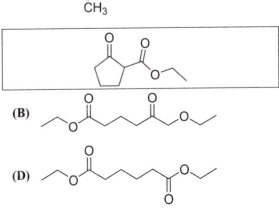

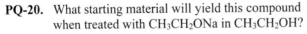

(A) 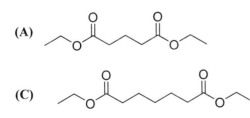 (B)

(C) (D)

PQ-21. What is the major product of this reaction?

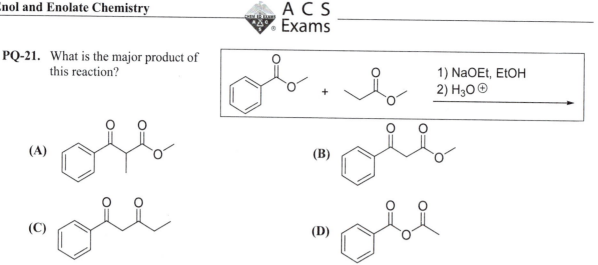

1) NaOEt, EtOH
2) $H_3O^{\oplus}$

(A)

(B)

(C)

(D)

PQ-22. Which compound when treated with $NaOCH_3$ followed by neutralization with aqueous acid will produce this β-diketone?

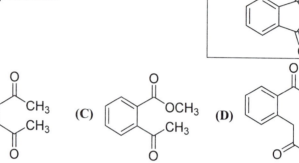

(A)

(B) CH_3 CH_3

(C) OCH_3 CH_3

(D) OCH_3 OCH_3

PQ-23. The self-condensation of a single ester in a Claisen reaction produces which of these?

(A) a β–diketone   **(B)** an α–keto ester   **(C)** a β–keto ester   **(D)** a β–hydroxy ester

PQ-24. If this steroid tetracarboxylic acid is heated, which carboxyl group will be readily lost as carbon dioxide?

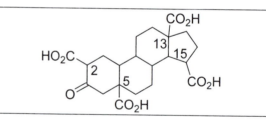

(A) CO_2H at C–2   **(B)** CO_2H at C–5   **(C)** CO_2H at C–13   **(D)** CO_2H at C–15

PQ-25. What is the major product of the reaction?

H_3CO OCH_3 + H CH$_3$ONa CH$_3$OH

(A) H H

(B) H_3CO H

(C) H_3CO OCH_3

(D) H

PQ-26. Which nucleophilic reagent will give the most 1,4-addition product with the given reactant?

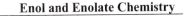

(A) LiAlH₄

(B) NaCN

(C) CH₃MgBr

(D) (C₆H₅)₃P⁺−CH₂⁻

PQ-27. Which reagent will accomplish this conversion?

(A) CH₃I

(B) CH₃MgBr

(C) CH₃Li

(D) (CH₃)₂CuLi

PQ-28. What is the major product of this reaction?

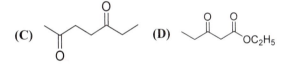

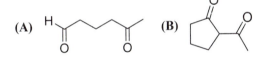

(A)

(B)

(C)

(D)

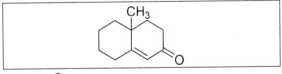

PQ-29. Which compound could be prepared using a Michael reaction?

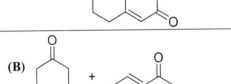

(A)

(B)

(C)

(D)

PQ-30. Which starting materials could be used to produce this product through a Robinson annulation?

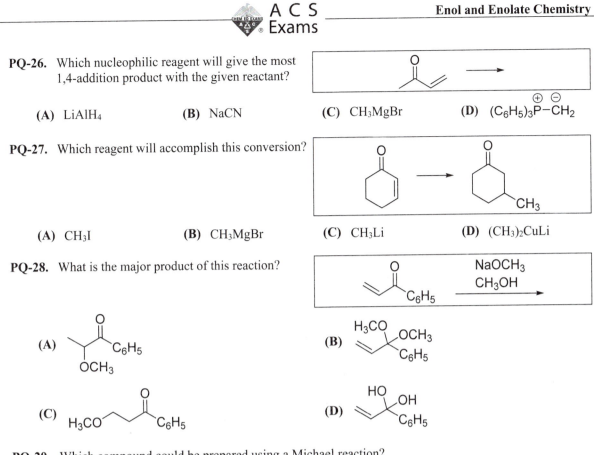

(A)   +

(B)   +

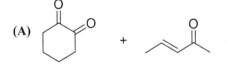

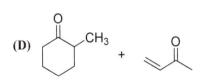

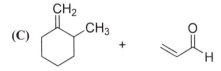

(C)   +

(D)   +

Answers to Study Questions

SQ-1.	D	SQ-4.	B	SQ-7.	C
SQ-2.	B	SQ-5.	C	SQ-8.	D
SQ-3.	C	SQ-6.	A	SQ-9.	B

Answers to Practice Questions

PQ-1.	D	PQ-11.	D	PQ-21.	A
PQ-2.	A	PQ-12.	D	PQ-22.	C
PQ-3.	B	PQ-13.	A	PQ-23.	C
PQ-4.	A	PQ-14.	B	PQ-24.	A
PQ-5.	C	PQ-15.	C	PQ-25.	C
PQ-6.	A	PQ-16.	B	PQ-26.	B
PQ-7.	B	PQ-17.	B	PQ-27.	D
PQ-8.	C	PQ-18.	D	PQ-28.	C
PQ-9.	B	PQ-19.	C	PQ-29.	A
PQ-10.	C	PQ-20.	D	PQ-30.	D

Chapter 15 – Application to Multistep Synthesis

Chapter Summary:
> This chapter will focus on combining multiple reactions to synthesize a new compound.

> Specific topics covered in this chapter are:
> - Predicting the product of a multistep synthesis
> - Choosing a multistep synthetic route to produce a desired product

> Previous material that is relevant to your understanding of questions in this chapter include:
> - Nucleophilic Substitution Reactions (*Chapter 5*)
> - Elimination Reactions (*Chapter 6*)
> - Addition Reactions: Alkenes & Alkynes (*Chapter 7*)
> - Addition Reactions: Alcohols & Ethers (*Chapter 8*)
> - Radical Reactions (*Chapter 10*)
> - Conjugated Systems (*Chapter 11*)
> - Aromatic Reactions (*Chapter 12*)
> - Carbonyl Chemistry (*Chapter 13*)
> - Enols and Enolates (*Chapter 14*)

Where to find this in your textbook:
> The material in this chapter typically aligns to "Synthesis" in your textbook. The name of your chapter may vary.

Practice exam:
> There may be practice exam questions aligned to the material in this chapter. Because there are a limited number of questions on the practice exam, a review of the breadth of the material in this chapter is advised in preparation for your exam.

How this fits to the big picture:
> The material in this chapter aligns to the Big Idea of "Reactions" (V) as listed on page 13 of this study guide.

Study Questions (SQ)

SQ-1. What is the product of this reaction?

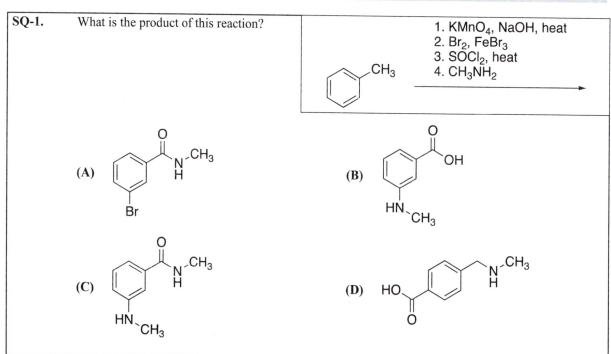

1. KMnO₄, NaOH, heat
2. Br₂, FeBr₃
3. SOCl₂, heat
4. CH₃NH₂

Knowledge Required: (1) Oxidation reactions. (2) Electrophilic aromatic substitution reactions. (3) Preparation of acid chlorides. (4). Formation of amide reactions.

Thinking it Through: You have been asked to predict the product of a multistep reaction. To solve this problem, you decide to predict the product for each of the reaction steps and, ultimately, select the choice that matches your predicted product.

You note that the first set of reaction conditions oxidizes alcohols and benzylic hydrogens. The starting material is toluene, which has three benzylic hydrogens that can be oxidized; you predict that benzoic acid is formed from these reaction conditions.

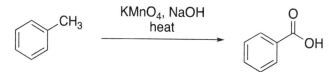

The next reaction is the bromination of an aromatic ring via electrophilic aromatic substitution. Because there is a substituent on the ring, you note that you have to determine if the substituent is an *ortho-para* director or a *meta* director. The substituent is a carboxylic acid group, an electron-withdrawing group; thus, the substituent is a *meta* director. You predict that 3-bromobenzoic acid is formed from these reaction conditions.

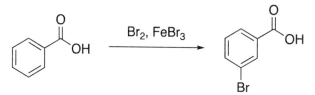

You note that the next set of reaction conditions transforms alcohols and carboxylic acids to alkyl chlorides and acid chlorides, respectively. Thus, you predict that 3-bromobenzoic acid will be transformed into 3-bromobenzoyl chloride from these reaction conditions.

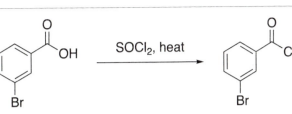

Finally, you note that methyl amine can react with acid chlorides to form amides. Thus, you predict that 3-bromobenzoyl chloride will be transformed into 3-bromo-*N*-methylbenzamide from these reaction conditions.

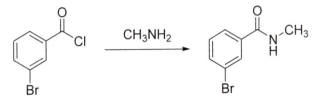

Choice (**A**) is correct.
Choice (**B**) is not correct because methyl amine does not replace bromine on the aromatic ring and sulfonyl chloride does not transform bromine into chlorine. Choice (**C**) is not correct because methyl amine does not replace bromine on the aromatic ring. Choice (**D**) is not correct because carboxylic acid is not a *para* director.

***Practice Problems:* PQ-1, PQ-2, PQ-3, PQ-4, PQ-5, PQ-6, and PQ-7**

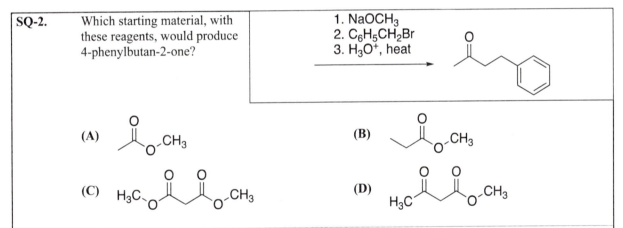

SQ-2. Which starting material, with these reagents, would produce 4-phenylbutan-2-one?

1. $NaOCH_3$
2. $C_6H_5CH_2Br$
3. H_3O^+, heat

(A) (B)

(C) (D)

Knowledge Required: (1) Acid-base reactions. (2) Substitution reactions. (3). Decarboxylation reactions.

Thinking it Through: You have been asked to determine which of four starting materials produces the desired product given a set of reaction conditions. One method for determining the correct answer is to conduct a retrosynthetic analysis of the product given the set of reaction conditions. Another method is to "predict the product" for each of the answer choices and choose the response that leads to the formation of the desired product. You decide to choose the second method to solve the problem.

Beginning with methyl acetate, you note that step one forms an enolate of the starting material. Step two uses the enolate as a nucleophile for a substitution reaction with 1'-bromomethylbenzene. Step three converts the methyl ester to a carboxylic acid. Thus, this is the product you determine would be formed from choice (**A**):

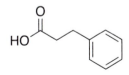

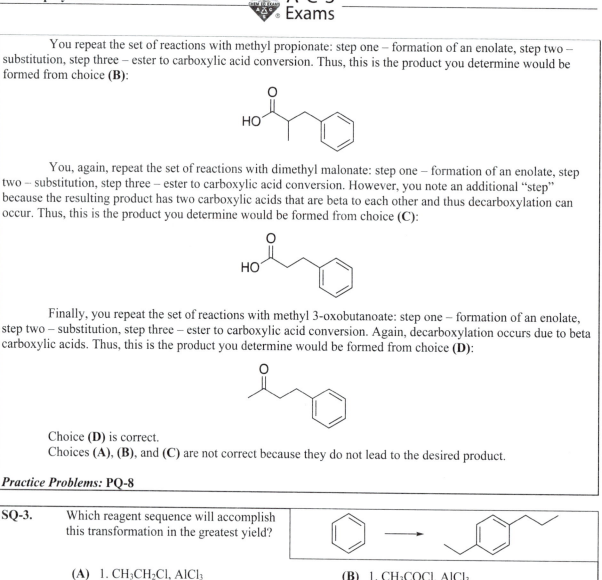

You repeat the set of reactions with methyl propionate: step one – formation of an enolate, step two – substitution, step three – ester to carboxylic acid conversion. Thus, this is the product you determine would be formed from choice (**B**):

You, again, repeat the set of reactions with dimethyl malonate: step one – formation of an enolate, step two – substitution, step three – ester to carboxylic acid conversion. However, you note an additional "step" because the resulting product has two carboxylic acids that are beta to each other and thus decarboxylation can occur. Thus, this is the product you determine would be formed from choice (**C**):

Finally, you repeat the set of reactions with methyl 3-oxobutanoate: step one – formation of an enolate, step two – substitution, step three – ester to carboxylic acid conversion. Again, decarboxylation occurs due to beta carboxylic acids. Thus, this is the product you determine would be formed from choice (**D**):

Choice (**D**) is correct.
Choices (**A**), (**B**), and (**C**) are not correct because they do not lead to the desired product.

Practice Problems: PQ-8

SQ-3. Which reagent sequence will accomplish this transformation in the greatest yield?

(**A**) 1. CH_3CH_2Cl, $AlCl_3$
2. $CH_3CH_2CH_2Cl$, $AlCl_3$

(**B**) 1. CH_3COCl, $AlCl_3$
2. CH_3CH_2COCl, $AlCl_3$
3. Zn(Hg), conc. HCl

(**C**) 1. CH_3CH_2COCl, $AlCl_3$
2. CH_3CH_2Cl, $AlCl_3$
3. Zn(Hg), conc. HCl

(**D**) 1. CH_3CH_2Cl, $AlCl_3$
2. CH_3CH_2COCl, $AlCl_3$
3. Zn(Hg), conc. HCl

Knowledge Required: (1) Friedel-Crafts alkylation reactions. (2) Friedel-Crafts acylation reactions. (3) Reduction of carbonyl reactions.

Thinking it Through: You are asked to determine which set of reaction conditions lead to the given transformation. You determine that the best method to solve this problem is to evaluate each set of reaction conditions with the given starting material to determine which reaction conditions lead to the desired product. Thus, you choose to treat this problem like a series of "predict the product" problems.
    Choice (**A**): You predict that benzene will react with chloroethane and aluminum trichloride in a Friedel-Crafts alkylation. Next, you predict that ethylbenzene will react with 1-chloropropane and aluminum chloride leads to a second Friedel-Crafts alkylation; the group will add *para* due to the directing effect of alkyl groups. However, you note that an isopropyl group will add to the aromatic ring, as the carbocation intermediate will rearrange to the more stable secondary carbocation.

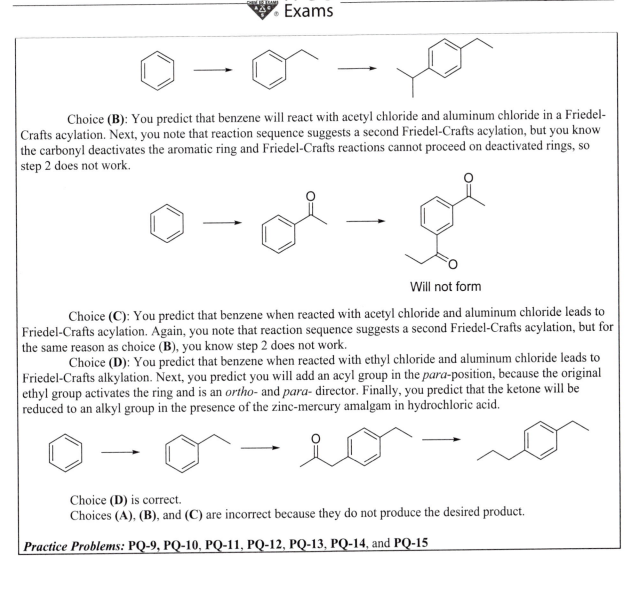

Choice (**B**): You predict that benzene will react with acetyl chloride and aluminum chloride in a Friedel-Crafts acylation. Next, you note that reaction sequence suggests a second Friedel-Crafts acylation, but you know the carbonyl deactivates the aromatic ring and Friedel-Crafts reactions cannot proceed on deactivated rings, so step 2 does not work.

Will not form

Choice (**C**): You predict that benzene when reacted with acetyl chloride and aluminum chloride leads to Friedel-Crafts acylation. Again, you note that reaction sequence suggests a second Friedel-Crafts acylation, but for the same reason as choice (**B**), you know step 2 does not work.

Choice (**D**): You predict that benzene when reacted with ethyl chloride and aluminum chloride leads to Friedel-Crafts alkylation. Next, you predict you will add an acyl group in the *para*-position, because the original ethyl group activates the ring and is an *ortho*- and *para*- director. Finally, you predict that the ketone will be reduced to an alkyl group in the presence of the zinc-mercury amalgam in hydrochloric acid.

Choice (**D**) is correct.
Choices (**A**), (**B**), and (**C**) are incorrect because they do not produce the desired product.

Practice Problems: **PQ-9**, **PQ-10**, **PQ-11**, **PQ-12**, **PQ-13**, **PQ-14**, and **PQ-15**

Practice Questions (PQ)

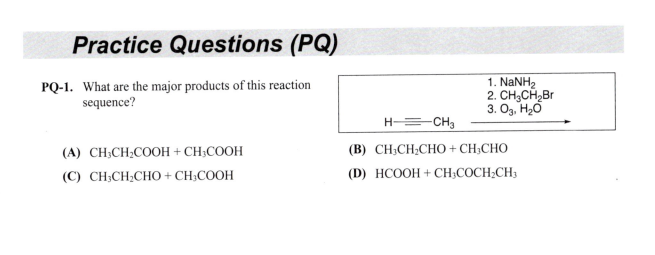

PQ-1. What are the major products of this reaction sequence?

1. $NaNH_2$
2. CH_3CH_2Br
3. O_3, H_2O

$H-\!\!\equiv\!\!-CH_3$ ⟶

(**A**) $CH_3CH_2COOH + CH_3COOH$

(**B**) $CH_3CH_2CHO + CH_3CHO$

(**C**) $CH_3CH_2CHO + CH_3COOH$

(**D**) $HCOOH + CH_3COCH_2CH_3$

PQ-2. What is the major product?

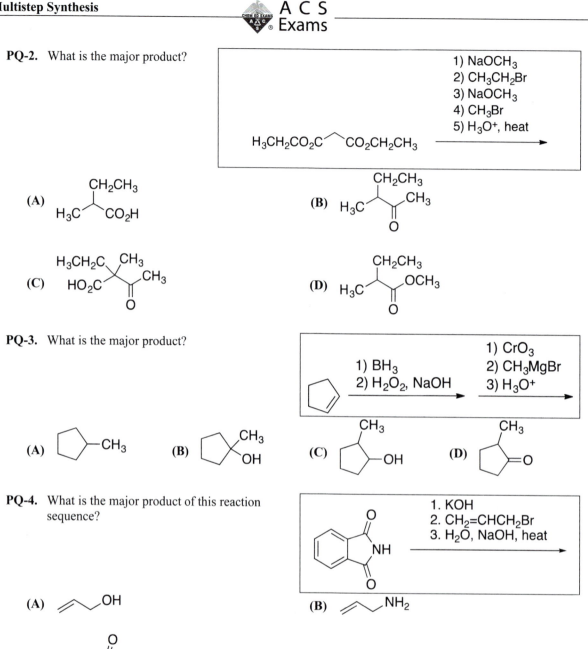

1) NaOCH$_3$
2) CH$_3$CH$_2$Br
3) NaOCH$_3$
4) CH$_3$Br
5) H$_3$O$^+$, heat

H$_3$CH$_2$CO$_2$C   CO$_2$CH$_2$CH$_3$

(A)

CH$_2$CH$_3$
H$_3$C   CO$_2$H

(B)

CH$_2$CH$_3$
H$_3$C   CH$_3$
O

(C)

H$_3$CH$_2$C   CH$_3$
HO$_2$C   CH$_3$
O

(D)

CH$_2$CH$_3$
H$_3$C   OCH$_3$
O

PQ-3. What is the major product?

1) BH$_3$
2) H$_2$O$_2$, NaOH

1) CrO$_3$
2) CH$_3$MgBr
3) H$_3$O$^+$

(A)   —CH$_3$

(B)   CH$_3$
OH

(C)   CH$_3$
OH

(D)   CH$_3$
O

PQ-4. What is the major product of this reaction sequence?

1. KOH
2. CH$_2$=CHCH$_2$Br
3. H$_2$O, NaOH, heat

O

NH

O

(A)   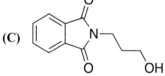   OH

(B)   NH$_2$

(C)

O

N

O
OH

(D)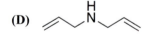
H
N

PQ-5. What is the major product of this reaction sequence?

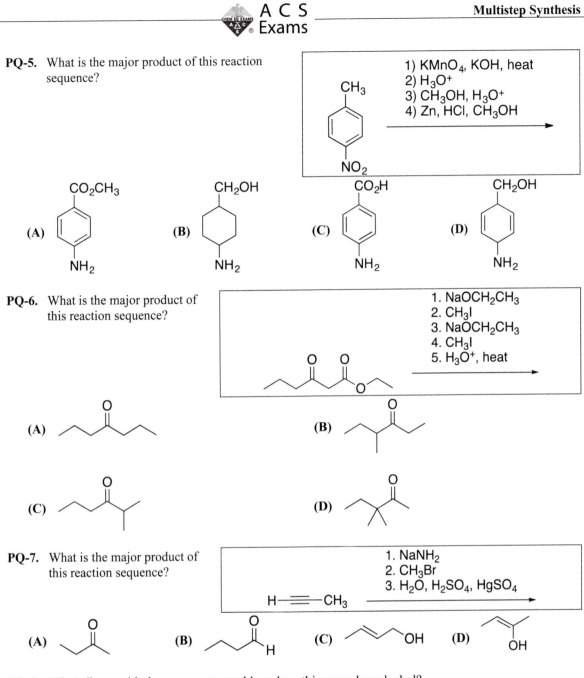

1) KMnO$_4$, KOH, heat
2) H$_3$O$^+$
3) CH$_3$OH, H$_3$O$^+$
4) Zn, HCl, CH$_3$OH

(A) CO$_2$CH$_3$ / NH$_2$

(B) CH$_2$OH / NH$_2$

(C) CO$_2$H / NH$_2$

(D) CH$_2$OH / NH$_2$

PQ-6. What is the major product of this reaction sequence?

1. NaOCH$_2$CH$_3$
2. CH$_3$I
3. NaOCH$_2$CH$_3$
4. CH$_3$I
5. H$_3$O$^+$, heat

(A)

(B)

(C)

(D)

PQ-7. What is the major product of this reaction sequence?

1. NaNH$_2$
2. CH$_3$Br
3. H$_2$O, H$_2$SO$_4$, HgSO$_4$

H——CH$_3$

(A)

(B)

(C) OH

(D) OH

PQ-8. What alkyne with these reagents would produce this secondary alcohol?

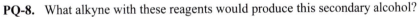

? → NaNH$_2$ / NH$_3$(l) → CH$_3$CH$_2$Br → Li / NH$_3$(l) → 1. Hg(OAc)$_2$, H$_2$O / 2. NaBH$_4$ → OH

(A) CH$_3$CH$_2$C≡CCH$_3$

(B) CH$_3$CH$_2$C≡CH

(C) CH$_3$C≡CH

(D) CH$_3$CH$_2$CH$_2$C≡CH

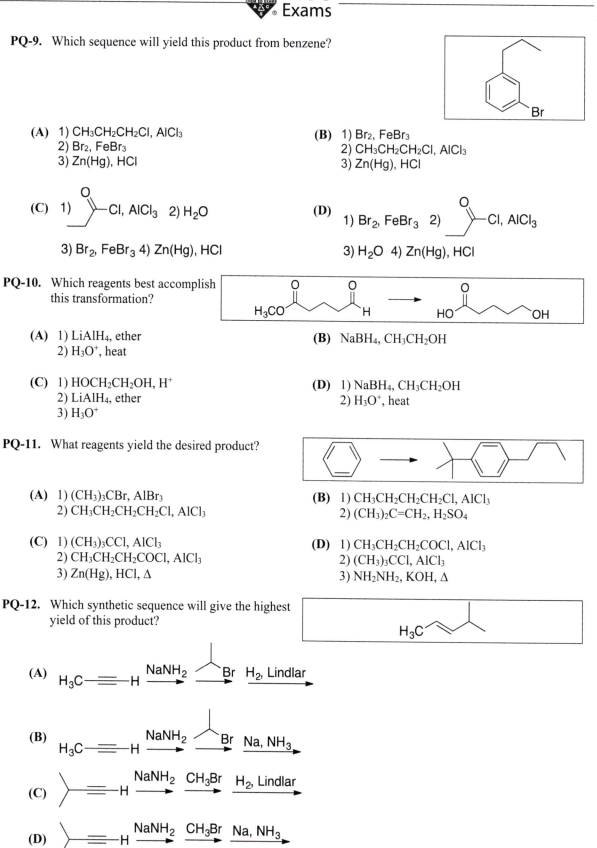

PQ-9. Which sequence will yield this product from benzene?

(A) 1) CH₃CH₂CH₂Cl, AlCl₃
     2) Br₂, FeBr₃
     3) Zn(Hg), HCl

(B) 1) Br₂, FeBr₃
     2) CH₃CH₂CH₂Cl, AlCl₃
     3) Zn(Hg), HCl

(C) 1) [structure] —Cl, AlCl₃   2) H₂O
     3) Br₂, FeBr₃ 4) Zn(Hg), HCl

(D) 1) Br₂, FeBr₃   2) [structure] —Cl, AlCl₃
     3) H₂O   4) Zn(Hg), HCl

PQ-10. Which reagents best accomplish this transformation?

(A) 1) LiAlH₄, ether
     2) H₃O⁺, heat

(B) NaBH₄, CH₃CH₂OH

(C) 1) HOCH₂CH₂OH, H⁺
     2) LiAlH₄, ether
     3) H₃O⁺

(D) 1) NaBH₄, CH₃CH₂OH
     2) H₃O⁺, heat

PQ-11. What reagents yield the desired product?

(A) 1) (CH₃)₃CBr, AlBr₃
     2) CH₃CH₂CH₂CH₂Cl, AlCl₃

(B) 1) CH₃CH₂CH₂CH₂Cl, AlCl₃
     2) (CH₃)₂C=CH₂, H₂SO₄

(C) 1) (CH₃)₃CCl, AlCl₃
     2) CH₃CH₂CH₂COCl, AlCl₃
     3) Zn(Hg), HCl, Δ

(D) 1) CH₃CH₂CH₂COCl, AlCl₃
     2) (CH₃)₃CCl, AlCl₃
     3) NH₂NH₂, KOH, Δ

PQ-12. Which synthetic sequence will give the highest yield of this product?

(A) H₃C≡H →[NaNH₂] →[Br (structure)] →[H₂, Lindlar]

(B) H₃C≡H →[NaNH₂] →[Br (structure)] →[Na, NH₃]

(C) (structure)≡H →[NaNH₂] →[CH₃Br] →[H₂, Lindlar]

(D) (structure)≡H →[NaNH₂] →[CH₃Br] →[Na, NH₃]

PQ-13. Which reagents would most successfully
complete this reaction?

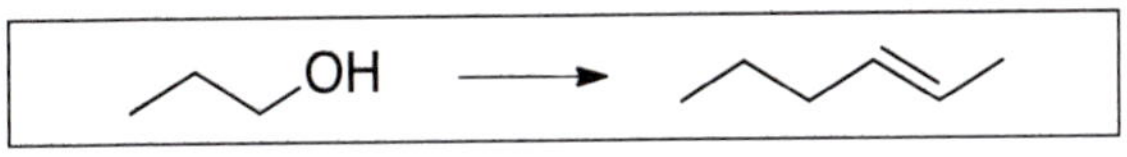

   (A) 1. $SOCl_2$, pyridine
          2. $NaCCCH_3$
          3. Li, $NH_3(l)$

   (B) 1. $NaCCCH_3$
          2. Li, $NH_3(l)$

   (C) 1. PBr_3
          2. $NaCCCH_3$
          3. H_2, Lindlar's cat.

   (D) 1. $SOCl_2$, pyridine
          2. $NaCCH$
          3. NaH
          4. CH_3Br

PQ-14. Which series of reagents would most
successfully complete this reaction?

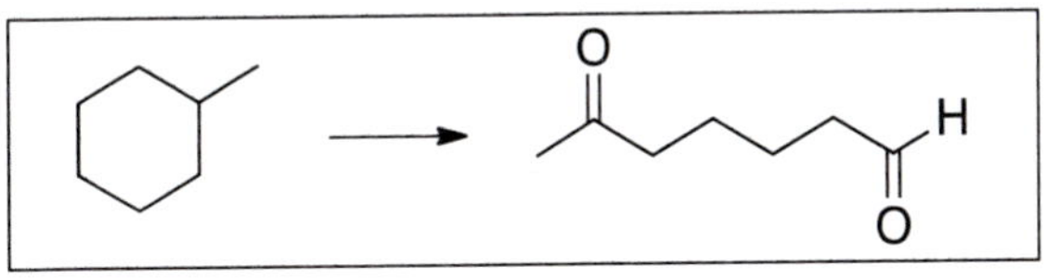

   (A) 1) Br_2, light
          2) KO*t*Bu, heat
          3) $KMnO_4$, heat

   (B) 1) Br_2, light
          2) $NaOCH_3$, heat
          3) $H_2Cr_2O_7$

   (C) 1) Br_2, light
          2) $NaOCH_3$, heat
          3) H_3O^+

   (D) 1) Br_2, light
          2) $NaOCH_3$, heat
          3) O_3
          4) CH_3SCH_3

PQ-15. Which reaction sequence will produce *m*-bromochlorobenzene?

   (A) 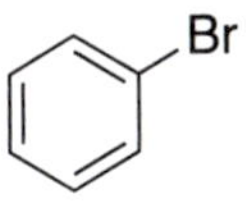
1. HNO_3, H_2SO_4
2. H_2, Pt
3. $NaNO_2$, HCl 0°C
4. CuCl, heat

   (B) 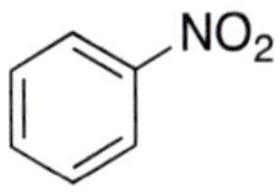
1. H_2, Pt
2. Br_2, $FeBr_3$
3. $NaNO_2$, HCl, 0°C
4. CuCl, heat

   (C) 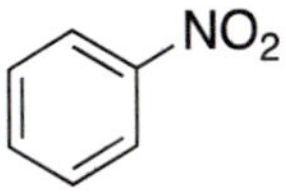
1. Br_2, $FeBr_3$
2. H_2, Pt
3. $NaNO_2$, HCl, 0°C
4. CuCl, Heat

   (D) 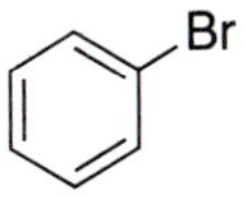
1. HNO_3, H_2SO_4
2. $NaNO_2$, HCl, 0°C
3. CuCl, heat

Answers to Study Questions

SQ-1.	A	SQ-2.	D	SQ-3.	D

Answers to Practice Questions

PQ-1.	A	PQ-6.	C	PQ-11.	C
PQ-2.	A	PQ-7.	A	PQ-12.	D
PQ-3.	B	PQ-8.	B	PQ-13.	A
PQ-4.	B	PQ-9.	C	PQ-14.	D
PQ-5.	A	PQ-10.	D	PQ-15.	C

Chapter 16 – Applications of Organic Chemistry

Chapter Summary:

This chapter will focus on applications of organic chemistry in polymers, biochemistry, green chemistry and spectroscopy. This chapter covers step-growth and condensation polymerization. Introductory topics in biochemistry are presented including carbohydrates, lipids, amino acids and proteins, and DNA/RNA. The principles of green chemistry are presented with special emphasis on atom economy. In addition, several spectroscopic methods are utilized to identify unknowns in this chapter.

Specific topics covered in this chapter are:
- Step-growth and condensation polymerization
- Carbohydrates
- Fischer and Haworth projections
- Lipids
- Amino acids and proteins
- DNA and RNA
- Principles of green chemistry
- Atom economy
- Identification of an unknown using spectroscopy

Previous material that is relevant to your understanding of questions in this chapter include:
- Atomic Masses *(Chapter 0)*
- Hydrophobic and Hydrophilic interactions *(Chapter 2)*
- Stereochemistry *(Chapter 3)*
- IR, ^1H and ^{13}C spectroscopy and mass spectrometry *(Chapter 9)*
- Polymer chemistry *(Chapter 10)*
- Acetals and hemiacetals *(Chapter 13)*
- Esterification reactions *(Chapter 13)*

Where to find this in your textbook:

The material in this chapter typically aligns to "Polymer Chemistry" or "Carbohydrates" or "Lipids" or "Amino Acids" or "Nucleic Acids" or "Spectroscopy" or "Green Chemistry" in your textbook. The name of your chapter may vary.

Practice exam:

There may be practice exam questions aligned to the material in this chapter. Because there are a limited number of questions on the practice exam, a review of the breadth of the material in this chapter is advised in preparation for your exam.

How this fits to the big picture:

The material in this chapter aligns to the Big Ideas of Structure and Function (III), Intermolecular Interactions (IV), Chemical Reactions (V) and Experiments, Measurement, and Data (IX) as listed on page 13 of this study guide.

How this may be covered on an ACS exam:

Because this is a chapter on applications or extensions of organic chemistry, it is reasonable that you may not have any formal questions on your ACS exams that are similar to the content of this chapter. However, as these applications are grounded in all of the previous material (the breadth of a standard two-semester organic chemistry course), it is also reasonable that this content could be applied in the contexts presented in this chapter. To the point, you may see questions on your ACS exam that include this content, but you also may not.

Study Questions (SQ)

SQ-1. What is the atom economy of this reaction?

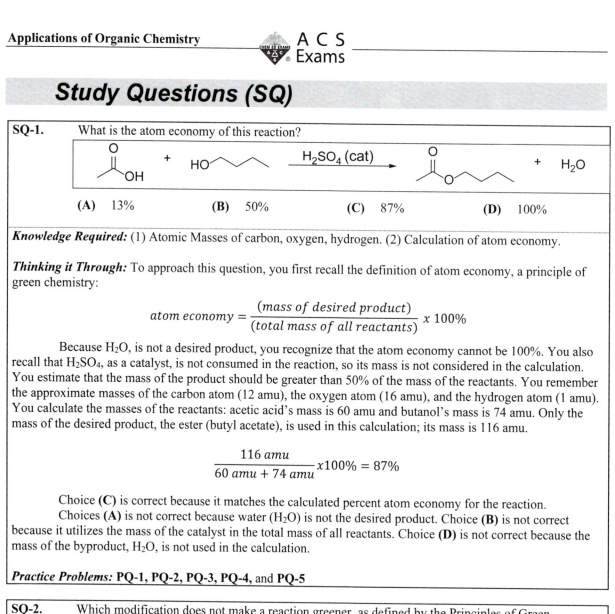

(A) 13% (B) 50% (C) 87% (D) 100%

Knowledge Required: (1) Atomic Masses of carbon, oxygen, hydrogen. (2) Calculation of atom economy.

Thinking it Through: To approach this question, you first recall the definition of atom economy, a principle of green chemistry:

$$atom\ economy = \frac{(mass\ of\ desired\ product)}{(total\ mass\ of\ all\ reactants)} \times 100\%$$

Because H_2O, is not a desired product, you recognize that the atom economy cannot be 100%. You also recall that H_2SO_4, as a catalyst, is not consumed in the reaction, so its mass is not considered in the calculation. You estimate that the mass of the product should be greater than 50% of the mass of the reactants. You remember the approximate masses of the carbon atom (12 amu), the oxygen atom (16 amu), and the hydrogen atom (1 amu). You calculate the masses of the reactants: acetic acid's mass is 60 amu and butanol's mass is 74 amu. Only the mass of the desired product, the ester (butyl acetate), is used in this calculation; its mass is 116 amu.

$$\frac{116\ amu}{60\ amu + 74\ amu} x100\% = 87\%$$

Choice **(C)** is correct because it matches the calculated percent atom economy for the reaction.
Choices **(A)** is not correct because water (H_2O) is not the desired product. Choice **(B)** is not correct because it utilizes the mass of the catalyst in the total mass of all reactants. Choice **(D)** is not correct because the mass of the byproduct, H_2O, is not used in the calculation.

Practice Problems: **PQ-1, PQ-2, PQ-3, PQ-4,** and **PQ-5**

SQ-2. Which modification does not make a reaction greener, as defined by the Principles of Green Chemistry?

(A) replacing the solvent, benzene, with toluene

(B) multiple recrystallizations from H_2O

(C) reducing toxicity of by-product

(D) recycling a metal catalyst

Knowledge Required: (1) Principles of green chemistry.

Thinking it Through: First, you recall the twelve principles of Green Chemistry:
1. Prevent Waste
2. Atom Economy
3. Less Hazardous Synthesis
4. Design Benign Chemicals
5. Benign Solvents & Auxiliaries
6. Design for Energy Efficiency
7. Use of Renewable Feedstocks
8. Reduce Derivatives
9. Catalysis (vs. Stoichiometric)

10. Design for Degradation
11. Real-Time Analysis for Pollution Prevention
12. Inherently Benign Chemistry for Accident Prevention

Next you consider the choices. Considering choice (A), you suspect that it falls under Principle 5, which calls for the use of benign solvents; although you note that though toluene is not benign, it is less hazardous than benzene. You note that while choice (B) may be necessary for a successful synthesis, it does not seem to fall under any of the categories and may violate Principle 1. You notice that choice (C) clearly falls under Principle 3, which calls for a less hazardous synthesis. Finally, you categorize choice (D) as fitting with Principle 9.

Choice (B) is correct because it does not follow one of the Principles of Green Chemistry.

Choices (A), (C) and (D) are not correct as they follow Principles of Green Chemistry.

Practice Problems: PQ-6, and PQ-7

SQ-3. What starting materials will lead to the condensation polymer shown below?

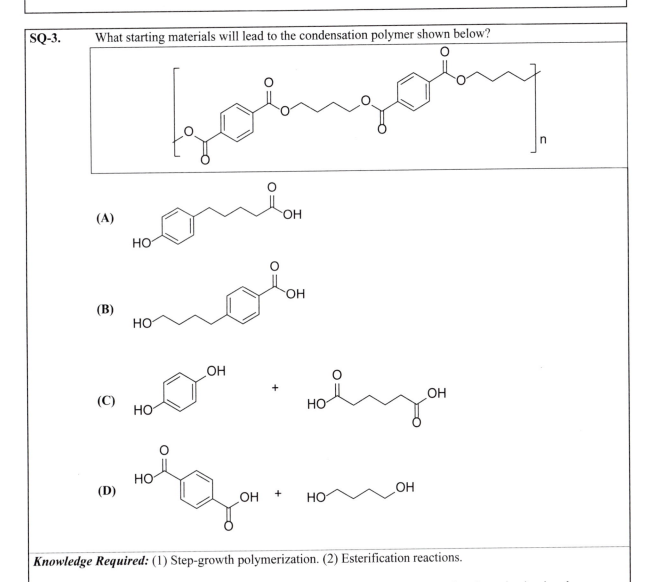

(A)

(B)

(C)

(D)

Knowledge Required: (1) Step-growth polymerization. (2) Esterification reactions.

Thinking it Through: To begin this question, you first remember that step-growth polymerization involves reactions between bifunctional monomers. You also recognize that the target polymer contains an ester functional group, so it is a poly(ester). The mechanism for the step-growth synthesis of an ester polymer follows the small molecule condensation reaction for the synthesis of an ester:

Next, you identify that in the target polymer, the ester carbonyls are both bonded directly to the aromatic ring, eliminating choices **(A)** and **(C)**. You note that while the structure in choice **(B)** has a carbonyl bonded to one atom of the aromatic ring, the *para* position is bonded to a –CH$_2$– group; this is different than in the polymer, which has two ester carbonyls bonded to the aromatic ring. To confirm that the answer is choice **(D)**, you count the carbons in both the aliphatic portion of the target polymer and the alcohol monomer and note that both contain four –CH$_2$– groups.

Choice **(D)** is correct because its starting materials will generate the given polymer product.

Choices **(A)**, **(B)**, and **(C)** are not correct because these monomers will result in different polymers.

Practice Problems: **PQ-8**, **PQ-9**, and **PQ-10**

SQ-4. Which molecule is consistent with these spectra?

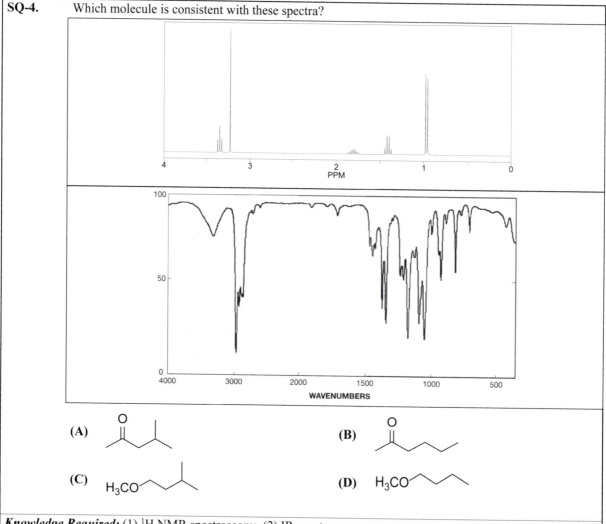

(A)   (B)   (C) H$_3$CO   (D) H$_3$CO

Knowledge Required: (1) ^{1}H NMR spectroscopy. (2) IR spectroscopy.

Thinking it Through: To begin this question, you first consider the IR spectrum and notice that there is not a signal in the 1770-1660 cm^{-1} region for ketone carbonyls, eliminating choices **(A)** and **(B).** You also remember that for many molecules that contain a C–O bond, there is an intense absorption between 1100-1300 cm^{-1}. Its presence supports that there is a C–O bond in the molecule, but it does not specify that there is an ether functional group.

Next, you consider the molecules in choices **(C)** and **(D)** and you think about how their structures will lead to different ^{1}H NMR spectra. The isopropyl group in molecule **(C)** will give a distinct doublet with an integration of 6. This signal will be upfield at 1.0 ppm. The presence of this doublet confirms that choice **(C)** is the correct answer.

Choice **(A)** is not correct because there is not a carbonyl absorption in the IR spectrum. Choice **(B)** is not correct because there is not a carbonyl absorption in the IR spectrum and choice **(B)** does not have an isopropyl group as indicated in the ^{1}H NMR. Choice **(D)** does not contain an isopropyl group as indicated in the ^{1}H NMR.

Practice Problems: **PQ-11, PQ-12,** and **PQ-13**

SQ-5. Identify the molecule consistent with the IR and ^{13}C NMR spectra.

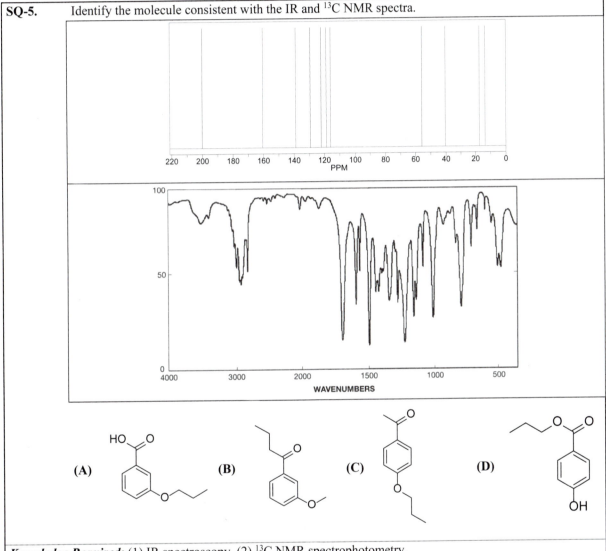

(A)   (B)   (C)   (D)

Knowledge Required: (1) IR spectroscopy. (2) ^{13}C NMR spectrophotometry.

Thinking it Through: To solve this question, you first note that the IR shows a carbonyl absorption. Because all of the molecules have carbonyls, none of the choices are eliminated.

Next, since the IR does not show an absorption at 3600 cm^{-1} indicating the presence of an –OH, you eliminate choices **(A)** and **(D)**. To determine if the molecule is choice **(B)** or choice **(C)**, you look at the ^{13}C NMR and note that there are eleven peaks in the spectrum, which is consistent with the number of carbon atoms in both choice **(B)** and choice **(C)**. However, you also notice that there are six separate peaks in the aromatic region, indicating that are six sets of homotopic aromatic carbon atoms. Choice **(B)** has six sets of homotopic aromatic ^{13}Carbon-atoms. Because of its symmetry, choice **(C)** only has four sets of homotopic aromatic ^{13}Carbon-atoms.

        Choice **(B)** is correct because it follows all the given IR and ^{13}C NMR data.

        Choice **(A)** is not correct because this structure is not consistent with the IR or ^{13}C NMR spectra. Choice **(C)** is not correct because this structure is not consistent with the ^{13}C NMR spectrum. Choice **(D)** is not correct because this structure is not consistent with the IR spectrum.

Practice Problems: **PQ-11, PQ-12,** and **PQ-13**

SQ-6.   What is the stereochemistry of the chiral carbons in D-glucose?

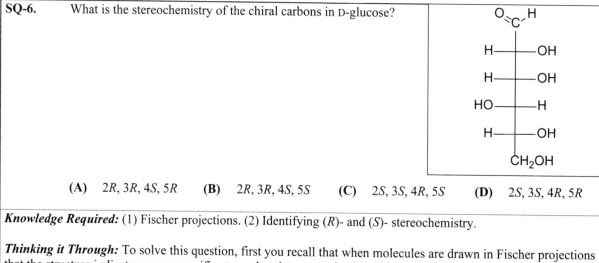

  (A)   2R, 3R, 4S, 5R   **(B)**   2R, 3R, 4S, 5S   **(C)**   2S, 3S, 4R, 5S   **(D)**   2S, 3S, 4R, 5R

Knowledge Required: (1) Fischer projections. (2) Identifying *(R)*- and *(S)*- stereochemistry.

Thinking it Through: To solve this question, first you recall that when molecules are drawn in Fischer projections that the structure indicates a very specific stereochemistry at each of the carbons in a cross hair as indicated below.

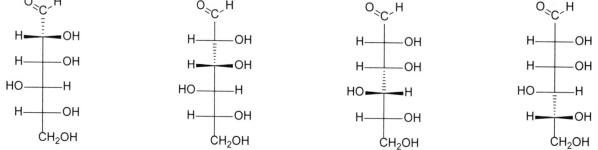

      Next, you recall the rules for rotating a Fischer projection's chiral carbon to maintain its chirality. A helpful rule for this structure allows you to rotate three of the groups attached to a chiral carbon clockwise or counterclockwise. For carbon-2, rotating the low priority hydrogen atom so it is pointing back assists with determining if carbon-2 has *(R)*- or *(S)*- stereochemistry.

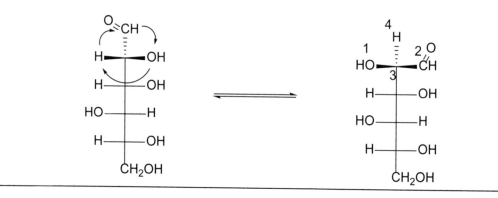

When this rotation is complete, you identify the priorities of the other groups attached to carbon-2 and note that this carbon has *(R)*-stereochemistry. This eliminates choices **(C)** and **(D)**. After you complete this process for the other chiral carbons on D-Gulose, you note that carbon-5 has *(R)*-stereochemistry, eliminating choice **(B)**.

Choice **(A)** is the correct answer because it contains all the correct stereochemical designations.
Choices **(B)**, **(C)**, and **(D)** are incorrect because each misidentified one or more stereocenter's chirality.

Practice Problems: **PQ-14** and **PQ-15**

SQ-7. Which is the Haworth projection for α-D-gulose?

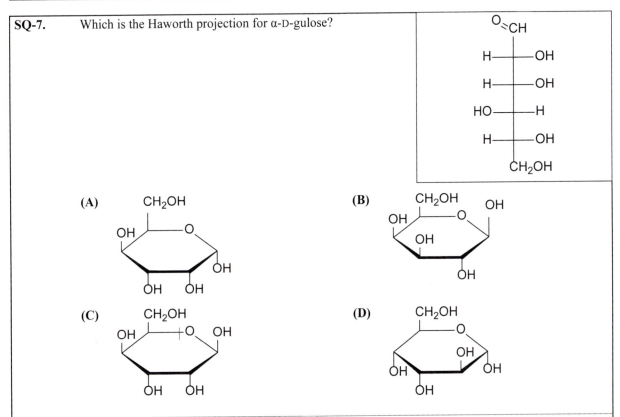

Knowledge Required: (1) Carbohydrate chemistry. (2) Fischer projections. (3) Haworth projections. (4) α- and β-anomers. (4) Identifying *(R)*- and *(S)*- stereochemistry.

Thinking it Through: You first recall that carbohydrates form cyclic hemiacetals. Gulose, an aldohexose, will form a six-membered ring after the chiral carbon furthest from the aldehyde attacks the carbonyl carbon to form the cyclic hemiacetal. You remember that the chiral carbons in the Fischer projection maintain their stereochemistry in the Haworth projection and a new stereocenter forms at what was the aldehydic carbonyl. You remember that in the cyclic structure this new chiral carbon is called the anomeric carbon. Because it is a new stereocenter, it has two different types of stereochemistry, indicated as α- and β- in carbohydrate chemistry. You recall that to maintain the correct stereochemistry, D-sugars, when drawn as Haworth projections often show the anomeric carbon to the right of the oxygen atom in the ring and the carbon-5 bond to the carbon-6 group (–CH₂OH) as "up" relative to the ring and left of the oxygen atom. You also remember that when the anomeric carbon's -OH group is *trans*- to the –CH₂OH group, it is identified as the α-anomer; when the anomeric carbon's –OH group is *cis*- to the –CH₂OH group, the anomeric carbon is identified as the β-anomer. The α- and β-anomers are in equilibrium with the acyclic form of the carbohydrate shown in the Fischer projection.

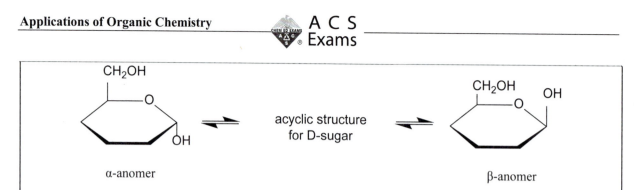

α-anomer   acyclic structure   β-anomer
                              for D-sugar

You notice that all of the choices show the carbon-6 –CH₂OH group as "up" relative to the ring but only choices **(A)** and **(D)** show the correct stereochemistry for the α-anomeric carbon. Next, you recognize that you need to identify the stereochemistry of carbon-2, carbon-3, and carbon-4, to ensure that it is maintained in the Haworth projection. While you may inspect the Fischer and Haworth projections to identify (*R*)- and (*S*)- chirality on these carbons, you recall that there is a protocol when drawing Haworth projections for D-sugars that show the above structure where the –CH₂OH group is "up." For the chiral carbons not involved in making the hemiacetal, the –OH groups on the right of the Fischer projection point "down" and those on the left point "up" relative to the ring. You remind yourself that, although it is not needed in this question, Haworth projections may flip and rotate, but their relative orientation to each other remains unchanged.

Choice **(A)** is correct because it correctly shows the stereochemistry of α-D-gulose.

Choices **(B)** and **(C)** are incorrect because they show the β-anomer of a carbohydrate. Choice **(D)** is incorrect because while this is the α-anomer structure of an aldohexose, it is not gulose.

Practice Problems: **PQ-16** and **PQ-17**

SQ-8.   Which disaccharide(s) test positive as reducing sugars when exposed to Benedict's reagent, Cu^{2+}?

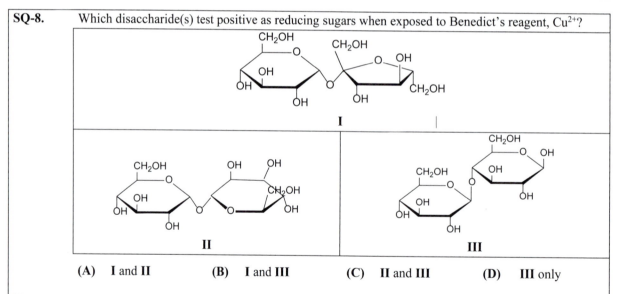

I

II   III

(A) I and II   (B) I and III   (C) II and III   (D) III only

Knowledge Required: (1) Haworth structures. (2) Glycosidic bonds. (3) Hemiacetal and acetal chemistry. (4) Reducing sugars.

Thinking it Through: You recall that an anomeric carbon in a Haworth structure forms from an intramolecular cyclization involving the carbonyl of a carbohydrate to form a hemiacetal. You remember that hemiacetals exist in equilibrium with their aldehyde or ketone counterpart. You recall that the blue solution of Benedict's reagent contains Cu^{2+}, a weak oxidizing agent that reacts with aldehydes to yield carboxylic acids. During the reaction, the Cu^{2+}, is reduced to Cu_2O, an orange precipitate. You recall that acetals act as protecting groups for aldehydes/ ketones. So, if the anomeric carbon exists as a hemiacetal, it is in equilibrium with the acyclic aldehyde and will reduce the Cu^{2+}; if the anomeric carbon exists as an acetal, it does not react.

Next, you identify the anomeric carbons on each of the carbohydrates in the disaccharides as the carbon bonded to two oxygens. Looking at molecule **I**, you identify the anomeric carbons:

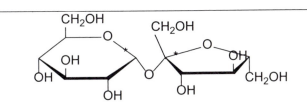

The anomeric carbon on the left is an α-anomer of its carbohydrate (glucose) and the anomeric carbon on the right is a β-anomer of its carbohydrate (fructose). You note that the glucose's anomeric carbon does not have an –OH group bonded to it instead it has a glycoside-bond to the fructose; you identify it as an acetal. Fructose's anomeric carbon also does not have an –OH group attached to it, so you identify that it is also an acetal. Because molecule **I** does not have a hemiacetal in equilibrium with a carbonyl, it is a non-reducing sugar. You eliminate choices **(A)** and **(B)**. You consider molecules **II** and **III** and identify the two anomeric carbons on each. Only the β-anomeric carbon on the right carbohydrate of molecule **III** has both an –OH group and an –OR group attached to it, making it a hemiacetal.

Choice **(D)** is correct as only molecule **III** contains a hemiacetal, making it a reducing sugar.

Choices **(A)**, **(B)**, and **(C)** are incorrect because they include molecules **I** and **II**, which are non-reducing sugars.

Practice Problems: **PQ-18** and **PQ-19**

SQ-9. What is the charge of glutamic acid at pH = 13?

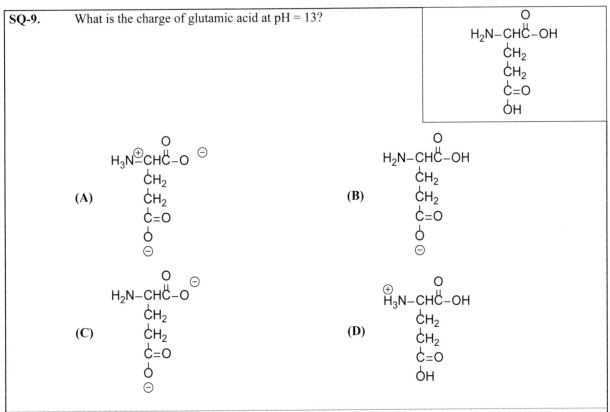

Knowledge Required: (1) Amino acid structure. (2) Isoelectric point.

Thinking it Through: When you solve this question, you consider the structure of amino acids and recall that they exist as a zwitterions at their isoelectric points (*p*I). You remember that the isoelectric point exists between the pK_a of two of the conjugate acids on the molecule. The pH for the *p*I is dependent on the structure of amino acid. Most amino acids' *p*I occurs in neutral solution, pH ≈ 7. You recall that the acid side chain for glutamic acid lowers the *p*I (its *p*I = 3.2).

At a low pH, both of the carboxylic acids and the amino group are protonated. As the pH rises, each acidic H-atom is lost, depending on its pK_a.

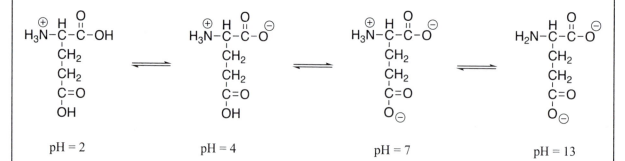

pH = 2   pH = 4   pH = 7   pH = 13

Choice **(C)** is correct because it correctly shows the loss of all acidic H-atoms in a highly basic solution. Choice **(A)** is incorrect because this is the structure of glutamic acid at pH = 7. Choice **(B)** is incorrect because glutamic acid cannot have this structure. Choice **(D)** is incorrect because this is the structure of glutamic acid at a very low pH.

Practice Problems: **PQ-20** and **PQ-21**

SQ-10.   Which factor has the least effect on the 2° structure of proteins?

(A)   Resonance in the peptide bond.   (B)   Interactions with other protein structures.

(C)   Hydrogen-bonding between the carbonyl and the amide's hydrogen-atom.   (D)   Hydrophobic and hydrophilic side chains.

Knowledge Required: (1) Protein structure.

Thinking it Through: To solve this question, you first recall the definitions of 1°, 2°, 3°, and 4° structures of proteins. The sequence of the amino acids comprises the 1° structure. The 2°, 3°, and 4° structures are concerned with the 3D arrangement of the protein in space. You remember that the 2° structure focuses on the local 3D structure and common types of local structure arrangements are the α-helix and β-pleat. You recall that the resonance structures of the peptide bond are a contributing factor in the α-helix and β-pleat structures:

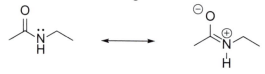

Additionally, you remember that hydrogen bonding between the carbonyl's oxygen and the amine's H-atom helps lock the protein into its 2° structure. Finally, the hydrophobic and hydrophilic interactions among the side groups on the amino acids, affect the loops and bends in the secondary structure. Of the possible answers, only choice **(B)** lists a factor that has little effect on the 2° structure of the protein. Interactions with other proteins, you recall, clearly affects the 4° structure of proteins.
    Choice **(B)** is the correct answer.
    Choices **(A)**, **(C)**, and **(D)** are incorrect because these factors all affect the 2° structure of proteins.

Practice Problems: **PQ-22** and **PQ-23**

SQ-11.   Which nucleoside is found in DNA?

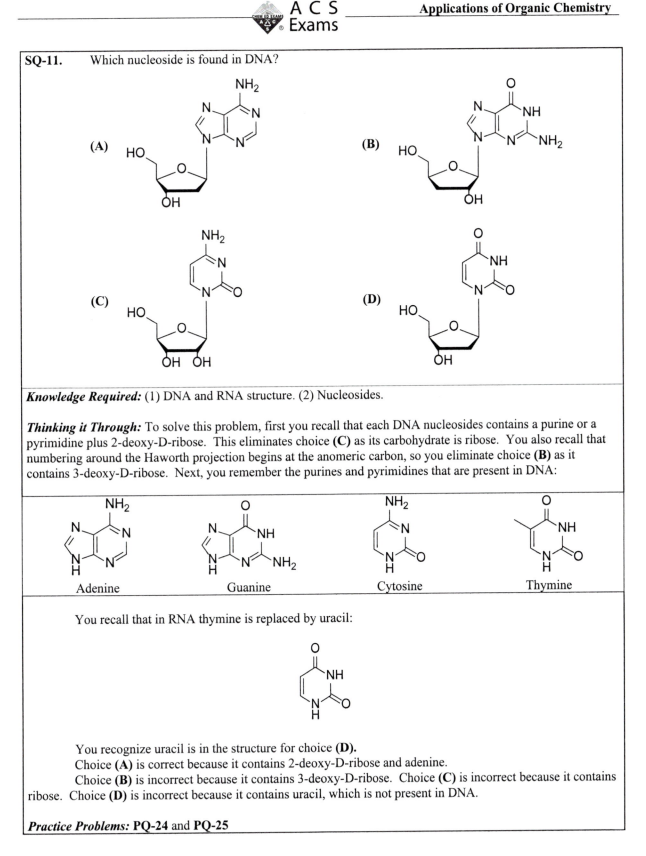

Knowledge Required: (1) DNA and RNA structure. (2) Nucleosides.

Thinking it Through: To solve this problem, first you recall that each DNA nucleosides contains a purine or a pyrimidine plus 2-deoxy-D-ribose. This eliminates choice **(C)** as its carbohydrate is ribose. You also recall that numbering around the Haworth projection begins at the anomeric carbon, so you eliminate choice **(B)** as it contains 3-deoxy-D-ribose. Next, you remember the purines and pyrimidines that are present in DNA:

| | | | |
| Adenine | Guanine | Cytosine | Thymine |

You recall that in RNA thymine is replaced by uracil:

You recognize uracil is in the structure for choice **(D)**.
Choice **(A)** is correct because it contains 2-deoxy-D-ribose and adenine.
Choice **(B)** is incorrect because it contains 3-deoxy-D-ribose. Choice **(C)** is incorrect because it contains ribose. Choice **(D)** is incorrect because it contains uracil, which is not present in DNA.

Practice Problems: PQ-24 and **PQ-25**

SQ-12.   Which structure is NOT classified as a lipid?

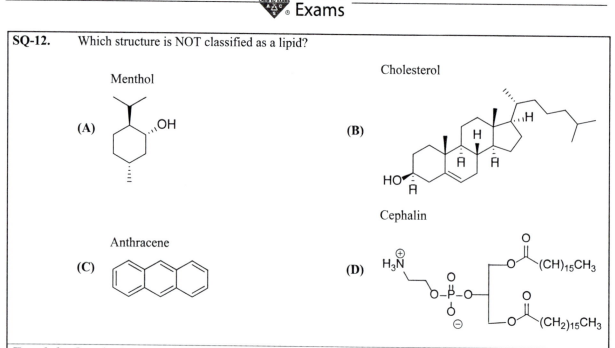

Menthol

(A)

Cholesterol

(B)

Anthracene

(C)

Cephalin

(D)

Knowledge Required: (1) Lipid structures.

Thinking it Through: To solve this question, you recall that the lipid family, unlike other biological molecule families, does not have a common structure among its members. Instead, the lipid family is composed of biological molecules that dissolve in nonpolar solvents. Next, you recall the common structural types that are classified as lipids: fatty acids and their esters, phospholipids, terpenes and terepenoids, and steroids.

You recall that fatty acids are acids whose long aliphatic chains make them insoluble in water. A common fatty acid ester form is a triacylglyceride, which you recall is composed of a glycerol backbone and three fatty acid esters. You recall that a phospholipid has a similar structure; it is composed of a glycerol backbone, two fatty acid esters, and an ester linkage to a phosphoric acid derivative.

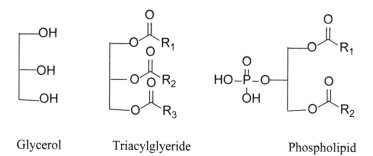

Glycerol   Triacylglyeride   Phospholipid

You identify cephalin as a phospholipid and eliminate choice (**D**). Next, you recall that terpenes and terpenoids are identified by the presence of five carbon units known as isoprene units. Terpenes and terpenoids usually contain 5n carbons broken into 5-carbon units that have the carbon skeleton of isoprene:

You notice that menthol has ten carbons and note its branching pattern that is characteristic in terpenes. You identify the two isoprene units in menthol and eliminate choice (**A**).

Finally, you recall that steroids and their derivatives have the specific four-ring backbone shown below that you recognize in choice (**B**).

Choice **(C)** is correct because while lipids may contain aromatic structures, anthracene does not belong to one of the structure types within the lipid family.

Choice **(A)** is incorrect because menthol is a terpene. Choice **(B)** is incorrect because cholesterol is a steroid. Choice **(D)** is incorrect because cephalin is a phospholipid.

Practice Problems: **PQ-26, PQ-27**, and **PQ-28**

SQ-13. Identify the picture that depicts a cross-section of how fatty acid carboxylates aggregate above a certain concentration in H_2O.

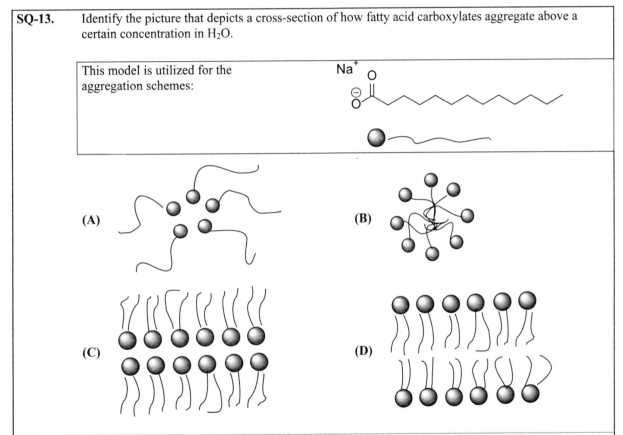

Knowledge Required: (1) Hydrophobic and hydrophilic groups. (2) Micelles and bilayers.

Thinking it Through: In thinking about this question, you first note that the ball (or headgroup) represents the ionic portion of the fatty acid carboxylate and are hydrophilic. The squiggly line represents the hydrophobic hydrocarbon chain (or tail). You eliminate choices **(A)** and **(C)** because you recognize that, in water, the molecules orient so the hydrophilic headgroup interacts with the water. Next you notice that the structures in choices **(C)** and **(D)** show two hydrocarbon tails but the carboxylate only has one tail. Also, you recall that fatty acid carboxylates form micelles in water, which is shown in choice **(B)**.

Choice **(B)** is correct because this scheme shows the micelle form.

Choice **(A)** is incorrect because the hydrophilic headgroups interact with the solvent, water. Choice **(C)** is incorrect because there are two hydrocarbon tails rather than one and the hydrophilic head groups interact with each other, while the hydrophobic tails are interacting with the solvent. Choice **(D)** is incorrect because there are two hydrocarbon tails rather than one.

Practice Problems: **PQ-29** and **PQ-30**

Practice Questions (PQ)

PQ-1. Which reaction synthesizes this molecule with the highest atom economy?

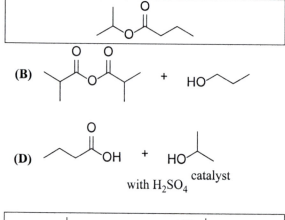

(A)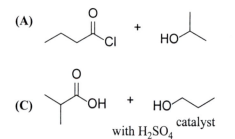

(B) + HO⌒

(C) with H₂SO₄ catalyst

(D) with H₂SO₄ catalyst

PQ-2. Which reagents complete this reaction with highest atom economy?

(A) BH₃/THF followed by H₂O₂/NaOH

(B) Hg(OAc)₂, H₂O followed by NaBH₄/NaOH

(C) H₂SO₄/H₂O

(D) OsO₄/NMO

PQ-3. What is the atom economy (ae%) for this reaction? (mass of Cl: 35.5 amu; mass of Na: 23 amu)

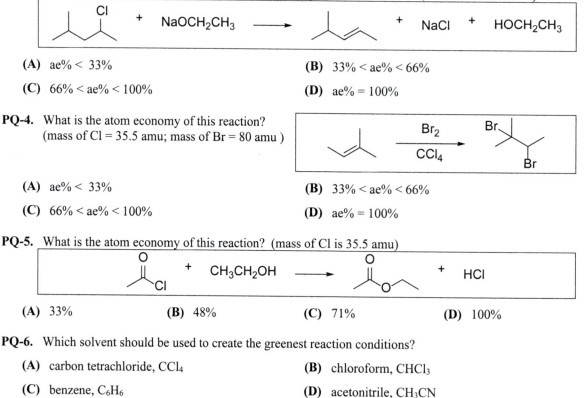

(A) ae% < 33%

(B) 33% < ae% < 66%

(C) 66% < ae% < 100%

(D) ae% = 100%

PQ-4. What is the atom economy of this reaction?
(mass of Cl = 35.5 amu; mass of Br = 80 amu)

(A) ae% < 33%

(B) 33% < ae% < 66%

(C) 66% < ae% < 100%

(D) ae% = 100%

PQ-5. What is the atom economy of this reaction? (mass of Cl is 35.5 amu)

(A) 33%   (B) 48%   (C) 71%   (D) 100%

PQ-6. Which solvent should be used to create the greenest reaction conditions?

(A) carbon tetrachloride, CCl₄

(B) chloroform, CHCl₃

(C) benzene, C₆H₆

(D) acetonitrile, CH₃CN

PQ-7. Which modification(s) to the extraction of caffeine from tea follow green chemistry principles?

I.	Replacing 30 mL dichloromethane as extraction solvent with 100 mL of 1-propanol.
II.	Heating the reaction to a high temperature to increase solubility of caffeine.
III.	Multiple sublimation steps to increase purity of product.
IV.	Use of a water bath for distillation of extraction solvent rather than a heating mantle.

(A) I only   (B) I, II, and III   (C) I, II, III, and IV   (D) II and IV

PQ-8. What step-growth polymer is formed from these two monomers?

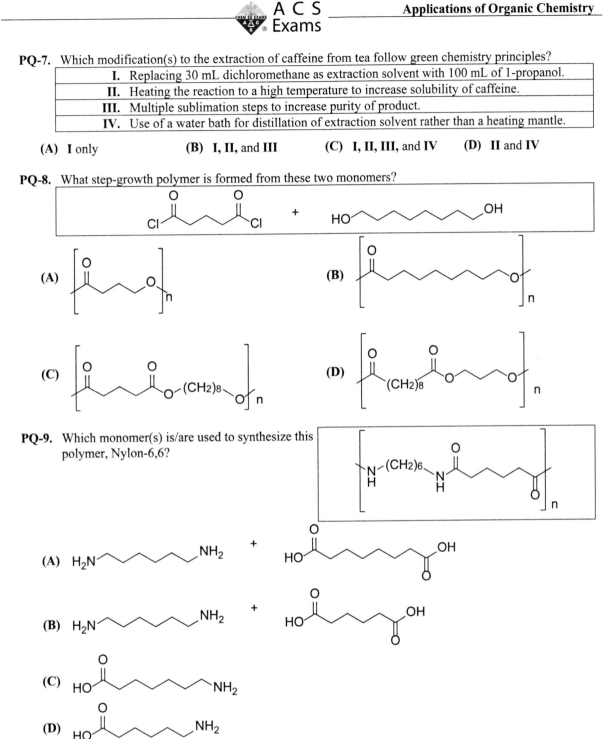

PQ-9. Which monomer(s) is/are used to synthesize this polymer, Nylon-6,6?

PQ-10. Which monomer(s) is/are used to synthesize this polymer?

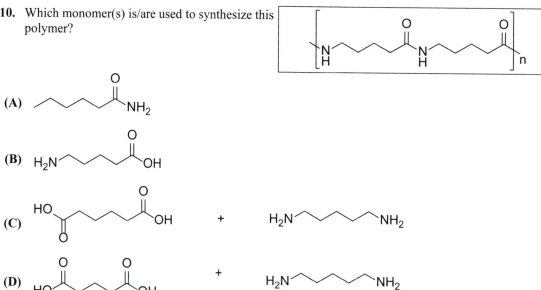

(A)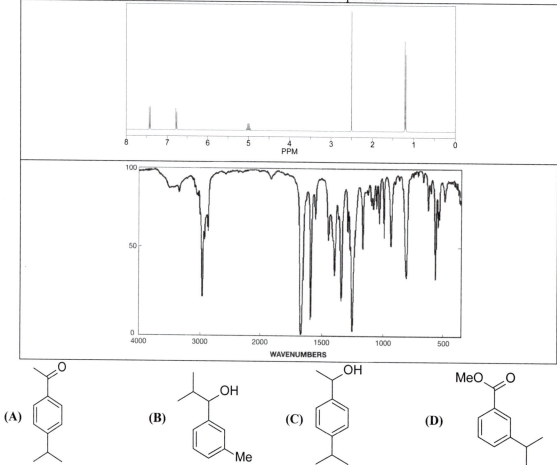

(B)

(C) +

(D) +

PQ-11. What molecule is consistent with both these IR and ^{1}H NMR spectra?

(A)   (B)   (C)   (D)

PQ-12. What structure is consistent with these spectra?

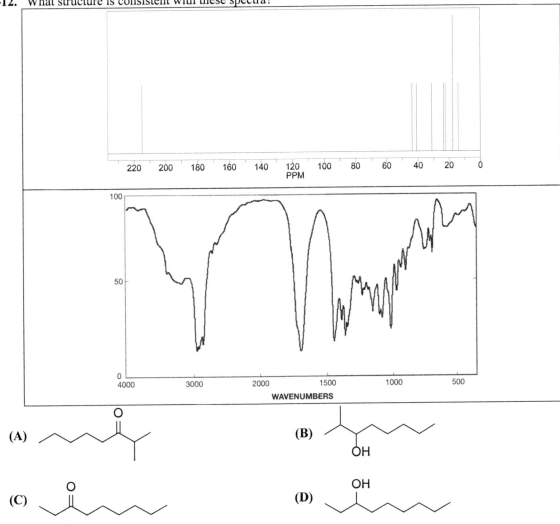

(A)

(B)

(C)

(D)

PQ-13. An unknown reacts with PCC and gives this ^{1}H NMR spectrum. Which structure is consistent with this data?

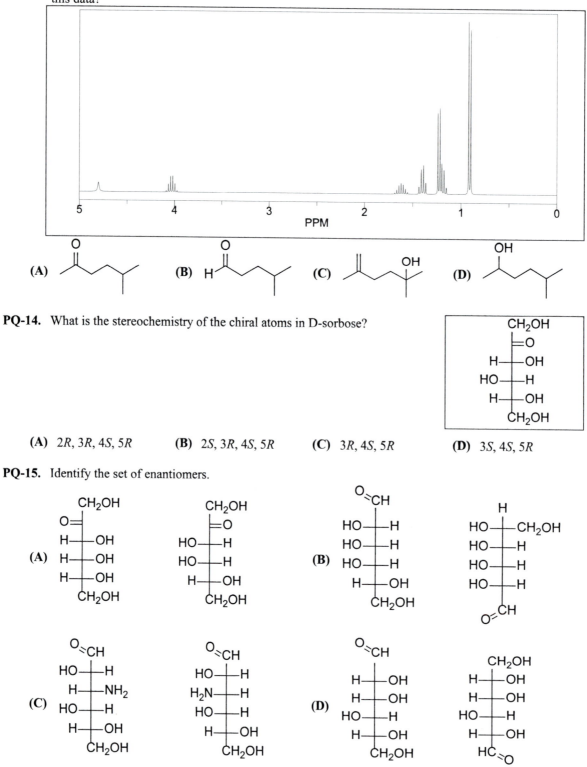

PQ-14. What is the stereochemistry of the chiral atoms in D-sorbose?

(A) 2R, 3R, 4S, 5R   (B) 2S, 3R, 4S, 5R   (C) 3R, 4S, 5R   (D) 3S, 4S, 5R

PQ-15. Identify the set of enantiomers.

PQ-16. What is the Haworth projection for β-D-galactose?

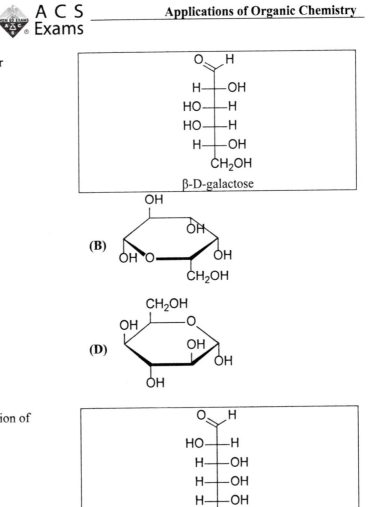

β-D-galactose

(A)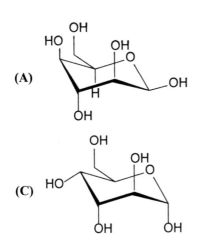

(B)

(C)

(D)

PQ-17. Which shows the chair conformation of α-D-altose?

α-D-altose

(A)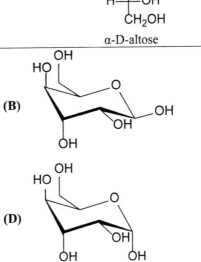

(B)

(C)

(D)

PQ-18. Which structure reacts with Cu^{2+}?

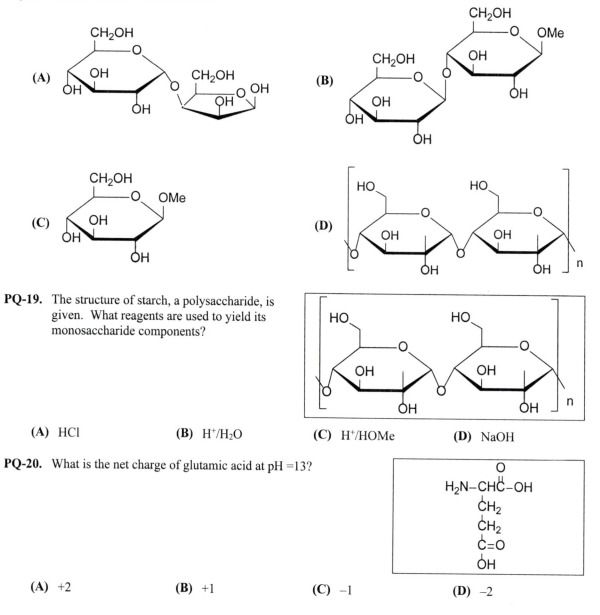

(A)

(B)

(C)

(D)

PQ-19. The structure of starch, a polysaccharide, is given. What reagents are used to yield its monosaccharide components?

(A) HCl

(B) H^+/H_2O

(C) $H^+/HOMe$

(D) NaOH

PQ-20. What is the net charge of glutamic acid at pH =13?

(A) +2

(B) +1

(C) –1

(D) –2

PQ-21. What is the primary structure of this protein at pH = 7: val·lys·ala·cys?

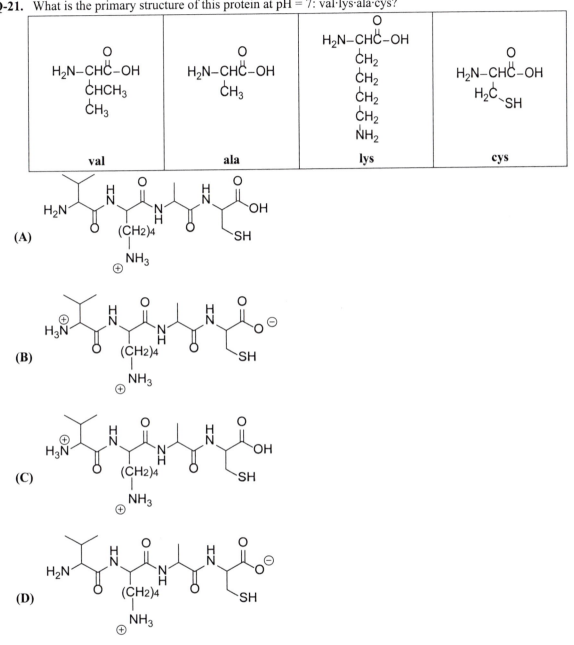

val	ala	lys	cys

(A)

(B)

(C)

(D)

PQ-22. Classify the reaction to form a disulfide bond.

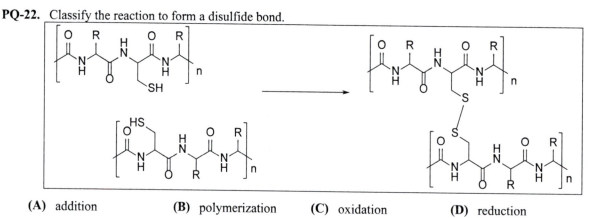

(A) addition   (B) polymerization   (C) oxidation   (D) reduction

PQ-23. The amide group in peptide bonds are planar. Which diagram explains this geometry?

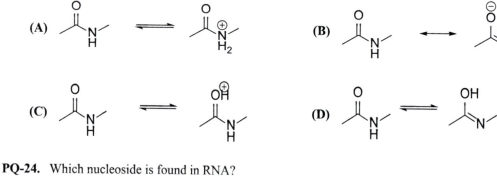

PQ-24. Which nucleoside is found in RNA?

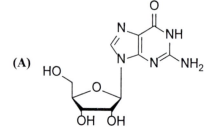

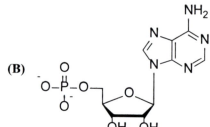

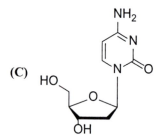

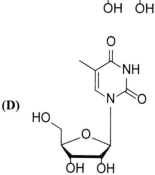

PQ-25. Which statements are true for DNA's 2° structure?

I.	H-bonding occurs between the purines and pyrmidines.
II.	The disulfide linkage formation causes the α-helix to change conformations.
III.	The phosphate linkage occurs between carbon-**3** and carbon-**5** atoms on the carbohydrate.
IV.	Thymine pairs with Guanine.

(A) I and II   (B) I and III   (C) I, III, and IV   (D) II, III, and IV

PQ-26. Rank these triacylglycerides by their melting points (lowest < highest).

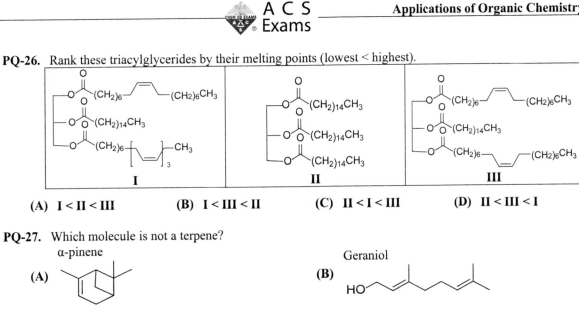

I   II   III

(A) I < II < III   (B) I < III < II   (C) II < I < III   (D) II < III < I

PQ-27. Which molecule is not a terpene?

(A) α-pinene

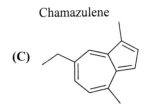

(B) Geraniol

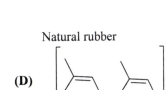

(C) Chamazulene

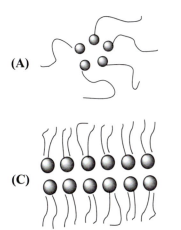

(D) Natural rubber

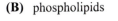

PQ-28. What do not exist as a biopolymer?

(A) proteins

(B) phospholipids

(C) DNA

(D) polysaccharides

PQ-29. Above a certain concentration, which picture depicts a cross-section of how phospholipids aggregate in H_2O? This model is utilized for the aggregation schemes:

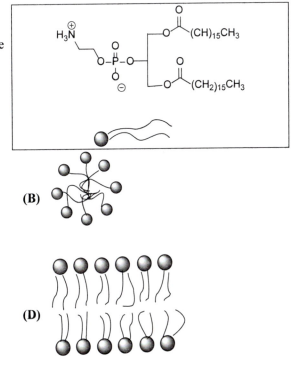

(A)

(B)

(C)

(D)

PQ-30. What are the products of this saponification reaction?

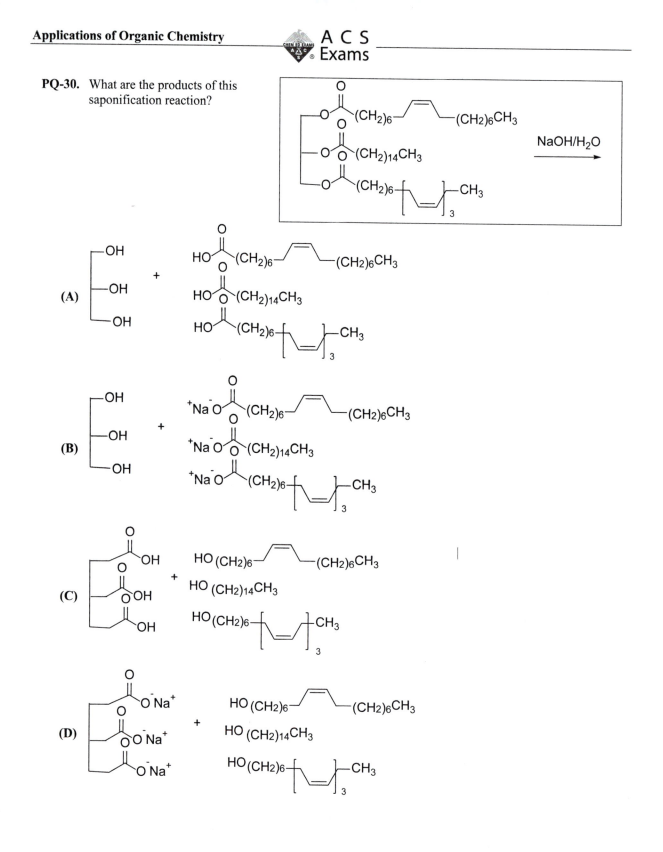

Answers to Study Questions

SQ-1.	C	SQ-6.	A	SQ-11.	A	
SQ-2.	B	SQ-7.	A	SQ-12.	C	
SQ-3.	D	SQ-8.	D	SQ-13.	B	
SQ-4.	C	SQ-9.	C			
SQ-5.	B	SQ-10.	B			

Answers to Practice Questions

PQ-1.	D	PQ-11.	A	PQ-21.	B
PQ-2.	C	PQ-12.	A	PQ-22.	C
PQ-3.	B	PQ-13.	D	PQ-23.	B
PQ-4.	D	PQ-14.	C	PQ-24.	A
PQ-5.	C	PQ-15.	B	PQ-25.	B
PQ-6.	D	PQ-16.	C	PQ-26.	B
PQ-7.	A	PQ-17.	C	PQ-27.	C
PQ-8.	C	PQ-18.	A	PQ-28.	B
PQ-9.	B	PQ-19.	B	PQ-29.	D
PQ-10.	B	PQ-20.	D	PQ-30.	B